RESTORING
TOURISM DESTINATIONS
IN CRISIS

Dr David Beirman, BA Hons Dip Ed MA Hons Phd, is the founding Director of the Israel Tourism Office Australasia & Southwest Pacific. He is the first non-Israeli contracted by the Israel Ministry of Tourism to run an Israel Tourism office and has held the position since 1994. He is also the founder and inaugural chairman of the Eastern Mediterranean Tourism Association (Australia) which was established in 2001 to market and promote the region between Italy and Jordan (including Israel) to the travel industry and public. He is a board member of ANTOR (Association of National Tourist Office Representatives), Australia. David has been professionally involved in the travel industry for over 20 years, including ten years working for Jetset Tours in a variety of roles ranging from travel consultant to personnel and in-service training manager. Since 1989 he has been the principal of his own training and management consultancy firm Struan & Associates, specialising in the travel industry.

Dr Beirman has extensive university lecturing experience in the fields of Tourism, Market Research, Middle East Studies and Sociology. He has lectured at the University of Technology Sydney, the University of Sydney and the University of New South Wales and has guest lectured at many schools of tourism and professional and academic conferences and symposia in Australia, New Zealand, Singapore, Hong Kong, Canada and Israel. His articles on tourism crisis management have been published by international publications including the *International Journal of Vacation Marketing* and PATA's publication *Compass*. In September 2002 PATA invited him to join their crisis management advisory board.

Outside the professional sphere, David enjoys travelling, bushwalking and exploring. He is based in Sydney.

RESTORING TOURISM DESTINATIONS IN CRISIS

A strategic marketing approach

David Beirman

CABI *Publishing*

First published in Australia and New Zealand by Allen & Unwin, 2003
Published simultaneously in the United Kingdom and United States by
CABI *Publishing*, a division of CAB *International*, 2003

CABI *Publishing* is a division of CAB *International*

CABI Publishing
CAB International
Wallingford
Oxon OX10 8DE
UK

Tel: +44 (0)1491 832111
Fax: +44 (0)1491 833508
E-mail: cabi@cabi.org
Web site: www.cabi-publishing.org

CABI Publishing
44 Brattle Street
4th Floor
Cambridge, MA 02138
USA

Tel: +800 528 4841
(Toll Free from US/Canada)
Fax:: +1 617 354 6875
E-mail: cabi-nao@cabi.org

A catalogue record for this book is available from the British Library, London, UK.
A catalogue record for this book is available from the Library of Congress,
Washington, DC, USA.

ISBN 0 85199 729 5

Set in 11/13 pt Spectrum by Bookhouse, Sydney, Australia
Printed by McPherson's Printing Group, Maryborough, Australia

10 9 8 7 6 5 4 3 2 1

CONTENTS

LIST OF FIGURES AND TABLES

ACRONYMS

ANC	African National Congress
ASTA	American Society of Travel Agents
ATC	Australian Tourism Commission
BTA	British Tourist Authority
CTB	Ceylon Tourist Board
EMTA	Eastern Mediterranean Tourism Association
FAA	Federal Airports Authority
FVB	Fiji Visitors Bureau
IATA	International Air Transport Association
ICTO	International Council of Tour Operators
IGTO	Israel Government Tourism Office
IHA	International Hotels Association
MAFF	Ministry of Agriculture, Fisheries and Food (UK)
MEMTA	Middle East and Mediterranean Tourism Association
MICE	meetings, incentives, conventions, exhibitions
PAL	Philippine Airlines
PATA	Pacific Asia Travel Association
PCVC	Philippines Convention and Visitor Corporation
SAA	South African Airways
SATOUR	South African Tourism
TAG	Tourism Action Group (Fiji)
TCSP	Tourism Council of the South Pacific
TIA	Tourism Industry Association
TPC	Tourism Policy Council
TT	Tourism Tasmania
USTTA	United States Travel and Tourism Authority

VFR	Visiting Friends and Relatives
WTO	World Tourism Organization
WTTC	World Travel and Tourism Council

ACKNOWLEDGMENTS

There are many people who have provided invaluable assistance to the completion of this volume. First and foremost, I would like to thank Allen & Unwin for having agreed to publish this book. A very special thanks to Elizabeth Weiss and Catherine Taylor who have so professionally and patiently guided me through the publication process. I have been fortunate in receiving generous cooperation from many of my fellow directors of national and state tourist offices based in Australia and some of their head office colleagues. A very special thanks to Erdal Aktan Turkish Tourism Office; Virginia Haddon; South African Tourism; Deirdre Livingstone and her crisis management team from the BTA's London office; Sharon Hannaford and John Koldowski of PATA's Bangkok office; and to Perry Hobson, Head of School of Tourism and Leisure at Southern Cross University, Lismore who, along with John Koldowski, read and appraised the manuscript. Thanks also to Josaia Rayawa of the Fiji Visitors Bureau, Elhamy Elzayat, CEO and chairman Egyptian Association of Travel Agents, Consuelo Garcia Jones, from the Philippines Department of Tourism, Malcolm Wells of Tourism Tasmania and Barry Schipplock, Visit USA (Australia) and Daniel Young of USTTA Associates who carefully appraised my United States chapter.

A very special appreciation to my own colleagues from the Israel Ministry of Tourism in Jerusalem and in eighteen cities around the world with whom I have shared the experience of managing Israel's own tourism marketing crises. Ruth Eilat, Suzan Klagesbrun and Noga Sher-Greco have been at the forefront of managing Israel's tourism marketing challenges from the Israel end. A very special thanks to my inspirational research assistant Liz Angus, whose invaluable contribution in the form of ideas, information sourcing and editing at the initial manuscript stage helped shape this book. To all these people and many others, some of whom preferred not be named but who willingly gave of their time, effort and expertise to assist me with this book, I extend a heartfelt thanks.

To all my professional colleagues in both the travel industry and tourism academia, I hope your crises are few but you are well prepared to manage them and market your way to restoration and recovery. If this book helps at all in achieving that goal then the effort has been well worthwhile.

PREFACE

No tourism destination is immune from crisis. Consequently, the global tourism industry requires strategies and a set of directions which enable and prepare destination tourism authorities to manage a crisis event from its onset and rapidly implement a recovery strategy. The field of tourism crisis management is in its infancy and my overriding motivation for writing this book was to help fill some of the many gaps which exist in the literature. There remains enormous scope for future research in this subject.

The prime research focus is an analysis of the marketing dimension as it applies to specific crisis events: war, terrorism, natural disasters, crime waves and epidemics, and the appropriate restorative approaches. There is no doubt that destination crises arise from many causes including business collapse and industrial dispute. Destination restoration also involves a multitude of factors other than marketing. The issue of retraining and redeploying people whose livelihoods are affected by a crisis, though significant, is outside the scope of this work. The field of crisis management is very broad in scope and I have sought here to cover only those areas where I have specialist knowledge. Although the main topic covered is tourism destination marketing in crises, the principles of crisis management and restoration marketing apply to every business in which marketability is vulnerable to external crisis.

This book addresses three major themes. First, a destination crisis is defined and the distinction between a destination crisis and a hazard is explained. The image and marketability of tourism destinations were seriously compromised in each of the case studies discussed, and the crises analysed were beyond the direct management control of local destination marketing authorities. The DESTCON system is introduced as a means to classify the severity of a crisis in terms of the threat to destination marketability, and to signal an appropriate strategic response.

Secondly, the reader is presented with a detailed guide to the strategic management of in-crisis and post-crisis marketing programs and their incorporation in contingency planning. Marketing restoration approaches emphasising the establishment of strategic alliances between destination authorities, airlines and all key principals of a destination's tourism infrastructure are outlined. The approach to restoration marketing involves a multi-track strategy including the communication of customised crisis response messages for specific audiences. Market recovery programs are designed to restore the marketability and positive image of the destination to the travel industry, consumers and the media. The management of security concerns is a recurring theme in all case studies discussed in this book.

Thirdly, and significantly, this book includes a broad range of international case studies, enabling the reader to assess how contemporary crises have been managed by various destination marketing authorities. Care was taken to select cases of prime relevance. Although every effort has been made to minimise error, any mistake in analysis or fact rests with the author.

As this book was going to press, the bombing of a nightclub in Indonesia's most popular tourist resort area on the island of Bali resulted in over 200 deaths and 300 wounded. Most victims were young tourists from Australia, New Zealand, Europe, Southeast Asia and North America. This incident was one of the deadliest attacks targeted at tourists in modern history.

The incident severely compromised many years of tourism infrastructure development and the successful marketing of Bali as one of the world's most desirable tourism destinations. Bali now joins the list of destinations forced to undertake the formidable task of restoring and recovering its marketing image.

As a professional destination marketer, I derived invaluable insights about destination crisis and restoration marketing from the case studies researched. Many proved to be inspirational learning experiences. It is my sincere hope that you will share some of the enlightenment I was privileged to gain during the course of my research.

David Beirman
Sydney, September 2002

AUTHOR'S NOTE

Our world has not yet witnessed the futility of all-out nuclear war. In 1945 the atomic bomb was dropped on Japan, obliterating the cities of Hiroshima and Nagasaki. This is as close as we have come, so far, to annihilation.

Once again, 40 years after the Cuban Missile Crisis of 1962, which brought the world to the brink of DEFCON 1, the highest state of military readiness, nuclear war remains an ominous threat. Attempting reconstruction of anything after a nuclear strike, let alone tourism infrastructure, is, to me, almost beyond imagination.

Those of us committed to the success of the tourism industry desire peace and harmonious international relations even above profits. Tourism professionals regard our work as building bridges of understanding between peoples, opening up the world and breaking down the barriers of ignorance and prejudice that are used to create conflict.

Most countries examined in this study suffered a terrible catastrophe which impacted upon their overall economies and tourism industries. Yet, they are testimony to the best qualities of the human spirit to endure and to rebuild.

The term DESTCON 1 used in this book describes the maximum level of crisis which can impact on the viability of a destination's tourism industry. I hope you never have to read that countdown.

Part I | OVERVIEW

1 | DEFINING TOURISM DESTINATIONS IN CRISIS

BASIC DEFINITIONS

The marketability of individual destinations and global tourism is vulnerable to sudden changes in market perceptions. Acts of man or nature can transform the reputation, desirability and marketability of the most popular tourism destinations overnight. The 1991 Gulf War involved a United States-led 30-nation coalition of forces against Iraq. The attacks on New York City and Washington DC on September 11, 2001, in which hijacked Boeing 767 and 757 commercial aircraft were engaged as flying missiles which blew up the World Trade Center in New York City and part of the Pentagon in Washington DC, massively disrupted global tourism. The 2001 attacks generated world-wide panic, compromising the security of commercial aircraft and global tourism safety with specific focus on the United States, Europe, Central Asia and the Middle East. Many cases outlined in this study demonstrate that a crisis in one country has a ripple effect on neighbouring destinations.

For the sake of clarification, a destination may be defined as a country, state, region, city or town which is marketed or markets itself as a place for tourists to visit. In most cases referred to in this book, countries will be the primary focus of attention.

For most international travellers, tourism is a discretionary act. Many countries have invested heavily in tourism and have acquired a high level of economic dependence on inbound tourism. Events which compromise the viability of a destination may result in considerable economic disruption to the country, state or region. For individuals, this situation could result in loss of income, unemployment and poverty. However, few tourists will consider these implications in determining their choice of destination. Their prime concern is to travel to a destination satisfying their own desires with a minimum of complications or threats to their safety and well-being.

Global tourism crises, including those mentioned above, are evidence that destination crisis marketing can no longer be treated as a problem confined to a few specific destinations; it is now a global issue. Since September 11, destination crisis marketing has been moved beyond the cloisters of academia to become a critical economic, political and social priority for many nations to which tourism is a significant industry.

A book dealing with destination crisis requires a contextually appropriate working definition of the term 'crisis'. Bill Faulkner and Roslyn Russell in their discussion of turbulence, chaos and complexity, refer to crisis and disaster. They mention that the common definition of crisis is 'an action or failure to act that interferes with the organisation's ongoing functions and the attainment of its objectives, viability, or survival . . . with detrimental effects as perceived by employees, clients or constituents'. This definition is more appropriate to managerial failure than the crises caused by external factors.[1] Certainly there are no shortages of travel industry crises resulting from mismanagement. However, the crises examined and analysed in this volume have all arisen due to events beyond the direct control of destination authorities. Faulkner and Russell's second definition of a disaster is more applicable to the cases discussed in this book. They define a disaster as a situation in which 'a tourism destination is confronted with sudden, unpredictable, catastrophic changes over which it has little control'.

To modify Faulkner and Russell's definition and relate it to the crises examined in this study the author defines a destination crisis in the following terms: 'A crisis is a situation requiring radical management action in response to events beyond the internal control of the organisation, necessitating urgent adaptation of marketing and operational practices to restore the confidence of employees, associated enterprises and consumers in the viability of the destination.'

The threat of terrorism is understandably a major issue in destination choice. The popularity and desirability of specific destinations is influenced by many factors. These include economic factors such as affordability, special events such as Olympic Games or World Expos and the vagaries of fads and fashions. A wide range of perceptions governs the desirability and appeal of a destination to the potential traveller. Seyhmus Baloglu and Ken W. McCleary define the forces which influence destination image formation as shown in Figure 1.1.[2]

Figure 1.1: Forces which influence destination image development

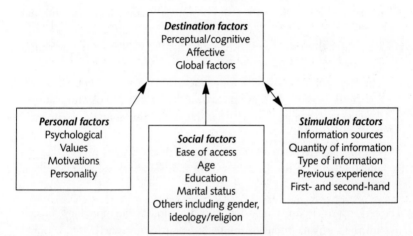

Figure 1.2: Path modules of determination of destination image

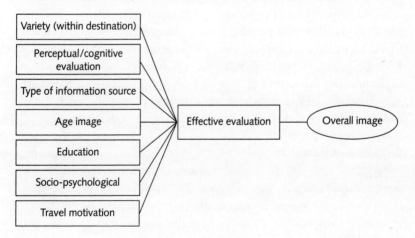

TRAVEL MOTIVATION

A major determinant in a traveller's decision to visit a destination is the perception of safety and security. Specific events or a series of events may undermine these perceptions of a destination. This book will examine five specific event typologies which undermine the safety and security image of tourist destinations and result in a destination crisis. These are:

- international war or conflict and prolonged manifestations of internal conflict;
- a specific act or acts of terrorism, especially those directed at or affecting tourists;
- a major criminal act or crime wave, especially when tourists are targeted;
- a natural disaster, such as an earthquake, storm or volcano, causing damage to urban areas or the natural environment and consequently impacting on the tourism infrastructure;
- health concerns related to epidemics and diseases; these may be diseases which impact on humans directly or diseases affecting animals, which limit access to tourist attractions.

These events or circumstances, individually or in combination, have a negative impact on perceptions of the safety, security or desirability of tourist destinations. Each circumstance poses challenges to tourism authorities and the tourism industry to implement appropriate strategies to restore the image of affected destinations. Certainly, those factors do not represent the totality of issues which can impact negatively on destination image; however, the core issue in this book involves analysing how a destination and its tourism industry conduct a marketing campaign to restore its image and recover its market from the damage caused by these events. A number of case studies are used to demonstrate that a properly focused marketing campaign plays a major role in restoring a destination's image and consumer perceptions of it. *Restoration marketing* is an integral element in the overall recovery of the destination.

Contingency management is discussed as a major component of tourism destination marketing. The specific contingencies examined—war, terrorism, crime waves, epidemic and natural disasters—have devastating impacts on any community, region, state or nation. This book focuses on their repercussions on eleven destinations around the world. Any destination is potentially vulnerable to one or more of the above threats to destination safety and market perception; consequently, it is imperative for all destination authorities to prepare and develop contingency plans to respond to varying levels of threats.

CASE STUDIES

Each of the eleven cases will focus on specific events and the responses of the tourism industries and local tourism authorities to them. The cases include:

- New York and global—the challenge to restore New York and the United States as a tourism destination following the September 11 terrorist attack and the subsequent global ramifications;
- Egypt—restoring confidence after terrorism directed at tourists in 1992–97;
- Israel—the marketing response to the conflict generated between Israel and the Palestinian Authority following the breakdown of the peace process since September 2000;
- Sri Lanka—marketing a destination during a civil war;
- Fiji—Fiji's response to the coup of 1987 and the George Speight rebellion of 2000;
- Turkey—Turkish tourism recovery after the 1999 Izmit earthquake;
- United Kingdom—response to the foot-and-mouth disease outbreak of 2001;
- South Africa—marketing a destination during the post-Apartheid crime wave;
- Australia—Tasmania's response to the Port Arthur massacre of 1996;
- Croatia—the Croatian tourism industry's recovery after the war with Serbia, 1992–96;
- the Philippines—restoring tourism after natural disasters, civil war and political instability during the 1990s.

While each case contains unique characteristics, there are a number of common elements which apply to these case studies. The above events resulted in a significant downturn in tourism numbers to the destination and created a climate of fear and concern about its overall safety and viability. In all cases, a marketing strategy was required to restore confidence in the destination. The duration of these strategies was subject to significant variations.

In the case of war and natural disaster, considerable time was involved in repairing physical damage to the infrastructure of the destination as a prerequisite to starting a marketing campaign.

It is an erroneous assumption that a restoration and recovery marketing campaign can be implemented only when the crisis is deemed to be over. In the case of Britain, Sri Lanka and Israel, marketing of the destinations continued during Britain's foot-and-mouth disease problems of 2001; the political conflict between Israel and the Palestinians since September 2000 (unresolved at the time of writing) and Sri Lanka's long-term civil war are examples of ongoing crises where marketing has been necessary. Some of these marketing strategies may be broadly defined as 'damage control'. Some of these marketing programs have involved an aggressive campaign to lure tourists by either highlighting alternative images to those disseminated by the mass media, or through the method of 'isolation'—that is, promoting parts of the destination unaffected by the existing problem. In all cases, marketing strategies were implemented to address the specific problems encountered and create public awareness of actions undertaken to redress them. In all case studies, a media and public relations campaign was directed at the travel industry with emphasis on prioritising promotions directed at key source markets. In the majority of cases examined, the restoration of tourism was regarded as a significant element in the overall economic, social and political recovery of the destinations concerned.

The field of destination recovery and restoration is an under-researched discipline within tourism studies and management practice. Yet it is a critically important element of tourism planning. The 'what if' or contingency planning aspect of tourism, especially destination management, has been a long-standing weak link in tourism destination management and marketing. By comparison, international airlines have well-established contingency measures in place in the event of crashes. However regrettable, aircraft sometimes crash, cruise ships sink and hotels can be destroyed by natural disasters or through the deliberate or accidental actions of human beings. The calmest, most orderly and tranquil locales can quickly descend into chaos through an act of nature, criminality, war or terrorism. A dramatic example of an aberrant, one-off crisis occurred in Tasmania, Australia at the historical site of Port Arthur in April 1996 when (according to the official version)[3] a young man armed with an automatic rifle killed 35 people, many of whom were interstate and overseas tourists. This event instantly plunged the Tasmanian tourism industry into crisis and engendered a marketing recovery process which is considered a role model for destinaton marketing management of a recovery program following a single-event crisis.

The case studies include countries as diverse as Israel and Sri Lanka, both of which have experienced repeated and prolonged episodes of war and inter-communal acts of terrorism. Although tourists have rarely been specific targets of terrorism in Israel, Israeli tourism authorities and marketers have endured a constant struggle to counter a widely held perception that Israel is a dangerous destination for tourists. Although most political violence has been confined to specific regions, Israel presents an especially interesting marketing case study of perception management. There are many parallels between the Israeli experience and that of Sri Lanka, where conflict between the government and Tamil separatists has largely been confined to the north-east of the country. Unlike the Israel situation, Tamil terrorists have occasionally targeted tourists within the broader context of their civil war tactics.

Political terrorism in Egypt specifically targeted tourism as a core strategy to undermine the national economy and the political system. Repeated acts of terrorism directed at tourists during the 1990s culminated in the Luxor massacre of November 1997. International tourism is the dominant source of foreign currency income for Egypt, so a slump in inbound tourism directly impacts on the Egyptian economy. Following episodes of terrorism, the Egyptian government, in association with the Egyptian Tourist Authority, embarked upon an intensive campaign to restore confidence in destination Egypt. The strategy incorporated two significant prongs: the correction of security lapses that made tourists a soft target for terrorism in Egypt; and a major PR and marketing campaign to incentivise tourism and restore inter-national confidence in Egypt as a major destination.

Croatia represents a notable example of a country which sought to inte-grate tourism within a national recovery strategy following prolonged warfare. Large regions of Croatia were off limits for international tourists during four years of conflict with neighbouring Serbia. In the Croatian case, the restora-tion of the tourism industry was integrated within a state-driven policy of economic recovery and was a major factor in attracting foreign investment and foreign currency. The signing of the Dayton Agreement in December 1995 was far more effective in restoring traveller confidence in Croatia than any specific marketing campaign.

In 1987 and 2000, Fiji experienced two episodes of political instability, which heavily impacted on its economically vital tourism industry. The 1987 coup, led by Sitiveni Rabuka, which overthrew an elected multiracial government, and George Speight's abortive attempt in 2000 to overthrow and take hostage the elected multiracial government, had a severe impact on the Fijian tourism industry. During the events and in their immediate *denouement*, the Fijian Ministry of Tourism and its marketing arm, the Fiji Visitors Bureau, mounted carefully planned campaigns in association with airlines and tour operators to restore tourism confidence in Fiji's tourism industry. During both crises, the Australian and New Zealand governments actively discouraged their citizens from visiting Fiji, which impacted heavily upon Fiji's two largest tourism source markets.

The Fijian case highlights the significance of government tourism advisories as a factor in shaping tourism perceptions of specific destinations. Aside from advisories that directly prohibit citizens from visiting a specific country or region, negative advisories about the safety or advisability of visiting a destination influence tour operators, travel insurance providers and travellers in their respective decisions to promote, provide insurance cover or visit a destination.

South African tourism has suffered significant image problems as a result of street crime in South Africa's major cities. However, the South African situation has not stopped tourism growth, with South Africa's tourism marketing authorities managing the impact of crime as a hazard to tourists rather than as a crisis.

There are certain regions of the world which, due to their climate, geographical and geological locations, are prone to specific forms of natural disasters. The tropics are in the path of hurricanes, typhoons and cyclones; parts of Turkey are vulnerable to earthquakes; San Francisco and Los Angeles in the United States, Tokyo and Kobe in Japan and Wellington in New Zealand are built on top of geological time bombs on the major fault lines of the earth's crust; and Naples in Italy is one of many cities in the world located in close proximity to active or potentially active volcanoes. Most technologically advanced countries and regions have well-established contingency plans for responding to natural disasters. However, many less-developed countries are under-prepared for major natural disasters and cannot cope, especially if the occurrence is located far from major urban and regional centres. There are also cases where the scale of a natural disaster is so vast that it is beyond established emergency contingencies. Intentionally, or unintentionally, media coverage often magnifies the extent of the impact of destruction within the actual disaster zone and turns it into a national problem. Two case studies dealing with the problem of marketing destinations in the wake of a natural disaster are examined here. The exceptional tourism recovery achieved by Turkey following the 1999 Izmit earthquake was an outstanding example of combining international sympathy for the plight of the victims with an effective PR campaign. This strategy clearly communicated the distinction between the damage wrought within the earthquake zone and Turkey's tourism infrastructure, which remained largely intact and unaffected by the disaster.

The Philippines has been beset by three types of crisis: terrorism, political instability and natural disaster. The 1991 eruption of Mt Pinatubo demonstrated that the Philippine government was able to effectively employ disaster-management methods to ensure the orderly evacuation of thousands of people prior to the eruption. The Philippine tourist authorities also managed this natural cataclysm in a manner which minimised the disruption to tourism growth during the period 1991–97, incorporating the Mt Pinatubo experience into the formulation of the country's tourism master plan.

Epidemic and disease are among the least researched areas of tourism crisis management. Yet this subject has for many years been an issue affecting the decisions of tourists to either visit or avoid specific destinations. Outbreaks of typhoid, cholera and other infectious diseases have always been a factor determining inoculation policy and entrance requirements for most countries in the world. The recent outbreak of the HIV virus has had a major impact on tourist participation in what is loosely described as the 'sex tourism' industry. The high incidence of HIV in Africa and Southeast Asia has had a significant impact on social policy in these countries and also influenced the nature of tourism attractions in them. The case study examined in this book does not, however, relate to human epidemics.

The blanket media coverage accompanying the outbreak of foot-and-mouth disease in the United Kingdom during the first half of 2001 impacted severely on the British agricultural sector and inflicted significant harm on the British tourism industry. The closure of farms and rural regions severely damaged the rural sector of Britain's tourism infrastructure, a sector which had been assiduously marketed for many years. The intensity and extent of media coverage generated an image of Britain as a country ravaged by this disease and severely compromised its overall image as a tourism destination.

The British Tourist Authority's approach to the foot-and-mouth epidemic crisis is particularly interesting, as it is one of the world's first cases in which the Internet played a major role in the management of destination marketing during and after a tourism crisis.

THE MEDIA AND DESTINATION CRISIS

A significant element in this study is an examination of the role of the international media in both publicising the actual crisis and in reporting (and in some cases ignoring) recovery and restoration programs. Globalisation of the media and their enhanced ability to report events as they occur give rise to a mixture of benefits and problems for tourist authorities. The international media appear to have a penchant for focusing upon a number of key elements which determine the newsworthiness of an issue. Favoured items tend to be defined under the following categories:[4]

- crime;
- crisis;
- conflict;
- conquest;
- corruption;
- catharsis;
- cataclysm;
- rescue;
- scandal;
- triumph over adversity.

Any content analysis study of media news reporting will ascertain that these elements dominate lead stories in print and electronic media. They tend to focus on what is broadly described as 'bad news'. The ingredient of magnification—the degree to which any of the above elements is exaggerated—determines whether the publication, television, radio program or website is deemed to be 'responsible' or sensationalistic. Issues such as editorial and political bias, in addition to accessibility of sources, will have a large bearing on the frequency, extent and nature of coverage.

Democratic countries committed to the broad concept of freedom of the press are open to uncontrolled reportage of variable accuracy. A crisis has a higher probability of being subject to media coverage than the recovery and restoration stages. The role of effective public relations management is critical for tourist authorities in democratic countries to ensure that recovery and restoration efforts are reported at all, let alone in proportion to the coverage of the actual crisis. Non-democratic countries impose far more control over media coverage; consequently, reporting of the crisis and the recovery process is often stage-managed by governments. Media relations remains one of the most critical elements in crisis management.

The supervision of media coverage of both the crisis and the crisis management process is a core issue for tourism authorities and tour operators. The establishment and maintenance of effective media relations is a critical function of destination tourist authorities. Media relations extend beyond developing a network of contacts with local media and usually require the development of global contacts. The November 1997 Luxor massacre, Israeli–Palestinian political violence and the 2001 foot-and-mouth disease crisis in the United Kingdom were all subject to worldwide attention and scrutiny. When foreign tourists are victims or are indirectly affected by a particular crisis, they are often subject to media attention in their home country. Conversely, the international pervasiveness of American, British and German global news networks such as CNN, BBC and Deutsche Welle meant that many local issues in those countries become globally disseminated.

It is arguable that an incident on the scale of the New York/Washington DC attacks of September 11, 2001 would have attracted extensive coverage had they occurred in any large city elsewhere in the world. However, their occurrence in the United States and the targeting of the military and financial symbols of American power and prestige guaranteed blanket worldwide media coverage. The instantaneous nature of news reporting, especially via the electronic media, requires that tourist authorities immediately implement their contingency plan, deploy their crisis management team and initiate communication with the media. Failure to prepare for a crisis scenario places the tourist authority consistently on the defensive when responding to reporters' questions at media press conferences. Tourist authorities must exercise maximum control during interviews and initiate the agenda of the media's coverage of the crisis.

Once a strong cooperative relationship is developed with the relevant media, it is also likely that the media will seek to cover the tourist authorities' management of the actual crisis and post-crisis developments. The Tasmanian government's sensitive and effective media management of the

Port Arthur massacre, coupled with an effective post-crisis tourism marketing program, resulted in Tasmania experiencing a relatively rapid tourism recovery following the Port Arthur massacre in 1996. The Egyptian Ministry of Tourism, the Fiji Visitors Bureau, the Turkish Ministry of Tourism and the British Tourist Authority all include examples of effective media management of specific recent crises which impacted on their respective tourist industries followed by relatively swift recoveries.

ALLIANCES BETWEEN TOURISM AUTHORITIES AND THE PRIVATE SECTOR

An integral part of effective marketing management of crises and their restoration phases is for tourist authorities to establish and maintain effective alliances with those private and government organisations sharing common vested interests. Airlines, hoteliers, resorts, museums, attractions and wholesale tour operators all depend on the successful selling and marketing of destinations which form all or part of their programs. In times of crisis, the effectiveness of these working relationships is often put to the test. It is a common element of a post-crisis recovery process for one or all of these organisations to engage in intensive marketing programs featuring temporary discounts or incentives as tactics in the recovery strategy. Tourist authorities and national carriers often subsidise blitz-marketing campaigns by the private sector. A tourist crisis in one destination often has regional implications. Cooperative marketing programs can potentially benefit neighbouring destinations.

Many of the case studies in this work demonstrate the significance of public–private sector alliances in managing marketing campaigns during the crisis period and in the recovery and restoration phases. One of the most important elements of this alliance is between national tourism authorities and flag carrier airlines. In many countries, the airline industry is privatised and some countries, including Britain, the United States and Australia, have more than one major international/domestic carrier. Nevertheless, in times of crisis either the flag carrier or the major carriers will band together to market the destination out of crisis. EgyptAir played a major role in Egypt's market recovery following the Luxor massacre in 1997. In the United States, Delta Airlines was one of a number of US carriers which encouraged travellers to visit New York City after the September 11 attack, through its offer to supply thousands of free tickets to Americans travelling to New York.

Airlines play a vital role in facilitating the travel of media and travel industry professionals making familiarisation visits. During a crisis period, the importance of familiarisation trips is greatly magnified. The travel industry is vital to any successful *push marketing* (directed at retailers) campaigns. Airlines traditionally work with tourist authorities in carrying travel journalists. The media are central to a successful *pull marketing* campaign (marketing directed at consumers). The Fiji Visitors Bureau provides a model of a highly effective alliance with the national carrier Air Pacific and major resorts in hosting large delegations of travel agents and travel writers after the 2000 coup.

CONCLUDING REMARKS

This book focuses on restoration and recovery of destinations in the field of tourism marketing. The author readily acknowledges that the repair of infrastructure, rebuilding, medical rehabilitation and financing are all necessary elements of the recovery process and constitute a field of study in their own right.

Many people readily dismiss marketing as the equivalent of 'spin-doctoring'—that is, adopting a selective approach to the truth. A successful recovery and restoration program should be conducted ethically. Consumers and travel professionals demand a truthful assessment of a crisis situation; failure by destination authorities to deliver may provide short-term gains, but in the longer term false reporting of a situation is easily exposed, calling into question the veracity of the tourist authority and reflecting negatively on the destination.

The British Tourist Authority (BTA)'s handling of the foot-and-mouth disease problem is an example in which open and honest management of marketing information has resulted in 'short-term pain for long-term gain'. During the foot-and-mouth crisis, the BTA's website informed travellers of event cancellations and the closure of parks, reserves, attractions, regions and accommodation. The website was frequently updated. While this information was clearly harmful to those places or events affected, the BTA information enabled travel agents and travellers to plan their visit to Britain in real time. As the epidemic waned, demand for travel to Britain quickly recovered and the BTA won the respect of many consumers and travel industry professionals for its reliable information.

It is often assumed that a crisis or complaint is something to dread. In fact, much good can come from a crisis. At its most base, the scene of a battle, crime or natural disaster often becomes a tourist attraction. In many parts of the world, scenes of natural disaster, battlefields and crime scenes have become tourist attractions. For example, the Alma Tunnel in Paris where Princess Diana died in 1997 became a focal point for tourists. The management of a crisis will (for unintended reasons) sometimes push a little-known destination into public prominence. Prior to Lebanon's civil wars and foreign invasions in the period 1975–95, many visitors regarded Beirut as the 'Paris of the Middle East'. Beirut has now undergone a gradual transformation, restoring its former ambience. The Croatian city of Dubrovnik suffered severe damage during the Croatian–Serbian war of 1991–95, but has since been fully restored and is once more Croatia's leading tourist attraction.

Lessons learned from a crisis should be incorporated into the day-to-day marketing of a destination. All case studies focus on the work of national/state or regional tourism authorities in the direction or coordination of crisis management. In many cases, the national, state or regional authorities work in conjunction with the private sector. In some instances, major operators and, in others, consultancy firms are contracted to provide independent management and marketing advice. There are specific cases in which the private sector plays a pre-eminent role in the restoration and recovery process. The United States is the most prominent example of this. Centralisation of decision-making and public relations is a common element in the more successful cases studies. Uniformity in the marketing approach does not necessarily apply to all source markets. The distance from the destination, together with demographic, sociological and political factors, will often determine the most effective marketing strategy applicable to each source market.

Professional marketers and marketing analysts are familiar with the concept of a SWOT analysis: Strengths; Weaknesses; Opportunities; Threats.

A SWOT analysis forms an integral part of each of the case studies examined. These crises have been managed with varying degrees of success. It is hoped that the reader may find some value in the concepts analysed and that the case studies will provide insightful illustrations of successful and unsuccessful applications of crisis management. Although the focus of this book is tourist destinations, these concepts have universal applications in the field of business and commerce.

While destination marketing during and following crises is a relatively new field of inquiry, a number of researchers have already made significant contributions in this discipline. Abraham Pizam and Yoel Mansfield are among the leaders in research relating to crime, war and terrorism.[5] In 1998, the World Tourism Organization published a *Handbook of Disaster Reduction in Tourism Areas*, which focused primarily on the management of destinations which had suffered from natural disasters.[6] Anthony Concil,[7] the Tokyo-based IATA (International Air Transport Association) Manager, Corporate Communications, has produced kits on marketing management for airlines following crashes and other incidents which might harm the airline's image. Globally, IATA's Communications division assists airlines in managing crises. Unlike airlines, much of the tourism and hospitality industry has belatedly realised that crisis management is a core rather than a peripheral aspect of its business.

This work seeks to add an extra dimension to the existing literature by analysing case studies of the major uncontrollable external factors which constitute a destination crisis. It also seeks to examine the marketing recovery and restoration of a destination, both during and following these crises. Academics including Bill Faulkner, Yoel Mansfield, Abraham Pizam, Linda K. Richter, Christian Nielsen and Michael Hall have been among pioneers of this field. They would all readily acknowledge that there is much research still to be done in this discipline.

The author wrote this book in the midst of Israel's long running destination crisis and the international crisis which arose from the New York and Washington DC attacks of September 11, 2001. The subject matter in this book presented a daily professional challenge and was far from a matter of theoretical research. The issues examined here apply to any reader involved as a teacher, student or practitioner of marketing tourism. The work is of universal relevance to all fields of marketing.

2 | MANAGING THE RECOVERY AND RESTORATION OF DESTINATIONS IN CRISIS

INTRODUCTION

The crises highlighted in this book were caused by external factors impacting negatively on the appeal and marketability of the destinations concerned. All were beyond the direct managerial control of destination authorities. The principal causes of crises covered here—war, terrorism, political/social unrest, crime waves, epidemics and natural disasters—fit the definition of a crisis as described in the opening chapter. There is no doubt that many other factors deter tourists from travelling to a destination. These include airline crashes, fatal accidents on tours, industrial relations breakdowns, chronically poor service and tourism infrastructure standards, business failures (especially of airlines, coach or tour companies, such as Pan Am in the United States, Laker Air in the United Kingdom or Ansett in Australia) which render some destinations isolated or under-serviced. The above examples represent the plurality of factors, which impact negatively on the marketability of a destination. Crises resulting from management failures, although relevant to destination crisis management, are not covered in this book.

The management of a destination crisis is greatly influenced by its duration. Most crises—especially one-off events such as the 1999 Turkish earthquake, an isolated terrorist or a criminal attack on tourists such as the 1996 Port Arthur massacre in Tasmania or the Luxor massacre in Egypt in 1997 —can be dealt with in two main stages: stage 1, involving the consolidation management of the actual crisis; and stage 2, the implementation of a post-crisis recovery program and strategy. However, longer-term crises such as the 'low–medium intensity political violence' experienced by Israel, the Philippines and Sri Lanka, can place destination authorities in a position where they are unable to indefinitely suspend destination promotion during the crisis and are forced to implement an in-crisis marketing strategy. In such cases, destination authorities are ready to implement a contingency plan to fully restore their markets after the crisis is deemed to be over. Specific such cases in this book, including Fiji's coups of 1987 and 2000, sporadic terrorist attacks against tourists in Egypt in the early 1990s and the 2001 foot-and-mouth problems in Britain, required a twin-track crisis-management policy. In these cases an in-crisis and a post-crisis marketing plan worked in tandem. The uncertainty of the crisis's duration necessitated a parallel approach.

The Philippines is a particularly challenging case because the country's tourism authorities have been obliged to maintain tourism marketing in the face of several external crisis types: simultaneous terrorism, natural disaster, crime and epidemics. The September 11 attacks against the World Trade Center in New York City and the Pentagon in Washington DC expanded from being a terrorist threat to the American tourist industry to a global tourism crisis. This particular event took the concept of crisis management in tourism far beyond issues of destination marketing to challenging the marketability of international air travel. Clearly, as the scale and complexity of a crisis escalates, more processes are required to manage its restoration and recovery.

THE DESTCON SCALE

Assessing the severity of a destination crisis

Global armed forces have rated the status of military readiness in times of threat to a nation's security on a five-point scale known as defence readiness conditions, DEFCON. The scale ascends from DEFCON 5: Normal peacetime readiness to DEFCON 1: Maximum force readiness. A comparable scale is relevant to identifying the status of a destination condition termed DESTCON.

In general terms, these are descriptions of DESTCONs:

- DESTCON 5: Normal marketing conditions;
- DESTCON 4: Normal, increased intelligence and strengthened marketing measures;

- DESTCON 3: Increase in marketing readiness, above normal readiness;
- DESTCON 2: Further increase in marketing readiness, less than maximum readiness;
- DESTCON 1: Maximum crisis marketing readiness.

The following expands on destination conditions:

- DESTCON 5: Minimal perceived threat to the marketability of the destination.
- DESTCON 4: Isolated problems within the destination: crime, low-level political disturbances, which may require avoidance of specific areas but have minimal impact on the overall marketability of the destination. South Africa is the prime example discussed in this study.
- DESTCON 3: There are major problems within identifiable regions in the destination which are well-publicised and present a credible threat to tourists in these areas. Threats include a major crime event/s, outbreaks of terrorism, a localised natural disaster or an epidemic. Major problems in a neighbouring destination may impact on the marketability of the principal destination. Cases examined matching this situation include Turkey, Fiji and Port Arthur. In most cases, these are one-off highly publicised localised crises which often deter tourists from visiting the entire destination.
- DESTCON 2: A crisis of this magnitude places large parts of the country at or under imminent threat of war or destruction from natural disaster. This stage includes widespread terrorism, natural disaster, disease or widespread disorder in which the safety of tourists is under measurable threat. Consequently, governments of source markets caution heightened levels of concern or insist on complete avoidance. Case studies analysed here which have reached this level include Croatia, Israel, the Philippines, Egypt and Sri Lanka. The problems experienced in these situations frequently have a negative impact on the marketability of neighbouring destinations.
- DESTCON 1: A crisis of this magnitude not only threatens the marketability of one destination but also has widespread global or regional repercussions on tourism. In most instances, this involves a major act of war or terrorism, which draws in many nations. The attacks on New York City and Washington DC on September 11, 2001 and their global repercussions most closely correspond to this level of crisis.

There are some instances in which a crisis situation exists according to the definitions outlined above. By muting the response, little attention is drawn to the situation as a *crisis*. South Africa's tourism authorities cannot be accused of ignoring the serious crime rate in the country; however, they treat it more as an avoidable tourist hazard than as a crisis, thus diffusing crime as a threat to the viability and appeal of the destination. Several countries have managed to treat endemic social and political problems in a similar manner. In the case studies examined here, low-level Tamil terrorism in Sri Lanka and multiple problems in the Philippines did not impinge on tourism growth during certain periods. However, when those problems crossed the invisible line from *background hazard* to crisis, tourism numbers often plummeted.

The level of media exposure influences the distinction between a tourist hazard, a crisis and even the DESTCON rating. The international media intensively cover the United States, Britain and Israel. Consequently, aberrant events are subject to intensive coverage and widespread dissemination. Terrorist attacks in Israel are routinely reported and disseminated in the international media. Conversely, there is relatively little international media attention given to terrorism in Sri Lanka unless it occurs in or near the capital, Colombo, or impacts directly on tourists and foreign nationals. Coverage is subject to the media's access to a conflict or crisis zone. Few international journalists are able to encounter terrorist groups in the Philippines, but journalists have almost unrestricted access to the flashpoints of the Israeli–Palestinian conflict. The extent of media access relates to the political system and the openness of the society. A factor contributing to the success of Egypt's tourism recovery after the 1997 Luxor massacre was the tight controls imposed by the Egyptian government and its tourism authority on media coverage and reporting. Conversely, there was far more discussion about the foot-and-mouth crisis in the United Kingdom. Whilst the British Tourist Authority was able to present an internally consistent media message during the foot-and-mouth crisis, other groups and organisations in Britain freely expressed contrary views. This was visibly evident in relation to defining suggested no-go areas for tourists.

A major factor determining the shifting status of a problem from a background hazard to a crisis impacting on international tourism is the international political impact of the issue. When terrorism in Turkey, Sri Lanka or the Philippines is restricted to an isolated localised crisis far away from major cities and tourist centres, it is largely ignored internationally. However, when terrorist attacks target foreign tourists or tourist infrastructure, then the matter becomes an international incident. If a government from a destination's strategically important source market issues a negative travel advisory, it can seriously harm inbound tourism and may attain destination crisis magnitude. During Fiji's abortive coup of 2000, travel advisories of the British, Australian and New Zealand governments calling on their citizens to defer travel to Fiji proved an effective political weapon when wielded by the governments of three of tourism-dependent Fiji's principal source markets.

The third factor which influences the management of a crisis affecting tourists is the degree to which the events are aberrant to the social norms of that society. The 1996 Port Arthur massacre in Tasmania was an incident so completely contrary to the late twentieth century Tasmanian social context that it constituted a tourism crisis. By comparison, a suicide bombing in Israel—which may have resulted in a similar number of casualties and is equally horrific—will not by itself trigger a tourism crisis for Israel, due to the fact that such events (especially since September 2000) have occurred on numerous occasions and reinforce the stereotype of Israel as a risky destination for tourists.

The preceding discussion provides a context for the destination crisis management and restoration steps outlined below. Each situation is very different, and there is no universal response to a crisis nor a contingency plan applying to every destination crisis. Each situation requires specific variations on the approaches outlined. It is hoped that the steps outlined below clearly explain the process of destination crisis marketing. They seek to take into account the various external crises impacting on tourist destinations and provide a logical series of management processes towards a restoration and recovery program.

Events which trigger a crisis are often aberrant, destructive and traumatic in the short term. Effective crisis contingency planning results in long-term benefits for destination authorities and the tourism industry. Detailed planning leads to improved infrastructure, security management, service, and more innovative and effective marketing programs. Highly trained and co-ordinated management and staff are required to implement crisis prevention policies. Well-prepared destination authorities will quickly move from crisis to recovery mode.

STEPS TO MARKETING MANAGEMENT OF A DESTINATION CRISIS

Summary

- Identify the event/problem as either a crisis or a hazard.
- Establish a crisis management team and define roles.
- Promote the destination during and after the crisis.
- Monitor recovery and analyse the crisis experience.

Step 1: Identify the event/problem as either a crisis or a hazard

The destination authority needs to ask the following questions:

- Will this event/problem be widely and negatively publicised in key source markets?
- Does it have the potential to threaten the safety or well-being of tourists?
- Were tourists directly affected?
- Have foreign governments altered or threatened negative travel advisories as a result of the event/problem?
- Have insurance companies deleted or limited coverage to the destination?
- Are airlines, shipping, rail or coach operators and tour operators considering withdrawing or limiting services and products to the destination?
- Are travel agents in source markets reducing bookings to the destination?
- Are the destination representatives overseas or interstate reporting a substantial growth of negative inquiries from the public and the travel industry? Is there substantial growth in cancellations and a reduction in forward bookings?
- Are media groups hosted by the destination grossly delaying publication, broadcast or screening of material about the destination with or without explanation?
- Is there a statistically significant (seasonally adjusted) drop in arrivals and hotel occupancy levels?
- Is there pressure within the tourism infrastructure to reduce employment levels?

- Is there a local sense of political urgency regarding the prospects of the tourism industry?
- Are tourism receipts significantly (seasonally adjusted) reduced?

If the answer to at least three of the above questions is 'yes', then the destination authorities should treat the situation as a crisis. This is not an absolute and definitive identification of a crisis; rather, the above questions constitute a representative list of key indicators.

If the answer is 'yes' to less than three of the questions, the situation should be treated as a hazard and the best means to manage hazards is with honesty and discretion. South Africa has a serious crime rate, acknowledged even in its own tourism promotional literature. While South African tourism authorities advise prospective travellers on how to minimise their exposure to crime, the warnings are given in conjunction with a broader range of travel advice. It is a matter rarely discussed in tourism promotion or advertising and, although subject to occasional media coverage, it is normally referred to within a broader context of destination coverage. Some foreign governments mention crime in South Africa in their advisories, but it is not regarded as a reason to avoid or defer travel. Hazard management is not a question of evading a problem, but placing it within an appropriate perspective.

Step 2: Establish a crisis management team

There are a number of elements involved in managing a destination crisis. At the management level (subject to the size of the organisation), there may be a requirement for several teams to manage the crisis. The overall responsibility for crisis management in any destination authority rests with the chief executive officer (CEO) or an appointed crisis manger, who will normally establish global guidelines. In the cases of destination authorities with representatives either within the country or in overseas source markets, there may be regional or national factors which require variations from the head office approach. The major elements, especially from a marketing perspective, include:

- media and public relations;
- relations with the travel industry in source markets;

- operations and situation assessment and dissemination focusing on internal national/international staff and the industry within the destination;
- destination response coordination with the local tourism and hospitality industry;
- liaison with local/regional and national government authorities;
- implementation of alliances with tour operators, airlines, shipping lines and/or land transport providers which service the destination.

Each team requires a single key spokesperson or point of contact, plus backup contact (where possible). In dealing with outside organisations, every effort has to be made to follow a consistent line. Even the most democratic organisations may internally debate the organisational position adopted during the crisis, but once determined it is important that recipients of the message perceive it to be from a united organisation.

Having established the crisis management team, it is important to determine the key roles of these teams.

Media and public relations
In the heat of a crisis it is a natural emotional inclination of destination authorities to treat the media as adversaries. As discussed in Chapter 1, a crisis is a media staple followed closely by corruption and official dishonesty. It is essential to be as honest and open with the media as circumstances permit. This does not imply that it is appropriate to be untruthful, but in circumstances where national or tourist security may be compromised, it is appropriate to be selective about what is revealed to the media. The media representatives of key source markets will primarily be concerned about the impact of a destination crisis on people from their home audience. Typically, if 50 tourists are killed in a terrorist attack in the Middle East, the *New York Times* will focus on victims from New York City, the United States and then other countries in that order.

Managing media coverage requires preparation to deal with the frequently localised concerns of media outlets. There are several common questions with which media managers should be familiar:

- What is being done to assist victims?
- What is the extent of the damage/casualties?
- What is being done to reduce, minimise or eliminate future risks?

- What can the government/destination authorities do to guarantee safety?
- Why did this event occur in the first place?
- Who is to blame?
- How long will the crisis last?

Destination authorities are rarely able to answer all of these questions, but it is important not to be perceived as evasive, glib or unhelpful. If the media contact cannot answer certain questions, then that person should direct the media to people or authorities who are qualified to do so. In an interview or press conference situation, it is a paramount requirement to control the interview and in some circumstances a prepared statement may be more useful than fielding questions. In crisis situations, tourism authorities work in conjunction with other government departments. Tourism authorities should have specific answers to the first four questions listed above. In the twenty-first century, it is increasingly essential to have the information readily available on a website and also in a format in which visual images and text can be rapidly communicated by email.

The website has begun to replace the printed press kit as a preferred tool of media communication and public relations, especially for instant news reports. In cases such as questions relating to blame and the original cause of a crisis, it may be more appropriate for authorities unrelated to tourism to deal with these issues. In virtually all crises discussed here, it is crucial to have a principal media spokesperson and contact point. The content should then be transmitted to the destination's interstate or overseas representatives and emulated as closely as possible.

In anticipating key questions, it is essential to maintain a series of simple bullet points. The electronic media are especially harsh on verbosity and the mastery of '30-second grabs' is a major responsibility for media managers. Press releases should be concise and limited to one page. Wherever possible, anticipate questions and be ready with answers. Preparedness to provide the media with relevant information makes a reporter's life easier and in most cases will engender an atmosphere conducive to cooperation between the destination authority and the media. Cooperation is then likely to extend to media coverage of the restoration and recovery process.

It is always worthwhile for the media to view both the crisis and the restoration and recovery process at first hand. A fine line can be drawn between familiarisation visits being perceived as an honest inspection or a staged PR exercise. Interviews with tourists from the source markets, local officials and local tourist and hospitality industry professionals should be included. The key message destination authorities seek to communicate is that, while a crisis has occurred, positive steps are being taken to return to normality.

At all stages, it is important to recognise the critical role the media play in shaping public attitudes to tourism destinations. Reporters should be treated with due respect and courtesy. Destination authorities should control the parameters of discourse with media professionals, thus ensuring that the media have as much access to information as possible.

The duration of a crisis is a key issue for media management. In most cases, the crisis is a short-term affair involving a brief consolidation phase followed by a recovery phase. In a short-term crisis, destination authorities can readily prepare the media for a recovery phase. When a crisis extends into months, media management becomes an entirely different proposition. A common crisis management practice is to isolate the problem area from the rest of the destination and point to the distinction between a 'trouble spot' and the remainder of the destination. In extreme cases such as Croatia's four-year war with the Yugoslav Federation (1992–1996) and Israel's conflict with the Palestinian Authority since September 2000, isolation strategies are more difficult to employ. Although violence may predominate in specific areas, random and unpredictable outbreaks can occur anywhere. In such instances, the issue of secure forms of tourism to these destinations needs to be stressed. There are instances where destination authorities adopt an approach in which they publicly refuse to acknowledge that a crisis situation exists and enter a phase of denial. This approach undermines the credibility of the destination authority for the media, but it sometimes works for the consumer market.

Relations with the travel industry in source markets

Successful marketing of tourism requires maintaining a balance between pull marketing (appealing direct to consumers) and push marketing (appealing to those who sell travel in a manner that will encourage them to sell a specific destination). Travel professionals, in common with the public are influenced in their perceptions of destinations by media coverage and this can result in travel consultants advising their clients on the merits of a destination based on their media-sourced impressions. Destination authorities frequently need to treat the travel industry in a similar fashion to the media. A high priority is to assist industry professionals to be more aware of the situation in destinations than their consumers. While informative and updated websites, industry updates and seminars are all valuable aids to communicating the situation in a destination in crisis, there is nothing more powerful than personal experience. Destination authorities should seek to identify those members of the travel industry in their source markets who are well respected by their colleagues and invite them to visit and inspect the destination, circumstances permitting. An independent testimonial carries far more *gravitas* than the spokesperson of a destination authority.

The Turkish Ministry of Tourism achieved a remarkable and rapid recovery of tourism following the 1999 earthquake. A factor enhancing this recovery was the policy of hosting large groups of travel industry professionals from most major source markets to witness the devastation of the earthquake and the fact that most tourist attractions were untouched. The Turks adopted a similar program with the media, and the message that Turkey was safe for tourists to visit was quickly disseminated in both the pull and push dimensions of the tourism market. Travel retailers and wholesalers who are confident and knowledgable about a destination are able to allay consumer concerns and sell the destination.

It is also valuable in a crisis for destination authority representatives to maintain regular briefings with the local travel industry to keep them up to date with the crisis and the recovery and restorative measures undertaken. Involving industry colleagues recently returned from the destination in providing testimonials is a most valuable enhancement during these briefings.

Operations and situation assessments with internal staff briefings
There are occasions during which destination authorities effectively disseminate information about a crisis to the market, but in so doing ignore the people closest to the crisis—their own staff. The effective management of a crisis is enhanced when staff and representatives of the destination authority are fully appraised of the operational and marketing implications of their own crisis management. They need to be aware of the line adopted in dealing with the media, foreign governments and the tourism industry. Internal communications and effective internal briefing are vital elements of successful crisis management. Staff must be fully briefed on the situation and on the roles of their closest colleagues, enabling them to alternate between roles when necessary.

It is a common practice for destination authorities to outsource consultancy services to assist in crisis management. Most countries examined utilised such services. This does not suggest that the destination authorities lack the internal expertise to fulfil this role, but rather it is prudent to obtain the expertise available from dispassionate professional outsiders able to draw on their company's experience in managing international tourism and other business crises. Expert consultants provide independent assessments of the extent to which the destination authority is managing the various facets of its crisis and recovery programs, free from the internal culture and politics of the organisation.

There is great value in many crisis situations for overseas or interstate representatives of the destination authority meeting together in the destination to exchange ideas and personally experience the impact of the crisis, recovery and restoration program. As discussed earlier, the most detailed and vivid written or audio-visual briefings are no substitute for first-hand experience. External representatives are also able to apply the marketing approach most relevant to their specific marketing environment.

In the United States, which abolished centralised national government tourism marketing authorities in 1996, the challenge of marketing destination USA after the New York City and Washington DC attacks of September 11 was largely in the hands of the private sector and was coordinated by the Travel Industry Association. The US case was an exception to the general rule of destination crisis management coordinated by centralised government-controlled destination authorities. Despite September 11, destination marketing of the United States remains the most pluralistic in the world. Consequently, maintaining a coordinated approach is a major challenge in establishing common terms of reference when marketing the United States globally.

Destination response coordination with the local tourism industry
A key measure of successful destination crisis management is the degree to which the various elements of the destination's tourism industry cooperate to manage the crisis and the subsequent recovery process.

This involves accommodation and transportation providers, tour operators, resorts and attractions, restaurants and food outlets, as well as regional and local tourist authorities. During a crisis there may be a requirement to transport and accommodate tourists from a crisis zone to a 'safe' zone at short notice and in a manner that minimises cost and inconvenience to the tourists. During the recovery phase, it is a common practice to offer reduced-price holidays or value-added special offers as incentives for tourists to return to a destination or former crisis zone. Destination authorities may need to subsidise these incentives. In the case of Fiji, the Fijian tourism industry formed an umbrella association called TAG (Tourism Action Group) to coordinate marketing and pricing policies of hotels, attractions, resorts, airlines and car rental firms during the recovery phases following the coups of 1987 and 2000. The Fijian case was an example of highly centralised and coordinated action on the part of both the government and the private sector of the tourism industry, to stimulate a value-added and price-driven recovery.

A less centralised, but nevertheless high, level of coordination existed within the British tourism industry during its recovery following the foot-and-mouth crisis in 2001. Following September 11, New York City's tourist authority was able to elicit massive support from airlines, hotels and attractions to encourage tourists to return to New York. However, the recovery process for the US tourism industry has varied throughout the country. While the Tourism Industry Association of America and Visit USA organisations have marketed destination USA energetically throughout key source markets overall, private sector coordination has been uneven.

Israel has experienced a long-term tourism crisis since September 2000. The Israel Ministry of Tourism closely coordinated marketing activities with the national carrier El Al Airlines. Conversely, Israeli hotels have adopted varying approaches to tourism pricing. Some have increased prices to compensate for lack of patronage, while others have reduced prices to attract patronage. The lack of consistency confuses consumers and travel professionals alike.

After the November 1997 Luxor massacre, the Egyptian Tourist Authority, EgyptAir, the local tourism and hospitality industry conducted a professionally coordinated campaign to stimulate recovery.

A crisis does not require the inhibition of private sector competition within the tourism industry. Although cooperation must be increased, a recovery phase tends to be more rapid and successful if the destination authorities and the tourism industry are seen to be working in concert rather than at cross-purposes. Fiji, Egypt, Turkey, Croatia and Tasmania exemplified highly coordinated and very rapid post-crisis recovery phases.

Liaison with local and regional tourism authorities and foreign governments

In most cases, a tourism crisis will affect an entire country. However, the epicentre of the crisis will be the most gravely affected. The Port Arthur massacre in the Australian state of Tasmania had a minimal impact on tourism to Australia as a country and a limited impact on Tasmania, but the tragedy's impact on the Port Arthur region was quite profound.

At the opposite end of the scale, the attacks on New York City and Washington DC impacted heavily on the two cities, especially New York, with a huge impact on tourism to the United States. The ensuing conflict in Afghanistan had a profound global impact on all facets of the tourism industry.

Destination authorities at the national level need to be supportive of the local and regional tourist authorities most directly affected by a crisis. Support may be in the form of direct grants or marketing subsidies, giving the region a higher marketing profile in advertising and marketing campaigns. The destination authorities should encourage a broader industry focus on an affected locality or region. In New York City, Delta Airlines provided 10 000 free seats to passengers from all over the United States to visit New York City. Global tour operator Insight Vacations, in conjunction with EgyptAir, value-added a one-week package in Egypt, including a tour of Luxor for the equivalent of US$1 in association with its European product as part of Egypt's recovery program following the 1997 Luxor massacre.

Regular liaison between national, local and regional tourism authorities is vital during a crisis. In Britain, rural tourism operators and regional bodies criticised the British Tourist Authority during the foot-and-mouth crisis. They felt alienated by what they claimed was the BTA's abandonment of rural Britain in favour of promoting urban attractions during the crisis. The Croatian Ministry of Tourism sought to subsidise the marketing programs of less-visited areas of the country during its postwar recovery phase from 1996.

Government advisories and travel insurance

A critical and often neglected area of crisis management is the establishment and maintenance of an ongoing liaison between destination authority representatives and foreign ministries in the governments of their source markets. A destination's image and tourist accessibility can be severely damaged by government advisories which caution citizens to avoid or defer travel to a destination or describe a multitude of threats which deter travellers from considering this destination. The primary significance of travel advisories is that travel insurance coverage for that destination is based on the wording of the advisory, which greatly influences the marketability and saleability of a destination.

A destination authority has little direct influence over another country's travel advisories, but they can adopt a consultative role and be treated as a credible source of information. Few nations have a diplomatic presence in every country, and foreign ministries sometimes rely on second- and third-hand advice in formulating a travel advisory. This sometimes results in serious inaccuracies. Effectively managing the delicate communication with foreign ministries requires consistency, persistence and a commitment to a long-term consultative relationship.

During a crisis, many destinations subject to a negative government advisory, especially from a strategically or commercially important source, react with anger and seek to overtly impose pressure or overturn the advisory. Confrontational tactics are rarely, if ever, successful. No government is prepared to defer to foreign pressures on matters relating to the perceived security of its citizens.

Alliances with tour operators, airlines and hospitality industry representatives servicing the destination in source markets

One of the most important tasks destination marketers undertake as an ongoing concern is the establishment, development and maintenance of business alliances with tour operators, travel agents, wholesalers, airlines, hoteliers, car rental firms and other principals which service, promote or sell the destination in key source markets. Most national, state and regional tourism offices work in conjunction with these allies at all times to promote the destination to the trade and the consumer market. During a crisis situation, these allies assume a pivotal role in assisting the marketing activities of destination authorities. They are the prime movers in facilitating a recovery.

Many destination authorities provide marketing subsidies to such principals based on product specifically directed to that destination. The policy of the Israel Government Tourism Office is typical. If an operator produces a brochure in which Israel content comprises 50 per cent of the brochure, then subsidy support will be assessed on that 50 per cent of the content. During Israel's crisis since September 28, 2000, the percentage of subsidy support available to tour operators marketing Israel has increased. Similar practices are common among national tourist authorities. Most destination authorities ensure that their allies are regularly briefed on the situation during a crisis. Where possible, briefing visits are offered to the management of key allied organisations, providing them with necessary first-hand knowledge.

The allied organisations play a critical role in transmitting information provided by the destination authorities to their client base. In turn, destination authorities rely on their allies to assist in hosting and facilitating familiarisation visits for media, key consumer opinion leaders and influential travel industry professionals who provide a source of credible testimonials stimulating pull and push marketing programs. Cooperative relationships between destination authorities and allied principals are based on the mutuality of self-interest. If a destination is a major source of income to the airline, operator or hotel, then it is manifestly in that company's interest to do whatever it can to boost confidence and demand in the destination during and after a crisis.

The effectiveness of the alliance between the destination authorities and their principal partners is a gauge of success or failure in restoring a destination's market following a crisis. The significance of these alliances is a common element in every case study analysed in this book. However, it is important to note that the most successful and rapid recoveries occur when there is a high level of unity of purpose and a commonality of recovery policy and tactics. In the area of media management, the role of liaison between destination authority and principal allies should be as centralised as possible.

All the elements discussed in Step 2 should be incorporated by destination authorities as integral elements of a crisis contingency plan. The crisis management team must be prepared to act immediately a crisis occurs. Delays in mobilising a crisis management campaign after the crisis has begun are detrimental to all parties with a vested interest in marketing the destination.

Step 3: Promoting the destination during and after a crisis.

The approach to the promotion of a destination during and after a crisis varies according to the duration. During short-term crises such as the August 1999 Izmit earthquake in Turkey, or the 1996 Port Arthur massacre, it is appropriate to suspend destination advertising briefly and to focus on a post-crisis marketing campaign. In both cases, the destination authorities actually redesigned their destination marketing to promote the subliminal message that the crisis had passed.

There are some cases in which the duration of a crisis situation is so lengthy that the destination authorities maintain a marketing profile despite the crisis. The underlying assumption of this approach is that the attractions of the destinations and tourism product will override the risk factors which tourists may face. Such approaches, especially when the destination refuses to acknowledge the crisis, are accompanied by ethical problems. This strategy remains and is still practised by some destinations.

In cases where the crisis is of indeterminate duration, several marketing methodologies may be employed. They include the following:

Isolation marketing

This methodology involves the separation of the trouble spot from the remainder of the destination, which is depicted as safe and attractive to visit. Israel took a further step when a specific region of the country (the Red Sea port of Eilat) was promoted as a destination in its own right. In Britain during the foot-and-mouth crisis, emphasis was placed on promoting urban and cultural attractions at the expense of rural Britain. The Turkish government, during its recovery phase after the 1999 Izmit earthquake, distinguished between the earthquake zone and the accessibility and safety of the major tourist attractions elsewhere in the country.

Segmenting the market into stalwarts, waverers and disaffected

During an extended crisis, some destination authorities will prioritise their marketing and promotional activities and budgets according to the propensity of specific market segments to visit or support the destination during challenging periods. There are three key categories. Their naming is arbitrary but easily understood.

1. *Stalwarts.* The stalwart market comprises those with a strong affinity or feeling of solidarity to the destination. During a crisis, many destination authorities seek to elicit the support of the domestic market. In the United States after September 11, 2001, the US travel industry sought to encourage American citizens to visit their own country and considerable emphasis was given to New York City. Some countries draw on specific foreign source markets with a special affinity to the destination. Israel has sought

to promote solidarity tourism from Diaspora Jews and Christian Zionists. The Philippine tourism authorities encouraged expatriates to make a home visit. VFR (Visiting Friends and Relatives) tourism has been a significant market for many destinations cited here, including Croatia, the United Kingdom and South Africa, all of which have large communities of nationals or former nationals living abroad. The expatriate population is often exhorted to visit a destination during a crisis, or as an expression of solidarity during the recovery phase. The stalwart market may be deterred due to the crisis, but if the destination is marketed effectively many will continue to visit. In most cases, such marketing will appeal to their sense of affinity while overcoming their major concerns. Clearly, this group would be subject to intense advertising and promotion during a crisis situation and the recovery phase.

2. *Waverers/fair weather friends.* In DESTCON 5 (normal) circumstances, this group would form the mainstay of the market to the destination. It comprises people who would normally visit or conduct business, and who have a broad sense of affinity with the destination short of an ideological, ethnic or spiritual commitment. The crisis situation casts a question over their decision to visit the destination at the time of the perceived crisis. This grouping is normally the first to resume travel after the crisis is resolved.

    In the event of a short-term crisis, destination authorities may wait until the crisis situation is deemed to be over and conduct an intensive marketing campaign to lure this market back by reassurances that the destination has returned to normal and offers of incentives. This group represents the prime target market in the post-crisis recovery and restoration phase. In the event of a long-term crisis, this group requires attention and assurance that the region experiencing the crisis does not necessarily compromise the safety or viability of travel to those parts of the destination which normally attract this segment. In the Croatian case study, many well-informed Europeans continued to visit Croatia's northern Adriatic resorts during the 1992–95 war because they were assured of the relative safety of this region.

3. *Disaffected or discretionary market.* Predominantly, this segment of the market chooses to see the destination as a holiday destination and will understandably be deterred by anything which may be perceived as complicating, undermining security or adding stress to their visit. Media

reporting of a crisis situation readily influences this market and until they can be convinced that the destination is trouble-free they will choose an alternative destination. This segment is the largest travel market in the world. The dramatic slump in international travel during the 1990–91 Gulf War and the last quarter of 2001 was largely based on a twin fear of air travel *per se* (especially in 2001) and the perception that a vast region of the world was a potential danger area. This did not mean that people stopped travelling. However, during both periods travellers tended to stay closer to home than usual and favour destinations perceived as far removed from any threat. These patterns were especially evident among US and Japanese travellers.

Destination authorities have a number of options in marketing to this large group of people. Ignoring this market is *not* an option. In the midst of a crisis, destination authorities need to signal to all sectors of the market that they are committed to their destination and have the confidence to promote it. The intensity of promotion during a crisis to the discretionary market may be reduced, but a visible presence should be maintained through advertising campaigns which counter negative perceptions and highlight the positive reasons to continue travel. A visible presence at consumer tourism promotional events where destination authorities can engage in dialogue with prospective travellers, coupled with utilising media coverage and positive testimonials, can help challenge negative perceptions. It is the disaffected/discretionary segment which provides the greatest potential for market growth, especially during the restoration and recovery phase.

Marketing campaigns isolate trouble spots from the overall appeal of the destination, and feature images that contradict the media's focus on the crisis. A special effort is required to instil the travel industry with confidence to sell and promote the destination.

Incentives to restore the market

Destinations which have experienced crisis need to ensure that the recovery process is as rapid as possible. A post-crisis marketing approach requires the ability to restore market confidence in the destination through positive media coverage, maintaining an informed travel industry and wide dissemination of the recovery process to the consumer market.

During the intensive phase of the recovery process, normally within three to six months of the actual or announced 'end' of the crisis, marketing incentives should be offered. These may come in the form of discounts, value-added extras, competitions with a trip to the destination as the main prize and other marketing and promotional tactics which will stimulate demand and create a sense of urgency to return to the destination. Ideally, the incentives should cover as wide a spread of tourism product as possible, including airfares, hotel accommodation, tours, attractions and restaurants. During a crisis, every aspect of the tourism industry will have shared in the downturn and the destination authority should show a commitment to encouraging all elements to benefit from the recovery phase. The most rapid market recoveries have taken place when *all* segments in the industry are seen to be acting in concert. This was effectively illustrated in both the Fijian and Turkish case studies.

Once the restoration process is advanced, incentives are gradually phased out. This process should implemented and closely monitored in accordance with the duration of the recovery process.

Maintaining an effective website

Many destination authorities now realise that an effective website is one of the most cost-effective marketing tools they have. It is an especially useful marketing aid during and after a crisis. The media are heavily reliant on websites with visuals as a source of news and feature articles on tourism. The British Tourism Authority is one of many national tourist authorities which have used websites as a means to transmit crisis management information to the media, the travel industry and a growing portion of the public. The website serves as an integrated marketing medium featuring information on sites, operators, special deals and events. The qualities of a good website are ease of access and the comprehensive and up-to-date provision of information. During a crisis and the recovery phase, the website is rapidly replacing the traditional press release as a means of updating all concerned parties.

Ensuring that opinion leaders in source markets see for themselves

During a crisis and in a post-crisis recovery phase, the most brilliant marketing campaigns and the most comprehensive websites are no substitute for first-hand independent testimonials from opinion leaders in source markets. Influential travel writers, travel-orientated television, radio programs and influential travel industry identities reporting a positive impression from eyewitness accounts of visiting the destination, especially during the restoration phase, are an important element in recovery stimulation.

Step 4: Monitoring recovery and analysing the crisis experience

Destination authorities need to carefully monitor statistical trends and the duration of both crisis and recovery process. In doing so, they should include as many factors as possible. Market research should be a continual task for destination authorities. Monitoring source market and segmentation within each provides an understanding of the market, and enhances the development of strategies to effectively target each market segment with the most appropriate message. For destinations in which tourism is a strategically and economically significant industry, effective market research and detailed statistical monitoring are vital.

During a crisis and recovery process, analysis of source markets which under- or over-performed during the crisis assists the destination authorities to determine the allocation of marketing resources to each market. Market research gauges the effectiveness of marketing campaigns on source markets and segments within those markets.

For all the negative aspects of a destination crisis, effective analysis of a crisis presents an opportunity for a destination authority to adjust and alter market strategies. The Tasmanian and Turkish case studies are examples in which a crisis led to a reimaging of a destination.

One critical aspect of monitoring destination crisis and restoration marketing management is understanding how other destinations managed their own crises. A common popular expression in business management is 'world's best practice'. This concept is simply applying the world's most effective practice used in a specific field of endeavour. It applies to all fields of business, and tourism marketing is no exception. Each of the following case studies includes initiatives worthy of emulation and application, and errors that should be avoided.

Destination authorities managing a crisis should undertake a regular SWOT analysis of the management of their crisis and recovery process. The analysis of their strengths, weaknesses, opportunities and threats enables them to assess their performance according to the criteria of crisis and restoration management discussed in this chapter.

Professional crisis and restoration management is based on the ability to treat these issues as an operational and management contingency. While it would be unreasonable for any destination authority to have a management scenario for all crisis typologies, they must have readily accessible plans prepared for implementation of the events they are most likely to encounter.

The DESTCON ranking and implementation of the steps outlined in this chapter will be a guide to effective crisis management. The ability of a destination authority to be prepared for any crisis scenario can impact on millions of people whose livelihood is dependent on or linked to a prosperous inbound tourism industry.

Certain countries such as Vietnam have successfully created an economic boom (following extended periods of warfare) based upon heavy reliance on the tourism industry as the fulcrum of their national economic recovery. The case study of Croatia reflects the importance of a tourism restoration strategy as a core element in its national economic recovery.

Part II | TERRORISM AND POLITICAL VIOLENCE

3 | UNITED STATES: SEPTEMBER 11, 2001 TERRORIST ATTACKS

The impact on American and global tourism

CRISIS RANKING: **DESTCON 1**

BACKGROUND

Until September 11, 2001, the United States was the world's most popular long-haul tourism destination, exceeded only by France, Italy and Spain in absolute number of foreign visitors per annum.[1] In 2000, some 50.9 million foreign visitors entered the United States, of whom 44 608 658 were defined as tourists. They generated US$103 billion in revenue, making tourism one of the largest export industries in the United States. American citizens have long been a prime source market for many destinations throughout the world, although on a per capita basis they are less inclined to travel internationally than citizens of many other affluent industrialised countries. Americans travel widely within their own country, utilising a comprehensive array of domestic air, rail and coach services and millions of private motor vehicles.

NYC and Company (formerly known as the New York City Visitors and Convention Bureau) actively markets New York City within the United States and worldwide. In 2000, some 37.4 million people from all over the United States and internationally visited New York, spending an estimated US$17 billion. Almost half of these visitors stayed for at least one night. Of this number, 6.8 million visitors were international visitors (representing 14 per cent of all international visitors to the United States).[2] According to NYC and Company, the total economic impact of tourism on New York City was

US$24.96 billion. Under the city administration of Mayor Rudolph Giuliani the rate of violent crime abated, to the overall benefit of New Yorkers and visitors. The tourism authorities of New York were optimistic about building upon steady past growth in tourism to the city throughout 2001 and into the future. The World Trade Center, which was administered by the New York City Port Authority, comprised a complex of buildings dominated by the twin 110-floor towers. New Yorkers, some of whom saw the twin towers as overbearing structures even on New York's grandiose urban skyline, did not universally love the World Trade Center. The complex opened in 1974, briefly holding sway as the world's tallest office towers, and despite local controversy it became a popular tourist attraction for visitors to the city.

The United States arguably enjoys the highest level of international awareness of any tourism destination on earth. US dominance of the international media, especially television, Internet and newspaper coverage, coupled with the vast output of American-owned and managed film studios and its

Skyline, New York City. Photo courtesy Insight Vacations.

dominance of many multinational business organisations ensures that the United States enjoys a high level of awareness. Economically, the United States is by far the largest economy in the world. Many major US companies are now global. Household corporate names such as Coca-Cola, Microsoft, McDonald's, American Express and IBM, to name but a few, exercise global dominance in their respective fields of enterprise. The US dollar is the world's dominant currency and the United States is readily acknowledged as the world's leading military and political power.

The pervasive worldwide power, influence and high profile of the United States elicits strong emotions, ranging from admiration, respect to envy, jealousy and fear through to outright hatred. For tourists, the sheer size and variety of the United States and the familiarity of its most popular natural and man-made tourist sites contribute to its wide attraction as a tourist destination. There is a high level of international awareness about major US tourist attractions: New York City, Disneyland, Las Vegas, Miami, Honolulu, the Grand Canyon, Hollywood and San Francisco represent some of the better known attractions of destination USA.

From an operational perspective, the marketing of destination USA has become increasingly pluralistic in recent years. Unlike most other countries, where destination marketing is largely coordinated by national government tourism ministries, the marketing of destination USA has undergone considerable devolution and privatisation. Each of the 50 states and most major cities have established their own tourism marketing authorities with representative offices in many key source markets such as the United Kingdom, Europe, Japan and South Korea. The US government abolished federal government-owned tourism promotional and information authorities in 1996, opting out of direct involvement in keeping with the free market ideologies of both the Democratic and Republican parties.[3] In most large source markets, these have been replaced by private marketing enterprises which coordinate destination USA marketing activities in association with state tourist authorities, airlines, hotel chains, car rental firms, transport services and tour operators. In most major source markets, the promotion of destination USA is coordinated by organisations known as Visit USA. These operate either as subsidiaries of marketing or communications companies or as non-profit associations, and were established as the result of a federal subsidy following the abolition of the federally funded United States Travel and Tourism Authority (USTTA). According to Barry Schipplock,[4] CEO of Visit USA (Australia), the subsidy was a nominal US$5000 in each country in which a Visit USA organisation was established. The operational funding would come from airlines, tour operators, hoteliers, state government tourist authorities and city-based CVBs (Convention and Visitor Bureaux) and other principals. According to Barry Schipplock, there were 30 Visit USA organisations operating around the world in 2001, located in key source markets primarily in Europe, East Asia, South America and Australasia.[5] In Austria, Visit USA is a division of a telecommunications firm, in Australia it is a division of a larger marketing firm, while in other countries it is a self-contained association.

The overall coordination of tourism policy was also privatised in 1996 and came under the overall banner of the Tourism Industry Association (TIA) a confederation of US tourism industry umbrella organisations including American Society of Travel Agents (ASTA) and the roof bodies of US tour operators, wholesalers, hoteliers, major international carriers and other principals. The TIA which has been established since 1940 formulates overall

American tourism marketing policy and liaises with the federal government. The crisis which eventuated from the events of September 11 would present the sternest challenge to the effectiveness of privatised tourism marketing in the United States.

The United States arouses admiration and fascination in millions of people all over the world. However, there is a contrary view held by many others that the United States has come to symbolise quintessential evil. During the Cold War, generations of Soviet and Chinese citizens were taught under the communist system to believe that the United States symbolised the twin evils of capitalism and imperialism. For radical Islamists today, the United States is depicted as 'The Great Satan'—a corrupt, amoral and evil empire inimical to everything that Islam (as these groups interpret it) represents. Many Third World governments in Latin America, Africa and Asia are suspicious of the United States and in some cases are openly hostile to what they perceive as US dominance of their economies and American interference in their internal affairs. A corollary to this hostility is the fact that many of the countries who criticise the United States are heavily dependent on US foreign aid. Within the United States itself, disaffected elements refer to the US government as an integral element of a malicious, conspiratorial cabal committed to global economic and political domination. In fact, a vast array of governments, political organisations, religious sects, environmentalists and other groups around the world claim cause to oppose the United States and the policies of its government.

The events of September 11

Prior to September 11, 2001, the United States (in terms of its size and diversity) had been relatively free of major threats to tourists on US territory. Urban crime in major cities has remained a background threat which tourists have had to take into account when visiting major urban centres. With the exception of a 1991 crime outbreak in Miami, crime (at least in its own right) has rarely figured as a major disincentive to tourism. The United States is occasionally prone to natural disasters: tornadoes, volcanic eruptions, earthquakes and hurricanes have threatened citizens and visitors alike in several parts of the country. But while the actual occurrence of a natural disaster impacts on tourism, the potential threat is rarely a disincentive and sometimes is viewed as an attraction.[6]

Terrorism has long been a potential threat in the United States. Many foreign governments and both American and foreign organisations claim ideological, religious and economic motives for supporting and carrying out an attack on the United States. However, acts of anti-government terrorism on US soil, whether politically, ideologically or religiously motivated, have been rare. During the past decade, the two most prominent terrorist incidents were the bombing of the basement of the World Trade Center in New York City on February 26, 1993 and the bombing of the federal government offices in Oklahoma City on April 19, 1995. The group convicted of the World Trade Center attack in 1993, which resulted in seven deaths, were members of a radical Islamic sect. The convicted Oklahoma bomber was an American citizen, Timothy McVeigh, who was executed in 2001. The Oklahoma attack resulted in 168 deaths.[7] Since the 1960s, there have been occasional hijackings of US domestic aircraft over US air space which have rarely resulted in casualties, and more cases of US aircraft hijacked overseas. The most destructive terrorist incident involving a US commercial aircraft was the 1988 bombing of Pan Am Flight 103 which exploded while in flight between London and New York over Lockerbie in Scotland, resulting in the loss of 300 lives. In the eyes of most Americans, terrorism was perceived as a far greater threat to their safety and security outside the United States than on home soil. Thus the destruction of Pan Am Flight 103 over Lockerbie had relatively little impact on the overall popularity of destination USA, although it was a major factor in the ultimate demise of the financially and operationally troubled carrier Pan American in the early 1990s.

The scale of destruction and the compromised state of airline security on September 11, 2001 altered every preconception about tourism safety in the United States. The events of that day were the catalyst for a sequence of events, which has had devastating implications for the American and the global airline and tourism industries.

The destruction of the World Trade Center in New York City, and the damage to the military establishment's headquarters at the Pentagon, Washington DC, were subject to blanket media coverage. New York and Washington DC are both centres of US politics and business and the headquarters of the world's largest media organisations, including News Ltd, Time Warner and its subsidiary CNN, NBC, ABC and CBS. Additionally, both cities are host to the greatest concentration of foreign correspondents in the world.

The series of events, which culminated in the attacks against the World Trade Center in New York and the Pentagon in Washington DC, began on the morning of September 11 when American Airlines Flight AA11, en route from Boston to Los Angeles, was hijacked. Hijackers allegedly took control of the aircraft and diverted it to New York City. The aircraft crashed into the north tower of the 110-storey twin tower New York Trade Center at 8.45 a.m. Eighteen minutes later, United Airlines Flight UA175, which was originally en route between Boston and Los Angeles, was allegedly hijacked and diverted by the hijackers to New York. The aircraft crashed into the south tower of the World Trade Center at 9.03 a.m. and exploded on impact. Immediately following the attacks on the World Trade Center, New York City authorities ordered the closure of bridges and tunnels linking Manhattan with the remainder of the city. By 9.40 a.m. the Federal Airports Authority (FAA) had ordered a halt to all flight operations at US airports, the first time such a measure had been taken in American history. American Airlines Flight AA77, originally scheduled to fly between Dulles (Washington DC) and Los Angeles, was allegedly hijacked and diverted from its original flight path to fly into the Pentagon, an event which occurred at 9.45 a.m. United Airlines Flight UA93, scheduled to fly between Newark and San Francisco, was also allegedly hijacked. According to media reports, scuffles broke out between the hijackers and some passengers. The aircraft flew out of control and crashed in Somerset County near Pittsburgh, Pennsylvania at 10.10 a.m. Reports from the media, based on monitored mobile calls allegedly made by passengers from the aircraft to their spouses and other close relatives, suggest that this aircraft was also targeted on Washington DC.

There is no debate about the massive destruction wreaked by the airline crashes. The identity of the perpetrators, most of whom were Saudi nationals, has been established. However, questions about the lack of US defence response to radical changes in flight plans monitored by air traffic controllers, even the possibility that the aircraft were modified or operated under remote control and other intriguing issues will long remain subject to speculation, debate and investigation. The United States had never before experienced this magnitude of human-made devastation and loss of life in a single day. By October 1, New York City officials, the Defence Department, American Airlines and United Airlines respectively estimated that some 5219 people out of the estimated 50 000 people who normally worked in the World Trade Center had been killed in the explosions and subsequent collapse of the twin towers and surrounding buildings. By December 2001, this estimate had been reduced to 2950. A further 189 were killed in the Pentagon and in the aircraft which crashed into it. Forty-four people died in the fourth hijacked aircraft which crashed near Pittsburgh.[8]

The quadruple hijacking of aircraft, three of which were employed as suicide weapons targeted at the symbols of American financial and military power, represented an unprecedented event in the annals of international terrorism. Until this incident, hijacking an aircraft was an act of terrorism in its own right. Hitherto, the most extreme consequence of this act was the destruction of the aircraft and the killing of some or all passengers.

An immediate impact of the hijacking and the destruction of the World Trade Center and part of the Pentagon was the grounding of all civil aircraft in the United States and the suspension of all international arrivals and departures, which were either diverted to Canada or returned to the point of departure. This was a drastic US response to an act of air piracy. It was a response mirrored to a large extent in Israel, where the government immediately curtailed international arrivals by all carriers except for El Al on the assumption that Israel may have been targeted for a similar attack. The grounding of civil aircraft in the United States, while an understandable preventative measure for averting other possible attacks, exacerbated an almost immediate crisis of confidence in the aviation industry which had been initiated by the incidents.

The apparent coordination of the hijackings, coupled with the allegations made by US intelligence that, on each aircraft, at least one member of the suicide hijacker squad was trained to fly and navigate a large Boeing passenger aircraft, led US authorities to assert that the quadruple hijacking of September 11 was meticulously planned and synchronised. In all four cases, the choice of a large domestic aircraft—either a Boeing 757 or 767—fully fuelled for a trans-continental flight and allegedly taken over at an early stage of each flight was further evidence that the hijackers sought to maximise destruction and casualties at each target.

While the Western world's political leadership and media anointed the Afghanistan-based, Saudi-born Islamist terrorist and leader of the *Al-Qaeda* (The Base) group, Osama Bin Laden, as 'suspect in chief', it is possible that other individuals, organisations and nations were involved or complicit in this act. Initial indications and the *modus operandi* strongly suggest that radical Islamist groups were involved, but the *publicly available* evidence pointing to a single mastermind was more circumstantial than conclusive. Evidence collected by US government agencies and made available to a very restricted circle of world leaders and intelligence agencies has satisfied those recipients that Bin Laden was a legitimate suspect, but little compelling evidence was made publicly available until December 2001, when a grainy videotape in which Bin Laden is quoted as having both approved and masterminded the attack was released. While the Western media were quick to describe the tape as compelling evidence, some critics described it as a fake.

Some conspiracy theorists alleged that the attacks were organised or tacitly approved by senior members of US intelligence and the Bush administration. They asserted that this was done in order to advance a global agenda to rule and subjugate the world and to gain control over Afghanistan to advance the corporate agenda of leading energy companies. US President George W. Bush and his Vice President Dick Cheney's long involvement in the oil industry has heightened such speculation. Certain elements in the Islamic world blamed the Israeli Intelligence Agency *Mossad* on the dubious grounds that Israel would be a political and military beneficiary of US military attacks directed at Islamic countries.[9]

The international repercussions of September 11 on global tourism

In the weeks following the New York and Washington DC attacks, the focal point of the United States-led multinational military response was Afghanistan, the country in which Osama Bin Laden was reported to have been in hiding and protected by Afghanistan's radical Islamist Taliban regime. The intense military activity in the region surrounding Afghanistan and the launching of military attacks against Afghanistan from October 7, 2001 aroused heightened safety concerns about travelling anywhere within the Middle East and Central Asia. In common with the 1991 Gulf War, tourism to Europe, the Middle East and the Indian Subcontinent fell under a cloud.

The political impact of the New York and Washington DC attacks was immediate. The US administration sought to enlist a broad coalition to strike at international terrorism, obtaining varying degrees of international support. Britain, continental Europe, Russia, Australia and Canada were fulsome in their support. In addition to its more traditional NATO and Western allies, the United States sought support from Arab and non-Arab Islamic states as a means of demonstrating that retaliation was not directed at Islam *per se*.

These overtures met with reactions ranging from outright support from Turkey and the Southern Islamic republics of the former Soviet Union to heavily qualified and reticent support from Iran and Saudi Arabia. Several Islamic states signalled that their condemnation of the attack against New York and Washington DC did not extend to support for military attacks against Muslim nations—even pariah states like Afghanistan. Pakistan found itself in a most sensitive situation as a military ally of the United States and as home to a large and voluble Islamist population. It was the only country in the world that maintained formal diplomatic relations with the Taliban regime in Afghanistan while granting permission to US and British military forces for overfly rights and military bases to attack the Taliban regime and its military infrastructure in Afghanistan.

The broader the coalition enlisted, the narrower the areas of unanimity. Without going into detail, the 'war against terrorism' was replete with anomalies centred largely on the attempt to define a politically expedient version of 'who is a terrorist'. In the context of courting allies in the Middle East, senior members of the Bush administration and British Prime Minister Tony Blair found defining terrorists and terrorist organisations an uncomfortably complex matter.

The focus of retaliatory attacks was the Taliban regime of Afghanistan and suspected Al-Qaeda bases in that country. By mid-December 2001, the Taliban regime had been toppled by a coalition of anti-Taliban Afghan groups and replaced by a coalition government. There were hints that future retaliatory action could involve other Middle East countries, including Iraq. The fear of a 'Gulf War' scenario resulted in a heightening of travel alerts extended to cover the Middle East, South and Central Asia. This aroused concern and fear in Europe that countries allied to the United States may become targets of terrorist attacks. By the end of October 2001, isolated outbreaks of anthrax delivered by mail and addressed to US government agencies, some Israeli and Jewish organisations and selected media organisations were alleged to be part of a continuing Islamist terrorist campaign directed at the United States, its allies and the media. In early November, Bin Laden issued a videotaped statement in which he claimed he had ready access to nuclear and biological weapons of mass destruction. Irrespective of the veracity of this claim, it maintained the psychological war between the Islamist extremists and the United States.

The most severe initial impact on traveller confidence was within the United States itself. Serious questions were posed about US airport security and the security of civil aviation in the United States and globally. There were further questions about the failure of the US defence system to protect its citizens. There was little debate that the incidents of September 11 represented the most severe challenge to US and global airline and airport security since World War II.

The issue of airline and airport security became one of the most important challenges facing the world tourism industry. Airlines and airport authorities worldwide had actively addressed this issue since air piracy first emerged as a terrorist tactic during the 1960s. Since the advent of air piracy, all major passenger airports in the world have adopted a range of security procedures for international and domestic passengers. Following the US attack, the International Air Transport Association (IATA) sought to implement enhancements to airline and airport security procedures.[10] In the United States and in other countries, the advisability of armed sky marshals was raised. Armed sky marshals have been a part of the crew on Israel's national carrier El Al since the late 1960s and have flown with Royal Jordanian Airlines since the 1970s.

The economic impact of the US attacks on the airline industry in the United States and elsewhere was swift and devastating. Brian Hale, Simon Mann and Michael Millett quoted Wall Street analyst predictions on September 11 that the US airline industry was expected to lose US$2.3 billion during 2001 as a consequence of a general slowdown in business during the year. The New York City and Washington DC attacks forced a revision of those estimates and the anticipated loss was expected to double. In the immediate wake of the attacks, American Airlines shed 20 000 jobs and cut 20 per cent of its scheduled flights, while United Airlines shed 20 000 jobs and cut 26 per cent of its scheduled flights. By November 2001, within the United States, some 116 000 jobs had been lost in the airline industry alone. Aircraft component manufacturers were also affected. General Electric's aircraft engine division alone abolished 4000 jobs, representing 15 per cent of its staff.

Outside the United States, during the last quarter of 2001, Air Canada collapsed with a loss of 20 000 jobs; British Airways cut 7000 jobs and closed off 10 per cent of its scheduled flights; Alitalia cut 2500 jobs, its September 2001 traffic fell 21 per cent and fifteen of its planes were grounded; and Virgin Atlantic cut 1200 jobs, grounded five aircraft and cancelled 20 per cent of its scheduled services. The above examples represent a small portion of the US and international carriers which announced job cuts, loss of revenue and reductions in schedules in the immediate wake of the September 11 attack. Airline manufacturer Boeing was expected to cut 15 per cent of its staff and scale back production. In 2001, the previously expected production of civil aircraft was scaled back from 538 to 500 and in 2002 production was expected to drop further to 400. While the statistics on passenger numbers may not be available for some time, it is already clear that passenger patronage of domestic flights within the United States and international service in and out of the United States has plummeted since September 11, 2001. Patronage of international flights throughout Eurasia has also plummeted, in anticipation of the US military response to the September 11 attacks.[11]

The impact of September 11 on the US and international airline industry was mirrored within the broader tourism and hospitality industry. In New York City, which bore the brunt of the September 11 attack, Mayor Rudolph Giuliani issued a statement on September 17 encouraging American and overseas tourists to register their support for his city in the most meaningful possible way by visiting, staying and spending some of their money in the city.[12]

Some people—mainly Americans—responded to this call. However, national and worldwide sympathy for New York and admiration for the Mayor's conduct in the face of the September 11 attack was not readily manifested in the form of a solidarity-induced tourism boom. Most support had been in the form of financial donations.

The hospitality and tourism industry in the United States was estimated in 2000 to be worth US$582 billion, employing 17 million people and generating US$100 billion in federal, state and local tax revenues. The industry was clearly under threat after the September 11 attack. The drop in both domestic and international airline patronage coupled with the reduction of scheduled air services was expected to flow through to patronage of hotels, resort and attractions within the United States.[13]

Of the eleven case studies in this book, the September 11, 2001 terrorist attacks against the United States had the most extensive global implications. The London *Financial Times* of September 24, 2001 reported that some of the world's largest hotel chains, including Six Continents (owners of the Holiday Inn and Intercontinental Chains), French-based Accor and the California-based Hilton International chain, had reported a sharp drop in trading. The implications of the attack had also spread to international shipping cruise lines including P&O, which derived 75 per cent of its income from the United States.

On October 7, 2001, the World Travel and Tourism Council (WTTC) issued a projection of the economic and employment implication of a 10 per cent drop in tourism, which in effect, represented the potential challenge the world tourism industry faced if the crisis created by the attacks against the United States were to be prolonged:

- United Kingdom: Decrease of 1.9 per cent total GDP of United Kingdom economy and 190 000 jobs lost;
- European Union: Decrease of 1.9 per cent total GDP of EU states, economy and 1.2 million jobs lost;
- United States: Decrease of 1.8 per cent of total GDP of the US economy and 1.1 million jobs lost.
- World: Decrease of 1.7 per cent of total GDP of the world economy and 8 million jobs lost.[14]

On September 25, 2001, in the immediate shadow of the US attacks, a meeting of the World Tourism Organization (WTO) General Assembly was held in Seoul, South Korea. WTO Secretary-General Francesco Frangialli called on the eradication of violence for tourism to prosper. He also said that tourism could play a role in generating peace and economic development. Earlier, on September 17 in Madrid, Mr Frangialli had expressed a belief that global tourism would experience a temporary downturn but recover quickly. He pointed out that in the first eight months of 2001 world tourism had grown by 2.5–3 per cent over 2000 levels. His optimistic assessment was based on what he recalled as a downturn during the Gulf War of 1991 followed by a robust recovery. He claimed that even in 1991—the year of the Gulf War—while there was a decline in airline passenger numbers, the actual number of international visitor arrivals grew and receipts increased by 2.1 per cent over 1990 levels. While such optimism was refreshing, Mr Frangialli's perspective on the Gulf War and its impact on global tourism was the product of some especially selective statistical analysis.

As the WTO stated in a brief report on the impact of the September 11 attacks on international tourist released on September 18, one week after the attacks: 'The attacks on US citizens have made more of an impact than any crisis in the past. The situation is exceptional and past experience can only partly help analyse the consequences of such tragic events.' The report then claimed that, although total tourism demand may not undergo a decline, there would be a redistribution in total demand. One of the possible scenarios the report identified was a growth of short-haul regional and domestic tourism likely to be at the expense of airline travel, especially long-haul airline travel.

During the US led campaign against the Taliban in Afghanistan and the Al-Qaeda, the Al-Qaeda group released a number of video messages threatening retaliation against the United States and its supporters. The governments of most nations warned their citizens to either defer or review their travel plans to South Central Asia and the Middle East. The government advisories were heavily publicised by the international media, especially in Western countries, and were a contributing factor to the buildup of international tension. The more sensationalist elements of the media depicted the situation as the beginning of World War III. Some would-be travellers interpreted the situation as a cue to avoid travelling to much of Europe, Asia, North Africa and the United States. In Australia, Japan and elsewhere, tour operators servicing Europe, North America and the Middle East experienced a decline in forward bookings despite the fact that most carriers with long-haul routes between Southeast Asia and Europe, which normally pass close to Afghanistan, had adjusted them in accordance with long-standing IATA contingencies to be no closer that 1200 kilometres from Afghanistan.

The international hotel industry also experienced a slump in bookings. The website <www.ehotelier.com> extensively reported the slump in hotel bookings in the United States and Europe during October after the US attacks. In the week following the attacks, US hotel occupancy levels nationally fell by 26 per cent compared with the same period in 2000. On October 24, UK consultancy firm PKF reported a plunge of hotel occupancy levels in London in September 2001 of 17.2 per cent compared with September 2000. The concerns of the lucrative meetings, incentives, conventions and exhibitions industry matched those of the hotel industry.[15]

The WTO report was partially correct in its overall analysis of redistribution in tourism demand. In Australia and New Zealand, in the last quarter of 2001, there was a marked decline in forward bookings to the United States, the Middle East and South Asia. This was a consequence of fear of terrorist actions in these areas, an escalation of war and, more overwhelmingly, a fear of air travel. The decline in long-haul international travel was partially compensated for by a growth in demand for domestic travel or international short-haul destinations in the South-west Pacific. South American operators in Australia reported a strong growth in demand for tourism to South America, which was removed from the conflict. The Australian experience was reflected by significant changes in patterns of tourism demand all over the world. However, one feature which distinguished this crisis from previous international global travel crises has been that many consumers, rather than changing destinations, chose to defer travel—especially air travel.

The US and global tourism industries faced a severe marketing challenge following the September 11 attacks and the fluid and unpredictable political and military response to them. On October 12, 2001, the World Travel and Tourism Council (WTTC) released a statement based on the collaboration of many international travel and tourism associations which said, in part:

> In the wake of the terrorist attacks against the United States we call on a multi-government partnership to ensure that measures to strengthen security are effective, harmonised internationally and applied globally, helping to restore consumer confidence in travel and tourism.

The statement pointed out the importance of the tourism industry to the global economy. WTTC president Jean-Claude Baumgarten called on all sectors of the tourism industry to share their collective experience in improving all aspects of tourism security. The other key point in the statement was that: 'The representatives believe their efforts will demonstrate unity and leadership to help restore public confidence and an early return to "business as usual".'[16] The statement pointed out that world tourism annually generates approximately US$4494 billion dollars in economic activity.

The call for unity was reflected in an October 11 statement by IATA, in which IATA Director General and CEO Pierre J. Janniot, speaking in Hong Kong at the International Aerospace Forum, warned delegates that the airline industry faced potential losses of US$7 billion during 2001 (up from original estimates of US$2.5 billion) and job losses of 120 000. Mr Janniot called for upgraded conventional security at airports and further advocated the worldwide application of biometric security methods such as iris scans stored on databases for airline employees and frequent flyers. Mr Janniot looked forward to a recovery in 2002 and stated that flying was still the safest form of transport.

The early responses of international tourism associations to the attack on New York and the subsequent growth of international political tensions were relatively generalised. The dominant issue on which broad agreement was reached was the upgrading of security, but there was no common ground on the measures to be implemented. In dealing with the more complex issue of marketing strategy, no prescriptive policy was initially formulated by international tourism bodies.

The anecdotal evidence suggested that the international travel and tourism industry tended to adopt a wait-and-see attitude to the development of the current crisis. In many parts of the world, tourism-orientated promotional activities were either cancelled or postponed in the wake of the crisis. In Australia, the country's largest tourism promotional expos, scheduled for October 2001, were postponed until February 2002. In the United States and Europe, a number of major travel industry promotions were either cancelled or postponed. There is always debate surrounding the concept of 'bunkering down'. One attitude to this approach was that 'bunkering down' was an overt demonstration of the tourism industry's lack of confidence in the future of tourism and therefore a sign of weakness. The other major view centred on a concern that promoting tourism to consumers during a period of uncertainty and negativity in the marketplace was an irresponsible waste of resources. Statements such as those by US President George Bush, who claimed 'the world has changed', followed up by more apocalyptic interpretations by sections of the media, frightened many people into avoiding or postponing travel and opting to stay at home.

THE UNITED STATES' TOURISM MARKETING CRISIS

The United States faced a particularly difficult task in implementing a fully coordinated destination crisis marketing approach because, as mentioned earlier, it is one of the few countries in the world which lacks a centralised national tourism marketing authority. One of the key premises of having a strong and centralised national tourist marketing authority is to promote destination awareness. In privatising tourism marketing, the US Congress argued that the United States did not really require a government authority to provide this service. The private sector, through airlines, tour operators and the media, had traditionally fulfilled this task effectively. In the United States, the devolution of tourism promotion at the government level had placed the prime responsibility of destination marketing with private enterprise, and state and local government.

During 'normal' or non-crisis conditions, destination marketing procedures such as those used by Visit USA in Australia and other middle-range source markets are normally highly effective. However, this effectiveness is largely based on the assumption of continuing high demand, which means participating principals and operators are willing to spend money to promote a strong and growing market. Once the market is threatened and the private sector has reduced financial and other marketing resources for promotional activity, then privatising destination marketing becomes less viable.

As most case studies in this work indicated national government marketing authorities during a crisis tend to:

- centralise the marketing policy and implementation of that policy in responding to a crisis and in mapping out a recovery strategy;
- centralise the actual dissemination of crisis response information to the media, the trade and consumers;
- take on a larger share of the financial burden of marketing the destination out of crisis and subsidise the marketing costs of those operators and principals who are actively promoting the destination.

Since 1996, the role played by the former USTTA was filled by TIA[17] which, as stated earlier, is a confederation of travel industry roof bodies which was formed in 1940. TIA has sought to implement a national tourism crisis management plan but it is handicapped due to the fact that it can only act on consensus and, although it can request government financial support, it is dependent on the unanimity and financial support of its membership. On October 29, 2001, Secretary of Commerce Don Evans convened a meeting of the Tourism Policy Council (TPC), which is an inter-agency committee devoted to making national recommendations on tourism matters. It was established in 1981, reauthorised in 1996 and had not met since 1997. Such was the moribund state of policy planning on tourism issues that, even during a profound crisis for the US tourism industry, it took six weeks for the TPC to actually meet—let alone implement any meaningful program of action. While TIA has sought to develop a recovery plan in the wake of the September 11 crisis, it appears there was no known contingency plan to deal with a national tourism crisis; further, the devolved state of tourism marketing in the United States meant that each state, city and region had to manage its marketing as best it could with limited reference to a national coordinating body.

It is characteristic of the US government's reluctance to centralise crisis marketing management that the proposed *Travel America Now Act*[18] introduced by the US Senate in the weeks immediately following the September 11 attacks included an admission that the travel industry was a major component of the US economy. It pointed out that the tourism industry employed 19 million Americans, was the third largest industry in the country, generated sales of US$582 billion, generated US$99.6 billion in tax revenues and produced a balance of trade surplus of US$14 billion per annum. The Bill proposed a range of tax relief measures for travellers and travel businesses to stimulate the travel market, but at no stage did it propose a national destination marketing campaign.

Based on the methodology employed by other national governments, such as those of the United Kingdom, Turkey and Egypt, to manage a national tourism marketing crisis, the US government urgently needed to implement the following minimum measures to deal with what was effectively a national marketing problem:

- Establish a federally funded central national tourism marketing crisis management team comprising representatives from the American Society of Travel Agents, airlines, airport authorities, coach companies, railway companies, insurance providers, state government and regional tourism authorities (with the special involvement of New York), hoteliers, car rental firms, cruise companies, federal authorities specialising in security, inbound tour operators, representatives of foreign tour operators which market the United States and selected marketing, media and public relations consultants.

  While TIA certainly fulfils this role to a large degree, as a consensus-based organisation it is limited largely by its reliance on funding from its membership. It has no guaranteed source of government emergency support. It is notable that, in the months following the September 11 attack, TIA sponsored an impressive marketing campaign using the services of a number of leading US personalities—including President George W. Bush himself—to encourage travellers to visit the United States.

- From this group, appoint a core of people to act as representatives in communicating a coordinated marketing message to the media, the national and international travel industry and the American and international travelling public.

This has been one area in which TIA has had some success. To translate a US industry-approved message to overseas source markets, TIA is heavily dependent on the support of Visit USA offices outside the United States. As each office operates as a separate entity it is difficult to ensure a unanimity of both message and the qualitative delivery of this message.

- Establish and actively promote a website to communicate the national measures being undertaken to address the primary concerns of travellers to and within the United States, including security measures, and to promote the positive benefits of travel to and within the United States. The website can be linked to other existing sites which will further the cause of advancing the marketing of destination USA.

TIA has established a useful website but, compared with the websites established by many government tourist offices, it is less effective in addressing crisis issues than those of many other countries.

- Wherever possible, to co-ordinate and communicate any overall marketing initiatives undertaken by the private sector. TIA is limited in achieving this aim by its need to establish a national consensus.
- Putting this new body in a position to provide financial support for private sector marketing of destination USA to the travel trade and consumer promotions in economically or strategically important overseas source markets.

TIA is very limited in its own ability to do this, except as a lobbyist for federal government financial support. TIA is dependent on membership subscriptions and has limited access to large-scale financial assets.

None of the above measures precludes any initiatives or actions undertaken by state and local tourism authorities or by private firms. The establishment of a government-funded and empowered national body could be treated as an emergency measure and act as part of a long-term contingency plan in the event that the United States may encounter future threats to its viability as a marketable destination. The above measures represent a minimalist approach to destination crisis management when it comes to marketing destination USA. It is appropriate to consider the re-establishment of USTTA as a permanent body devoted to the development of a national tourism marketing strategy. The above measures can and should be implemented rapidly.

The pre-September 11 assumptions that the United States could dispense with a centralised tourism marketing policy body have been found wanting. The federal government has made large financial commitments to assist airlines and the Federal Airports Authority since September 11, 2001. In the 1980s, the Reagan administration found it necessary to intervene in solving an air traffic controllers' dispute and the administration of George W. Bush in 2001 was obliged to intervene in the airline industry. While it is contrary to the philosophy of a Republican administration, the economic fallout of the September 11 attacks required the US government to play a role in co-ordinating the national marketing of destination USA.

The September 11 crisis also required a review of marketing destination USA to key foreign source markets. The privatised Visit USA organisations in most source markets were an effective 'fair weather' marketing mechanism based on the propensity of privately owned principals and wholesalers to spend money to market their USA product. When demand was perceived as falling or under threat, marketing budgets were threatened, in turn threatening the whole rationale underpinning the privatisation of marketing destination USA outside the country.

NEW YORK CITY'S APPROACH TO CRISIS MARKETING SINCE SEPTEMBER 11, 2001

Since September 11 the New York City Tourism Authority, as well as NYC and Company, have benefited greatly from the actions of Mayor Rudolph Giuliani in seeking to highlight tourism as a means of boosting the morale and economic viability of New York City. The Mayor's plea on September 17 to Americans and international visitors to show their support for New York by visiting, staying and spending was an effective call for solidarity tourism. Giuliani's October 1, 2001 speech to the UN General Assembly (an honour to address the UN General Assembly is rarely accorded to any city official) was especially powerful as it identified the attack on New York as an attack on the entire international community. Since 1945, New York has housed the main headquarters of the United Nations and, as Giuliani was able to point out, the city includes citizens and residents speaking virtually every language and originating from every member state of the United Nations.[19]

Mayor Giuliani was nationally and internationally recognised as a symbol of strength and determination in the face of the September 11 attacks against New York City. His stalwart defiance set the tone for the remarketing of the city. The local tourism authorities did a great deal to entice tourists to New York. Much of the marketing appeal was directed towards Americans on the basis of solidarity and patriotism. Many of the city's hotels and attractions offered substantial discounts and value-added offers. The Waldorf Astoria Hotel dropped its nightly tariff from US$449 to US$232 and included tickets to many of New York's key attractions. Delta Airlines made 10 000 domestic tickets to New York available for promotional purposes. The NYC and Company's website <www.nycvisit.com> included many promotions of restaurants, attractions, events and hotels. The Company introduced an active campaign to host American and foreign travel writers to see the city for themselves. As in other case studies in this book, the Internet became a key means of communicating real-time information and was used as a prime source of tourism information by the media, the travel industry, consumers and academic researchers.[20]

NYC and Company and the city administration of New York actively sought to address safety and security concerns raised by the public and the travel industry. Tactically, they focused on the domestic market as the main priority and the international market as a secondary priority. New York attracts a larger number of visitors from the United States than from abroad, although the spending per capita of overseas visitors is far greater. However, it appeared that, with the downturn in demand for transatlantic air services—the primary source of international visitors—the New York City tourism authorities made a correct strategic choice in prioritising their marketing campaigns to focus on the American domestic market. In short, the essence of the campaign was reassurances of safety and an appeal to solidarity, backed by discounts and value-added incentives. The approach to international travellers included a combination of reassurance and incentives, but it needed to adopt a more subtle and varied approach in terms of psychological motivation. Some may be amenable to identifying with the courage of New Yorkers as citizens of the world courageously living life in the face of threat. However, NYC and Company predicted that many tourists and corporate travellers would respond to a business as usual message tagged with a cheaper than usual 'hook'. However, for international air travellers, the attraction of New York would need to be matched by a sustained confidence in airline safety and security.

THE US CRISIS AND ITS GLOBAL CONTEXT IN LATE 2001

The tourism crisis generated by the September 11 attacks extended far beyond the borders of the United States. From a purely tourism perspective, long-haul travel to the United States, the Middle East, Western Asia, the Indian subcontinent and Europe declined during the last quarter of 2001. The World Travel and Tourism Council and Pacific Asia Travel Association (PATA) indicated that there was evidence of a shift in the tourism market. Some regions would benefit from this—indeed, there were already indications that Southern Africa, South America, East and Southeast Asia (with the significant exception of Indonesia), Australia and the Southwest Pacific may have been affected positively by the US crisis. Domestic and short-haul travel within the United States/Canada and Europe was also likely to increase as many travellers chose to stay close to home during a period of international uncertainty. Hotel bookings and conferences which relied on international patronage were likely to suffer in the short to medium term.

PATA published a strategic forecast on tourism to East Asia and the Pacific on October 14, 2001. The report, produced by Stratfor (Strategic Forecasting), highlighted the political and security uncertainty which had emanated from the US attacks and the military response. The report suggested three possible scenarios for tourism in East Asia and the South Pacific during late 2001 and into 2002. The 'best case analysis' was that airline travellers would rapidly return to flying as measures to improve security were announced and visibly implemented. If the US attacks on Afghanistan resulted in the rapid capture of Bin Laden and the fall of the Taliban regime and its replacement with a more stable leadership, it may inspire Indonesia and the Philippines to crush some of the militant Islamist separatists in their countries.

Provided United States-led military action was confined to Afghanistan and was relatively fast, recovery could proceed quickly. Tourism to Asia, especially with the World Cup in Japan and Korea in mid-2002, could be a major economic boost to the East Asian region and hasten the recovery of global tourism. The 'worst case' scenario would have involved a collapse in the

United States-led coalition and follow-up attacks by militant Islamist groups around the world. Added to this was the possibility of increased instability in Egypt, Indonesia and Pakistan. Instability in Egypt and Indonesia posed a threat to international trade and shipping using the Suez Canal and the Straits of Malacca. A growth of secondary terrorism in the West and the rise of Islamic radicalism in Indonesia, the Middle East, Malaysia, Pakistan and Central Asia could threaten the viability of tourism throughout much of Southeast Asia and deter Australia-bound air travellers. This would be exacerbated in the event of any attacks on international carriers. If this scenario were to eventuate, many airlines would either mothball aircraft or go out of business, resulting in reduced demand and higher airfares. The impact of a global crisis on heavily tourism-dependent economies in Southeast Asia—such as Thailand—would be catastrophic.

The Stratfor report claimed that the most likely scenario would be that the Arab and Muslim countries associated with the United States-led military coalition would marginalise themselves or abandon support for the United States as the United States-led campaign became longer and more inconclusive. Military campaigns targeted at groups labelled as terrorists could become increasingly covert and increasingly global. George W. Bush, in the days following the strikes on New York and Washington, spoke of a ten-year war against terrorism which he envisaged as taking place in many parts of the world. The prime destinations which would suffer tourism decline resulting from a continuation and a geographical spread of war would be the Middle East and Central Asia. American and other Western business travellers may consider cutting discretionary travel. Tourism to Eastern Asia and Southeast Asia would remain strong with the exception of Indonesia and the Philippines, both of which—independently of the US situation—have long suffered internal dissension. Japanese travellers, who represent a key source market for many destinations in the Pacific rim, were expected to defer travel to the United States, Guam and Hawaii in favour of Europe, Asia, Australia and New Zealand.

The report pointed out that, for Asia and the Pacific, the post-September 11 situation promised a possibility of tourism growth. There was an opportunity to aggressively promote this region to selected markets and highlight its relative freedom and distance from the major sources of international instability.[21]

By the end of 2001 the United States-led campaign against the Taliban and Al-Qaeda was proceeding in accordance with the best case analysis, but the uncertainty of future developments—both in expanding the scope of the war against terrorism to Iraq or other targets and the possibility of a desperate terrorist response—have made prediction a treacherous exercise. Most destinations out of the direct path of the conflict sought to depict themselves as removed from it. It was already clear that the Middle East and the Eastern Mediterranean, which have frequently been referred to as 'danger zones' or 'no-go zones' by many professional and media observers, were anxious to distance their individual destinations from the conflict in Afghanistan, in common with tourist authorities in East Asia and the Pacific. Certainly, in the first months following September 11 and during the early phase of the United States-led response, tourism to a large proportion of the world, including the United States, underwent a hiatus.

CONCLUSION

The events of September 11, 2001 and their repercussions on the travel industry of the United States and global travel patterns are yet to be fully analysed. There is no doubt that the overriding issue has been the new and enhanced threat to travel security exposed by the September 11 hijackings. Governments and airline authorities were quick to address the security concerns, although the cost involved was clearly damaging to the international airline industry. The US government was forced to inject large sums of public money to assist its airline industry.

However, the issue of traveller security extended far beyond the airline industry. Hoteliers, conference venues, tour coaches and operators all had to visibly address consumer concerns about tourism safety in the wake of the September 11 attacks. International bodies such as the World Travel and Tourism Council, the World Tourism Organization, the International Hotels Association, the International Council of Tour Operators, IATA and similar supra-national bodies needed to address the global concerns through a co-ordinated information campaign. It is noteworthy that, despite the rapid support offered to the airline industry, little tangible support was forthcoming from the US federal government for travel industry marketing of destination USA, especially outside the United States.

The methodology of marketing destination USA as a pluralistic, semi-privatised enterprise with a consensus-based national umbrella body has been exposed as vulnerable to a national crisis and consequently as lacking the power necessary to respond optimally during this crisis. Despite the highly professional efforts of New York City's tourist authority, NYC and Company, and those of many state and private organisations to boost tourism to the United States, a crisis of the magnitude of the September 11 attacks requires a nationally coordinated marketing approach and the relative absence of any tourism crisis coordinating body in the United States is a major handicap to facilitating the most effective recovery. New York City implemented all the appropriate measures, but the crisis for the US tourism industry extends far beyond New York City. To date, the US government has enacted legislation which has provided subsidies and tax reductions to airlines and other segments of the tourism and hospitality industry. However, it appears to have failed to fully support the necessary national marketing approach to restore domestic and international confidence in destination USA.

The attacks on New York and Washington DC on September 11, followed by the United States-led military response to that attack and the outbreaks of mail-delivered anthrax which occurred combined to fuel a media frenzy. People in large parts of the word were panicked into speculation about a worldwide apocalypse. This sense of fear, to a very large extent, was directed to the international travel and tourism industry. Governments, and to some extent even travel agents, were infected by this fear, which manifested itself in governments issuing negative advisories about the safety of countries in which the objective threat was minimal and many travel industry professionals providing consumers with advice on destinations based on media-fuelled perceptions rather than reality. Figures released by the US Department of Commerce's Office of Travel and Tourism Industries in June 2002 revealed that inbound tourism numbers dropped by 11 per cent during 2001 to 39.8 million compared with just over 44 million in 2000. The impact of the September 11 attack was the single biggest factor, with last-quarter figures dropping over 25 per cent.[22]

The international travel industry faced a challenge in which it needed to restore global confidence—not in any specific destination or region, but in travel as a form of leisure and as a means of conducting business. Adopting a 'sales-orientated' approach and mouthing glib, generalised statements that all would be well if we kept our chin up was not sufficient. There are several specific actions that the international travel, tourism and hospitality industry is able to implement relatively quickly to assist in the task of marketing world tourism to a frightened public:

- Establish an international marketing crisis team with representatives from the international tourism industry bodies such as WTO, IATA, WTTC, International Hotels Association, PATA and International Council of Tour Operators. This body would liaise and engage with the media, national governments and the United Nations. Its mantra would be to ensure that the interests of the international tourism industry are effectively represented to the international media and governments.

- Mount an information campaign through a coordinated website to provide reliable and verifiable information on security measures being undertaken throughout the world by airlines and the tourism industry. This site should be developed as an international travel industry perspective of country-by-country advisories, maintaining a data bank of testimonials by tourists who have just completed their visits or real-time testimonials of tourists currently on tour.

- Develop a global marketing strategy which effectively promotes tourism as a path to world peace and reconciliation, and encourage all national tourism bodies to incorporate this theme as an integral part of their marketing.

- Review the current status of travel insurance coverage for international travellers. The 'general exemption' through which travel insurance companies refuse to extend coverage for loss arising from acts of politically motivated violence is an unfair impost on travellers who are victims of a random act of terrorism such as the New York attack.

These measures represent some of the key issues that can be managed globally during times of crisis. Tourist authorities in many parts of the world must tailor their own marketing programs in accordance with their specific needs. Clearly, the events of September 11 and their emerging impact on global tourism will have a significant influence on destination marketing well into the future. In order to maximise the business benefits of destination marketing, it is important to recognise the fact that no destination is an island. As September 11 demonstrated, a terrorist attack on one internationally sensitive target has global ramifications. Regional marketing of tourism—and indeed global marketing of the benefits and the concept of international tourism—will be required to stimulate the recovery of social and financial confidence in tourism.

4 | EGYPT: TERRORIST ATTACKS AGAINST TOURISTS, 1990–98

Restoring confidence in tourism

CRISIS RANKING: **DESTCON 2**

BACKGROUND

The Great Pyramid of Giza and the Sphinx are the unofficial emblems of world tourism. Powerful symbols of Ancient Egypt, they encapsulate the lure of exotic, mysterious and ancient places, unfailingly enticing tourists to spend large amounts of money and travel long distances to explore and experience Egypt. The tombs and temples of Pharonic Egypt along the Nile have always been the mainstay of the Egyptian tourism industry. In Egypt, tourism is economically critical to the nation and the tourism industry is the most important source of Egypt's foreign exchange earnings.

The tourism industry in Egypt displays many contradictions. There is a high level of government involvement at all levels: the national carrier, EgyptAir, is government owned; Misr Travel, one of the largest Egyptian tour operators and accommodation-booking agencies, is also largely government owned; and Egypt's tourism marketing is coordinated by the government-owned Egyptian Tourist Authority. However, members of a parallel private tourism infrastructure comprising Egyptian- and foreign-owned tourism enterprises actively compete and trade with each other alongside the government-controlled operations.

Adding to the contradictions of Egypt as a tourism destination is the inconsistency of its infrastructure. Until 2000, the major international gateway entry to Egypt, Cairo Airport (especially the terminal for the national carrier,

EgyptAir), was a substandard facility. The main terminal was poorly maintained, and the handling of passenger documentation and baggage was at best primitive. For a country heavily dependent on international tourism, Cairo Airport left a deflating first impression—a problem Egyptian tourist authorities and EgyptAir were anxious to change. Away from the airport, Egypt's tourism infrastructure and services offer a mixture of standards ranging from world-class excellence to Third World chaos. The highest echelon of hotels are of international standard, but quality rapidly plummets below the four-star level. Budget accommodation meeting the requirements of Western travellers is relatively scarce in Egypt.

Tourists visiting the pyramids of Giza on the outskirts of Cairo. Photo courtesy Tempo Holidays Australia.

Egypt's internal transport system is comprehensive and, for the most part, reliable. Travellers seeking Nile cruises have a choice ranging from luxuriously appointed air-conditioned cruises at the top end of the market to sailing the Nile on an authentic *feluca* at the budget level. EgyptAir runs a world-class standard of service on long-haul international routes and on services to European countries. The airline provides a basic level of service on domestic and short-haul services as EgyptAir or under the branding of its subsidiary, Air Sinai.[1]

The sites of Ancient Egypt, Cairo and its environs, Luxor, Karnak, Abu Simbel, temples and tombs along the Nile River and the Mediterranean port city of Alexandria are still the main attractions for tourists to Egypt. However, the Egyptian tourism industry has actively promoted other destinations within

Egypt, including Hurghada on the Red Sea, the Sinai Peninsula and parts of the Western Desert. The completion of Israel's withdrawal from Sinai in 1982 led to substantial private and government tourist investment, which facilitated the development and establishment of several high-quality tourism resorts in the Sinai, which are popular among tourists from Europe and neighbouring Israel.

The 1979 Camp David Peace Agreement between Egypt and Israel bestowed many economic benefits on Egypt. These included self-sufficiency in oil (most of Egypt's oil production comes from wells in the Sinai) and a reduction in military expenditure. Peace guaranteed income from transit fees charged for the use of the Suez Canal, which was closed to sea traffic between 1967 and 1975. The Egyptians expanded substantially on the rudimentary tourism infrastructure established by Israel during its occupation of the Sinai from 1967–82. The attraction of Mt Sinai, the coral-fringed Red Sea coast, small local Bedouin settlements and spectacular desert scenery led to Sinai's growth in popularity as an all-year, ecotourism and soft adventure destination for Europeans and Israelis. Sinai's isolation from the rest of Egypt and the strictures of Islamic laws facilitated a more 'Western-friendly' attitude to alcohol and dress standards at Sinai's coastal and beach resorts than in the more heavily populated and traditional regions of Egypt.[2]

Twenty-first century Egypt has made considerable progress in marketing a more diverse image of the destination. The Egyptian Tourist Authority, while recognising the overriding attraction of 'Ancient Egypt', has sought to market alternative images of Egypt to appeal to niche markets including conferences and conventions, ecotourists, war veterans and their descendants, among others. The decentralisation of infrastructure and tourist attractions spreads the economic benefit of tourism throughout the country.

Since the end of hostilities between Egypt and Israel following President Sadat's visit to Jerusalem in November 1977 and the 1979 signing of the Camp David Agreement, Egypt's tourism industry has been relatively free from the impact of international conflict. Egypt's wars with Israel in 1948, 1956 and 1967, the War of Attrition between 1967 and 1971 and the October 1973 war collectively retarded tourism growth both in terms of infrastructure development and the potential marketability of Egypt as a tourism destination.

As mentioned, Egypt's return to Sinai provided many economic benefits for Egypt, opening up new, large inbound markets of curious Israelis followed by a substantial growth in European tourism. On the negative side, from 1979–82, many Arab countries which opposed the Egyptian–Israeli accord subjected Egypt to political isolation. Consequently, tourism from the Arab world slumped during this period. Following the assassination of President Anwar Sadat in October 1981, and his replacement by the more politically cautious Hosni Mubarak, Egypt was again gradually accepted within the Arab fold.

Domestically, the Camp David Agreement between Egypt and its former enemy, Israel, reignited a traditional source of opposition to many regimes in Egypt. The Muslim Brotherhood, which had long advocated Egypt as a state observing Islamic law, began to reassert itself following the agreement. Supporters of the Brotherhood were responsible for the assassination of Anwar Sadat. Sadat's successor, President Hosni Mubarak, had been engaged in a long struggle during his presidency to suppress the influence and support of the Muslim Brotherhood and its affiliated groups. In common with many Islamist groups in the Arab world, the Muslim Brotherhood in Egypt is characterised by hostility to European and American influence. A significant portion of its funding has come from foreign governments, including Iran.

The Iraqi invasion of Kuwait in August 1990, and the subsequent 'Gulf War' (Operation Desert Storm) in January and February of 1991, had a negative impact on tourism to Egypt in common with virtually all countries in the Eastern Mediterranean and Middle East. The Egyptian government committed a substantial military force in support of the United States-led coalition which expelled Iraqi forces from Kuwait, and was (apart from Saudi Arabia) the largest Arab force in the coalition which included Syria, the Gulf states, Saudi Arabia and Morocco. Despite the support of the Egyptian government for the anti-Iraq coalition, there was vocal Islamist opposition to Egypt's Gulf War involvement.

ISLAMIST ATTACKS AGAINST TOURISTS 1992–94

During the 1980s and throughout the Gulf War, Islamist protest was directed at government agencies, the military and the police. However, from 1992 the Islamist groups, including al-Jama'a al-Islamiyya and Jihad—splinter elements which had broken away from the larger Muslim Brotherhood—began to target the largest and most vulnerable sector of the Egyptian economy, tourism, as an expression of their opposition to the Egyptian government.[3]

During the period 1992–97, a series of attacks were directed at Western tourists and groups which terrorists identified (incorrectly) as Israelis. The attacks normally occurred in clusters over specific timeframes. This often gave Egyptian tourist officials the opportunity to market a recovery program after a cluster of incidents, only for this recovery to be derailed by another set of attacks against tourists.

Salah Wahab stated that, in a period of 22 months from early 1992–94, there were 127 terrorist attacks in Egypt directed against tourists, resulting in nine tourists killed and 60 injured. While Wahab points out that tourist casualties in these attacks were fewer in number than terrorist attacks against tourists in many Western countries, the 'over-enthusiastic' international media coverage of these incidents resulted in some tourist-generating countries issuing statements that travel to Egypt was considered unsafe.[4]

There were several motivations behind the targeting of tourists in Egypt by radical Islamists. Many Islamists resented what they saw as the culturally intrusive influence of mass tourism on Egyptian society in general, and on Islamic piety and observance in particular. The Islamists were well aware that tourism represented a major source of foreign exchange earnings for Egypt and for the Egyptian government. Thus undermining the tourism industry would lead to deterioration in Egypt's existing low standard of living and fuel social and political discontent, which might lead to the overthrow of the Egyptian political leadership.

Members of al-Islamiyya and Jihad believed that the economic benefits which tourism did bring to Egypt were monopolised by a small elite in Egyptian society and did not filter down to the average Egyptian. In order to win support from Egypt's poor, the Muslim Brotherhood and other Islamist groups established clinics, welfare centres, food distribution depots and other welfare activities directed at poverty-stricken Egyptians. These activities built up support for the Islamists and heightened domestic hostility towards the Egyptian government and foreign influence in Egypt, including tourists— a visible symbol of the ills afflicting Egyptian society as defined by the Islamist groups. The Mubarak government sought to repress the activities and the members of the radical groups. During the 1990s, thousands were arrested and imprisoned and many were killed as part of a crackdown on activists and supporters of the Islamist groups. Mubarak accused Egyptian Islamist activists of being linked to Iran and Sudan as a means of depicting them as traitors to Egypt rather than as internal opponents to his government's authority.[5]

The Egyptian government's initial response to the spate of attacks against tourists was confused and *ad hoc*. The government's initial response to the media and the international travel industry was a mixture of silence, evasions and bland assurances that the incidents were isolated and that tourists had nothing to worry about. These responses were clearly ineffective, and by the end of 1993 it was apparent that a professional approach to restoring confidence in destination Egypt was required.

As Table 4.1 clearly indicates, tourism receipts represent almost one-quarter of Egypt's measurable foreign exchange income. However, money spent by tourists in markets, stores, restaurants, on tips to tour guides, hotel staff and drivers, and on other cash transactions to providers of tourism-related services is not measured in government statistics. Consequently, the actual economic impact of tourism on Egypt is far higher than official statistics could possibly reveal. The Egyptian government quickly realised that it could not afford to ignore events which had the potential to erode such a significant source of foreign currency.

Table 4.1: Foreign exchange earnings, Egypt, 1993–98 (US$ millions)[6]

	1993/94	1994/95	1995/96	1996/97	1997/98	% share 1997/98
Tourism revenues	1779	2298	3009	3646	2941	24.4
Workers remits	3489	3455	2991	3354	3660	30.4
Suez Canal fees	1990	2058	1885	1848	1777	14.8
Petroleum	1362	2175	2226	2557	1728	14.9
Agriculture	275	616	321	271	244	2.0
Manufacturing	1223	2166	1314	1304	1685	14.0

The government upgraded security for buses, trains and tourist sites while at the same time devising a massive public education campaign to discredit the Islamists. It also sought to address the social problems the Islamists had highlighted by improving access to social welfare.

PLANNING EGYPT'S TOURISM MARKETING RECOVERY STRATEGY AFTER 1993

In October 1993, the Egyptian Ministry of Tourism, under the direction of Tourism Minister Mamdouh El Beltagui, centralised the remarketing of Egypt. Mr Fouad Sultan of the ministry then sought the assistance of international consultancy firm Burson-Marsteller. Mr Martin Langford, the company's Asia-Pacific Vice-Chairman, was appointed as principal adviser to the Egyptian Ministry of Tourism and Civil Aviation in the project to restore travel industry and consumer confidence in destination Egypt.[7] Langford was quoted as stating: 'Fear is the single biggest de-motivator of tourists to visit any destination.' In the case of Egypt, this was the key issue which needed to be addressed.

In 1993, Burson-Marsteller conducted a survey of 1000 US travellers on their key travel fears. The results identified that 56 per cent cited crime, 42 per cent airline safety, 41 per cent terrorist activity and 32 per cent lack of access to professional medical facilities. Of specific relevance to the Egyptian situation, but equally germane to all cases in this study, 75 per cent of respondents said that news reports were either a very or extremely important determinant in forming their opinion on whether a destination was safe or unsafe to visit.

Langford's guidelines on managing Egypt's tourism problems were quoted:

- Define the real problem, short- and long-term.
- The media, however hostile, is rarely the real problem; rather, he suggested that Egypt focus on measures to restore confidence.
- Centralise and control the information flow by appointing one spokesperson. Avoid lies and distortions, respect media deadlines, avoid speculation and control interviews and press briefings.
- Isolate a crisis management team from extraneous business concerns.
- Contain the problem. In the case of terrorism define the actual extent of the problem.
- Depend on no one individual fully and ensure that the management team is accountable to the tourism ministry or head office.
- Resist the urge to adopt a combative stand in media briefings and understand that the media is looking for the cause or a party to blame for the crisis. This involves resisting the temptation to give leads in this direction.
- Identify allies with whom you can work and who will support your case.
- Clarify what measures are being taken to address the problem.

In Egypt, efforts were made to ensure that foreign correspondents had ready access to fully briefed Egyptian officials. This was important, as Egyptian government officials are not traditionally amenable to media questioning.

The Egyptian Ministry of Tourism quickly established a crisis-management team. Cairo and London became the chief coordination offices between Burson-Marsteller and the Egyptian government, with satellite branches in key source markets including the United States, Spain, Italy, France and Germany. The Egyptian Tourism Minister conducted well-publicised visits to seven countries in North America and Europe. The Egyptians increased promotion of 'safe zone' regions within the country, including Red Sea resorts in the Gulf of Suez and Sinai, which were isolated from major population centres. Western students returning from study tours in Egypt were encouraged to act as spokespeople and providers of testimonials in their home countries. These measures, in addition to widespread media and travel agency familiarisation visits, all combined to aid in Egypt's recovery after 1994. Egypt-Air expanded its network in Western countries in the early 1990s, which enabled the airline to facilitate online services for these visits.

Wahab pointed out that, following the 1992–93 incidents, many Western governments introduced advisories warning tourists of the dangers of visiting Egypt. However, these were rescinded quite rapidly after Egypt's remedial measures were enacted.[8]

PRELUDE TO THE 1997 LUXOR MASSACRE

The problem vexing Egyptian tourist authorities was that the 1992–93 wave of terrorist incidents represented the first cluster of these attacks. According to Fawaz Gerges, radical and mainstream Islamist groups in Egypt were subjected to arrest and government restrictions were imposed against their activities. At the same time, the Mubarak government sought to adopt a more overtly Islamic political profile and to address some of the welfare concerns the Muslim Brotherhood had raised. The Egyptian government's carrot and stick approach to Islamist opposition led to a brief hiatus of attacks against tourists. Terrorist attacks against tourists were opposed by many Egyptians who derived their livelihood directly or indirectly from tourism, and also alienated some Egyptians who would otherwise have supported the Islamist radicals.[9]

Adrian Swincoe has identified the major incidents attributed to Islamist terrorists which would result in cyclical episodes of crisis and recovery in Egypt's tourism industry during the 1990s:[10]

- October 1992: British nurse killed in bus attack near Cairo.
- February 1993: Two tourists (one French and one American) killed outside a Cairo hotel.
- October 1993: One US and one French tourists killed outside a Cairo hotel.
- March 1994: One German tourist killed on a Nile cruise boat.
- September 1995: Two Germans and two Egyptians killed in the Red Sea resort city of Hurghada.
- October 1995: One Briton killed and one wounded with one Egyptian killed and five wounded in an attack on a tourist mini-van in the Nile Valley.
- April 1996: Eighteen Greek tourists killed and sixteen wounded in an attack on a tourist Coach near the Pyramids at Giza. It is believed the Greeks were incorrectly assumed by their attackers to have been Israelis.
- September 1997: Ten German tourists killed in an attack outside the Egyptian Museum in Cairo.
- November 1997: Fifty-eight tourists massacred in the area of the Luxor Temple. Victims of this worst massacre of tourists in Egypt during the 1990s included French, Swiss, British and Japanese nationals.

THE NOVEMBER 1997 LUXOR MASSACRE AND THE POST-MASSACRE TOURISM MARKETING RESTORATION OF EGYPT

The November 1997 Luxor massacre represented the climax of the Islamist attacks against tourists and resulted in wide-ranging changes to Egypt's management of tourism—far more radical than the measures taken in late 1993. The massacre was the last major Islamist attack against tourists in Egypt during the twentieth century. The perpetrators were subjected to universal condemnation, even from Islamist states such as Iran. The massacre so alienated radical Egyptian Islamists from the support of their fellow Egyptians that large-scale attacks were officially delegitimised as a tactic of Islamist opposition in Egypt.[11] Because thousands of Egyptian people dependent on tourism for their livelihood (especially in Luxor) were deprived of their incomes, Islamist radicals lost support of the very people who they claimed to represent.

Table 4.2: International visitor arrivals to Egypt, 1989–2000[12]

Year	Arrivals (000s)	% Annual change	Spending (US$m)	% Annual change
1989	2503	+27.1	2058	+15.4
1990	2603	+ 3.9	1944	–5.5
1991	2214	–14.8	2029	+ 4.4
1992	3207	+44.8	2730	+ 34.5
1993	2508	–21.8	1927	–29.4
1994	2582	+ 3.0	2000	+ 4.1
1995	3133	+21.4	2686	+33.9
1996	3975	+26.9	3288	+22.4
1997	3961	–0.4	3801	+15.6
1998	3456	–12.7	2801	–26.3
1999	4405	+27.5	NA	NA
2000	5116	+13.9	NA	NA

Table 4.2 demonstrates the cyclical nature of international tourism to Egypt during the 1990s and the impact of specific cycles of terrorism on inbound tourism to Egypt.

Table 4.2 demonstrates the negative impacts on overall inbound tourism to Egypt of the 1990–91 Gulf War; the commencement of terrorist attacks against tourists in 1992–93; and the impact of the Luxor massacre in particular in late 1997. The overall impact is amplified by Table 4.3. which demonstrates trends from source countries. As most of the attacks were directed at Western tourists, visitors from the Arab and Muslim countries in Africa and Asia were far less subject to variations in inbound numbers than tourists from Europe, East Asia/Oceania, Israel and North America. From a more positive perspective, the table clearly demonstrates that the recovery period after a crisis takes about a year to return to growth. After the Luxor massacre, tourism recovery to Egypt (which surged in 2000) was aided by a combination of the implementation of the Burson-Marsteller recovery mode coupled with heavily increased internal security and an intensive marketing campaign by the Egyptian Tourist Authority which portrayed Egypt as a core millennial destination.

It is notable that one of the biggest source-market declines after Luxor occurred in Japan. Japanese tourists are particularly sensitive to safety concerns, especially as Japanese visiting 'exotic destinations' such as Egypt tend to travel in groups. Egypt had become a very popular 'exotic' destination for Japanese

Table 4.3: Major regional sources of tourism to Egypt in selected years ('000s)[13]

	1982	1995	1996	1997	1998
Middle East	618	1038	1150	1186	1021
% of total	43.4	33.1	29.5	29.9	31.0
Americas	193	299	259	257	207
% of total	13.6	7.3	6.6	6.5	6.0
Europe	524	1515	2022	2102	1970
% of total	36.8	48.4	51.9	53.1	57.0
Others (includes Asia/Oceania)	88	351	465	416	207
% of total	6.2	11.2	11.9	10.4	6.0

due to direct air connections from Tokyo and an infrastructure that lent itself to relatively short-duration package tourism. When Japanese were among the victims of the 1997 Luxor massacre, this market rapidly declined.

In addition to the Burson-Marsteller approach to marketing Egypt out of crisis, the Egyptian Tourist Authority and EgyptAir worked very closely with the private sector to entice tourists from major markets to return to Egypt. Major international tour operators, including Insight Vacations (formerly Insight International), Trafalgar Tours and others, offered heavily discounted packages to Egypt in conjunction with clients purchasing another Insight product. In 1993, $1 one-week packages to Egypt could be purchased over a limited period provided the purchase was made in conjunction with a full-priced Britain and Europe package. Such deals had a major impact in boosting long-haul source markets such as Australia and New Zealand. These offers were subsidised by the companies, the carriers and the Egyptian Tourist Authority.

One issue not fully addressed after the terrorist incidents of 1992–94 was the overall improvement of security. While the Egyptian government had made improvements to traveller security, it remained far from adequate. A factor that contributed to the high death toll of the Luxor massacre in November 1997 was the fact that a lone elderly guard was assigned to protect one of Egypt's most visited tourist sites. After Luxor, the Egyptian government massively increased security details assigned to all major tourist sites and this was accompanied by a relentless crackdown on Islamist groups. The Islamic Brotherhood was stung by outrage within Egypt and internationally over the Luxor massacre and officially disavowed attacks against tourists after Luxor. Five years later, there had been no reports of lethal attacks against tourists in Egypt by Islamist groups.

During previous outbreaks of terrorist attacks, many Western countries, including Europe, the United States, Canada, Japan, Australia and New Zealand, issued travel advisories warning tourists of the dangers associated with Luxor and other tourist sites in Egypt. In most cases, these advisories were quickly rescinded once the Egyptian government could demonstrate remedial measures had been taken. The Egyptian tourism authorities treated the advisories very seriously and were anxious to encourage their early revocation. The Egyptian Tourist Authority went to considerable lengths to invite foreign diplomats to inspect the upgraded security regime in tourist centres, which included enlarged police contingents and electronic surveillance at entry points.

In long-haul source destinations such as the United States, Canada, Japan and Australia, Egypt began to experiment in joint marketing exercises, especially with the travel industry, from 1995. In Australia during 1996, Misr Travel (the government-owned Egyptian travel operator), in association with the Israel Government Tourism Office, inaugurated a series of successful joint product seminars in all major Australian cities.[14] The Sydney Hilton function attracted 600 travel professional and 28 presenter companies and ranks as one of the largest ever destination travel industry functions staged specifically for travel agents held in Australia. The evening featured cultural performances and speeches by the ambassadors of both countries. These functions also served as an opportunity to launch EgyptAir's direct Sydney–Cairo services which had commenced in late 1995. The joint Egypt–Israel travel industry promotions would begin a trend towards the regionalisation of travel industry marketing for the Eastern Mediterranean and Middle East in Australia and New Zealand. Egypt also continued with destination specific promotions in its key source markets.

The joint marketing of Israel, Egypt, Jordan and the Palestinian Authority also became a feature of marketing Egypt to the travel industry in the United States, Canada and Japan. During the American Society of Travel Agents (ASTA) conventions from 1998–99, there were several joint presentations by Israeli, Egyptian and Jordanian travel industry officials.

Following terrorist incidents during the 1990s, the Egyptian Tourist Authority, EgyptAir and Misr Travel realised that there was an urgent need to actively market Egypt to the trade. There were many synergies between the Israeli, Egyptian and Jordanian travel industries, which made it mutually beneficial for them to cooperate on joint marketing exercises, especially from long-haul source markets. Many operators from long-haul source markets, notably the United States, Canada and Australasia, marketed Egypt and Israel as a dual-destination and occasionally Egypt, Israel and Jordan as a triple-destination combination, especially after the Israel–Jordan peace agreement of October 1994. Both Egypt and Israel had to overcome an image of being dangerous destinations for tourists; the nature and targets of terrorism were different between the two countries but both suffered equally in terms of their perception. In Europe, the Egyptian Tourist Authority, EgyptAir, the Egyptian Association of Travel Agents and Misr Travel embarked upon a massive marketing campaign to lure Europeans to Egypt. Pricing was an integral element of the campaign: by offering limited but heavily discounted lead-in prices on Egyptian tourism product, coupled with an information campaign to demonstrate that Egypt had addressed the security concerns of travellers, the market in Europe recovered quite rapidly during late 1998 and through-out 1999.

One marketing factor which hastened the recovery of the Egyptian tourism industry after the Luxor massacre of November 1997 was the prospect of a millennial tourism influx. Egypt was able to promote tourism on two levels. First, it had a legitimate stake in promoting itself as a pilgrimage destination to Christians commemorating Christianity's bi-millennium, based on the belief that Jesus and his family (as quoted in the New Testament) spent three years in Egypt. Among the early Christian communities established outside the Holy Land, Alexandria was one of the first major centres of Christian life. Many of Egypt's 7 million Copts (an Egyptian Christian denomination) claim ancestry from these early Christians—and indeed further back to Pharonic Egypt. The Egyptian tourist authorities played an active role in developing promotional material to appeal to the Christian market, as the bi-millennial would be a one-year event. In March 2000, Egypt was part of the Pope's visit to countries regarded as the birthplace of Christianity, including Jordan, Israel and the Palestinian Authority areas. In 1999, many tours were marketed to link the last Christmas of the old millennium in Bethlehem and

Jerusalem with ushering in the new millennium at the foot of the Pyramids in Cairo.

Egypt's other marketing coup was related to a more traditional attraction—the Great Pyramid. During 1999, there was intense speculation fuelled by the international media (with the tacit blessing of the Egyptian tourism industry) which spurred passionate internal debate within Egypt that a top, including a massive crystal, would be placed on the apex of the Great Pyramid at the stroke of midnight to usher in 2000. The 'completion of the Pyramid' was thought to culminate in a range of bizarre scenarios which encompassed everything from Armageddon, a takeover of the world by the Illuminati, the New World Order, the collapse of the world through the Y2K bug, the coming of the Messiah, the second coming of Jesus, the reptilian ascendency, the arrival of an alien invasion and the reincarnation of the Pharaohs, depending on which seer or conspiracy theorist was regarded as the appropriate authority on this matter. It eventuated that the Egyptian government acceded to local Islamic complaints that this event was 'un-Islamic'. There was a tacit superstition that the pyramid ritual would trigger one or all of these unwelcome manifestations and the government cancelled this event, ensuring that none of the above scenarios was vindicated. However, because cancellation of the Great Pyramid's ceremony occurred at the last minute, Egyptian tourist authorities and private firms were able to promote this belatedly truncated ultimate millennium event with full vigour.

The only part of the Pyramid extravaganza which proceeded was the massive rock music concert behind the Great Pyramid which was supposed to climax in the placing of the Pyramid's apex. The rock concert did go ahead, although it was something of an anti-climax partially due to fog which prevented a laser display. Of course, the spectre of this 'ultimate event' and the frenzied media-manufactured excitement it created about Egypt contributed substantially to reactivating traveller enthusiasm for Egypt during 1999.

According to an Egyptian tourism official interviewed for this study,[15] Egypt's tourism industry had fully recovered from the impact of the Luxor massacre by 2000. The only significant source market which had not been restored was Japan, largely due to the fact that a substantial portion of the casualties at Luxor were Japanese and there was a lingering reluctance to return. The largely secular and overwhelming non-Christian Japanese market was not interested in Christianity's bi-millennial.

Aside from the Japanese market, Egypt has been able to expand and upgrade its tourism infrastructure and increase prices for tourism product since 1999. Since late September 2000, it has been a relative beneficiary of Israel's tourism problems and while there were some initial cancellations from travellers on combined Egypt–Israel packages, Egypt has distanced itself from Israel's problems. The marketing cooperation between the Egyptian tourism authorities and Israel, which was a feature of the period 1996 to early 2000, had evaporated by the end of the millennium year.

PRIVATE AND PUBLIC SECTOR MARKETING COOPERATION IN EGYPT IN RESPONSE TO THE CRISES OF THE 1990s

One factor which distinguishes the Egyptian tourism industry from Israel's (discussed in Chapter 5) is the high level of government control. EgyptAir and the country's largest land tour operator, Misr Travel, are both government owned and together exercise strong influence on matters such as hotel pricing. In times of crisis, including the Luxor massacre, they are in a position to exert strong price pressures on privately-owned hotel chains and other private operators.

Part of the Egyptian recovery strategy included a reduction in prices to induce tourists to return after the three main waves of terrorism in 1992–93, 1996 and 1997. There was far stronger uniformity of price restraint in Egypt than in other countries with a stronger tendency to a free market economy. Special deals were directed to key source markets in the Arab world, Israel, North America, Europe and Oceania.

EgyptAir, the Egyptian Tourist Authority and Misr Travel were also able to combine to facilitate large-scale hostings of travel agents and travel journalists from the electronic and print media. EgyptAir had to overcome a major image problem following the crash of an EgyptAir flight from New York to Cairo in late 1999, resulting in the deaths of over 200 passengers. In response to the disaster, the carrier's management rapidly implemented techniques introduced by Burson-Marsteller in 1993–94. While the crash's impact on the carrier's reputation was considerable, its overall impact on the destination marketing of Egypt was manageable.

The 1990s was a decade in which Egypt returned to the business and political mainstream of the Arab world. Tourism from such key source markets such as the oil-rich Persian Gulf states, which had diplomatically isolated Egypt in the late 1970s and early 1980s, had fully restored ties during the 1990s. The resurgence of Arab tourism to Egypt has compensated for the reduction in tourism from Israel during the second half of 2000 and during 2001, a consequence of the cooling of relations between the two countries throughout this period.

In common with most other countries in the Eastern Mediterranean and the Middle East, Egypt suffered a brief downturn in tourism following the September 11, 2001 attacks on New York City and Washington DC.

CONCLUSION

Terrorism directed against tourists is one of the most severe challenges a tourism destination can face. While the causes of these acts derived from internal religious/political disputes between the Egyptian government and Islamist groups, the expression of dissent by targeting international tourism had the potential to cripple the Egyptian economy—an economy in which tourism is a critical and financially significant element. The Egyptian government's response to actual security threats was only partially successful after the events of 1992–93 and 1995. After the massacres of 1997, the security response appeared to have forestalled any major outbreaks.

From a marketing perspective, the Egyptian response to the acts of terrorism was successful. The centralised nature of Egypt's tourism marketing facilitated the employment of a national marketing strategy. The strong synergy and coordination between public and private sectors of Egypt's tourism industry facilitated a relatively disciplined and focused marketing response to the terrorist outbreaks.

The utilisation of Burson-Marsteller's consulting services in 1993 enabled the Egyptian tourism industry and the Egyptian Tourist Authority to implement a highly professional and structured marketing response and recovery strategy following the terrorist incidents.

After the Luxor massacre of November 1997, the marketing opportunities presented by the millennium and Christianity's bi-millennial provided a positive marketing focus, which assisted the hastening of Egypt's recovery process. However, the employment of a centralised and focused recovery program was the foundation of Egypt's largely successful recovery from a potentially crippling and challenging threat to the viability of its tourism industry.

5 | ISRAEL: THE PALESTINIAN UPRISING, 2000–02

Promotion of tourism during an ongoing crisis

RANKING: **DESTCON 2**

BACKGROUND

Israel's 3000 years as a tourism and pilgrimage destination should, by the twenty-first century, have qualified it as one of the world's most popular international tourist destinations. The holy sites within its borders, especially Jerusalem, are venerated by half the world's population—3 billion adherents of Christianity, Islam and Judaism. The Israeli port city of Haifa is world headquarters of the 5 million-strong Baha'i faith. Israel is a small country, equivalent in size to the US state of New Jersey or Wales in the United Kingdom, with a tremendous variety of scenery, terrain and climate, ranging from snow-capped mountains to barren desert. The country has shores on four very different bodies of water: the Mediterranean Sea; the sweet-water Sea of Galilee; the lowest point on earth and the world's saltiest and most buoyant body of water, the Dead Sea; and, in the south, the Red Sea, with its abundance of coral and marine life. Israel stands at the crossroads between Europe, Asia and Africa. The known human history of 250 000 years has bequeathed a wealth of archaeological treasures from the numerous civilisations which dwelt in ancient Israel and those left by foreign invaders during 23 000 years of civilisation. In September 2001, archaeologists digging on the drought-exposed shores of the Sea of Galilee found the remains of a 23 000-year-old village; it existed 13 000 years before any previously known urban centre.

Israel has a sophisticated and advanced tourism infrastructure, excellent roads and transport facilities, a wide range of well-maintained accommodation options, a highly educated, multilingual and multi-ethnic population with rich and varied cultural backgrounds. It is a maximum of five hours' flying time from any point in Europe and is easily accessible from North America, Africa and Asia. From the more distant source markets of Australasia and South America, flying time to Israel is no more than 22 hours. The main sites of the country can easily be visited within one week. Yet, despite its strong

Approaching the Western (Wailing) Wall, with the Dome of the Rock in the background, Jerusalem. Photo courtesy Israel Ministry of Tourism.

destination image, Israel has rarely attracted the numbers of tourists its infrastructure can manage.

The growth of Israel's tourism industry has been subject to frequent interruptions due to outbreaks of external threats and internal inter-communal violence. Conflict between Israel and its neighbouring countries has been limited since 1990 to the Iraqi missile attacks during the 1991 Gulf War and outbreaks of tension on Israel's frontier with Lebanon. However, the moves towards a resolution of the Israeli–Palestinian conflict have fluctuated between periods of relative calm and outbreaks of fighting between the nascent Palestinian Authority and splinter groups within the Palestinian population and the Israeli government. During the 1990s and the first years of the twenty-first century, tourism has been a barometer of Israeli–Palestinian relations. During periods of calm, tourism to Israel and the Palestinian territories has surged. During times of conflict, however, tourism numbers have severely contracted. Although conflict has been a recurring pattern in Israel's modern history, tourists are rarely targeted. Since 1972, when 22 tourists—most of whom were Christian pilgrims from Puerto Rica—were killed by terrorists at Ben Gurion (formerly Lod) International Airport, the only other case of tourists killed by terrorist action occurred on August 8, 2001 when two tourists were among fifteen people killed by a suicide bomber at a pizza café in Jerusalem, and two were killed in a suicide bomb attack in Netanya on March 27, 2002. Unlike Egypt in the 1990s, where tourists were the prime target of Islamist terrorists, in Israel the targeting of tourists is rare—a fact rarely mentioned by the vast international media contingent of at least 350 foreign correspondents permanently based in Israel. The Israeli–Palestinian 'peace process', which officially began with the televised handshake between Israeli Prime Minister Yitzhak Rabin and PLO leader Yasser Arafat on September 13, 1993, heralded a sense of confidence that tourism would be an integral part of the peace process and a tangible peace dividend. There were periods in which this optimism was justified. During 1995, Israel experienced a record year for tourism numbers, with over 2.5 million tourists visiting the country.[1]

Until November of that year, significant progress had been achieved in the Israeli–Palestinian peace process. Israel and Jordan established full diplomatic relations in October 1994, and during 1994 diplomatic ties were established between Israel and the Vatican. In September 1995, significant additions had been made to territories under the control of the Palestinian Authority (PA)—including Bethlehem, the birthplace of Jesus, thus providing PA control over one of Christianity's most revered sites. Israel was gradually accepted as an economic partner within the broader Middle East, with diplomatic or quasi-diplomatic ties established with seven Arab countries.[2]

In September 1995, Rabin's Labour-led coalition government hosted the 'Prime Minister's Conference for Peace Tourism', a major international conference for tourism industry leaders. Israel promoted 1995 as its Peace Tourism Year.

The assassination of Israel's Prime Minister Yitzhak Rabin by a Jewish extremist in November 1995, followed by a series of Islamist-inspired bombings in Jerusalem and Tel Aviv during February–March 1996, undermined the peace process. The election of a right-wing government in May 1996, led by Benjamin Netanyahu, and the reignition of conflict between Israel and the Palestinians, resulted in Israel experiencing a substantial reduction in tourist numbers during 1996.

During 1997–98, tourism to Israel was affected by anti-Netanyahu sentiment in the Arab world which was echoed internationally. In 1997, there was an outbreak of Israel–Palestinian fighting over widely reported false claims made by the PA that an archaeological tunnel leading from the Western Wall to the Via Dolorosa in Jerusalem was undermining the Muslim holy sites on the Temple Mount. In late 1998, there was international concern over the possible outbreak of war centred on Iraq and the fear that Iraq may have targeted Israel for missile attacks.

Throughout 1999, optimism returned to the Middle East political scene, with the election of a Labour Party-dominated coalition led by Ehud Barak. Mr Barak was committed to finalising a peace agreement with the Palestinian Authority and Israel's Arab neighbours. Barak's election was met with cautious optimism internationally and within the Middle East. In 2000, both Israel and the PA were preparing to host their greatest-ever influx of foreign tourists arriving to commemorate Christianity's bi-millennial. The highlight of the year was the Papal visit to Egypt, Jordan, Israel and the PA areas in March 2000. In the lead-up to the year dubbed by Israel as Holy Land 2000 and by the PA as Bethlehem 2000, there had been substantial improvements in tourism infrastructure. The Israeli government committed considerable funding to the beautification of Nazareth, Christian pilgrimage sites in Jerusalem and the Galilee. The Palestinian Authority made major improvements in Bethlehem and international hoteliers had invested large sums of money to build new hotels and improve existing hotels throughout Israel and the PA-ruled cities of Bethlehem, Jericho and, to a lesser extent, in Gaza. In the PA-ruled city of Jericho, the first legal casino in the Middle East had been opened in the expectation of a gambling-led windfall. Israel had also made considerable improvements to Ben Gurion International Airport, 13 kilometres from Tel Aviv, enabling the airport to handle a substantial increase in passenger numbers.[3]

There were plans for tourism cooperation between Israel and Jordan, including a joint airport facility for the Red Sea ports of Eilat in Israel and

Aqaba in Jordan and joint eco-tourism developments on the shores of the Dead Sea, in which Israel controlled the western shores and Jordan controlled the eastern.

In February 1999, the Israel Ministry of Tourism, in cooperation with the Palestinian Ministry of Tourism and Antiquities, hosted a delegation of 400 senior Christian ministers from all over the world as part of a broader campaign to attract Christian pilgrimage groups before, during and after 2000. In Europe, North America and Australasia, Israel Government Tourist Offices (IGTOs) engaged in joint promotions to the travel industry and consumers with their Egyptian, Jordan and Palestinian colleagues or representatives. In the United States, the Jordanian Tourist Board, the Palestinian Ministry of Tourism and Antiquities and the Israel Ministry of Tourism placed joint advertisements in major US newspapers, inviting Americans to come to the region and experience a year of peace. In Australia, leading tour operator Ya'lla Tours persuaded the resident Israeli, Egyptian and Jordanian ambassadors to sign a joint invitation inviting Christians to visit all three destinations.

In June 1999, the Israel Ministry of Tourism invited all its overseas personnel responsible for public relations (including the author) to gather for a final PR planning conference to market Holy Land 2000. The major decisions made at the conference were to intensify the targeting of Christian communities and church leaders; invite record numbers of travel journalists and TV crews to promote Israel in the respective source markets; and intensify the Holy Land 2000 message to the travel industry and public. The delegates were shown the developments in major pilgrimage sites in Israel and in PA-controlled Bethlehem to enable them to base their promotions on first-hand experience. Simultaneously a cooperation conference was held between Israeli and Palestinian tourism industry leaders. In 2000, the Israel Ministry of Tourism was preparing to host about 3 million tourists. Four peak periods were expected: the March Papal visit; Easter in April; the Feast of Tabernacles in September 2000; the Christmas/New Year period of December 1999–January 2000; and Christmas, December 2000.

The marketing lead-up for 2000 involved the Israel Ministry of Tourism and its overseas representatives since 1994. The normalisation of diplomatic relations between Israel and the Vatican in that year facilitated the commitment of the Catholic Church as the largest single Christian denomination (a billion adherents) to support and encourage Catholic pilgrimage to the Holy Land.[4]

During the first nine months of 2000, the tourist authorities of Israel and the Palestinian Authority had every reason to feel confident. In the period January–September, each month registered an all-time record number of tourism arrivals. The Papal visit in March to Jordan, Israel and the Palestinian Authority cities of Bethlehem and Jericho was an outstanding success in terms of attracting pilgrimage tourism. Over 100 000 foreign visitors arrived in Israel during one week in March 2000, primarily to witness the Papal visit. Accommodation facilities were stretched beyond capacity. Pope John Paul II visited all the major sites of Christian significance and Judaism's holiest site, the Western Wall. The Pope was present at a service at Jerusalem's Holocaust memorial centre, Yad Vashem. The Pontiff also visited the Temple Mount, known to Muslims as the Haram El Sharif, a place of supreme spiritual significance to Jews and Christians (and Islam's third holiest site). It is arguable that the Papal visit, which was covered by a massive international media contingent, achieved more in focusing positive attention on Israel and the PA territories as a prime millennial tourism destination than all the marketing activities of the Israel Ministry of Tourism worldwide in the six years prior to the event.[5]

As the year 2000 continued, statistical indicators showed that Israel's annual inbound tourism numbers were set to exceed 3 million for the first time in the country's history. However, political events were to puncture the mood of optimism. By July 2000, US President Bill Clinton was nearing the end of his second and final term in office. Israeli PM Ehud Barak and Palestinian Authority Chairman Yasser Arafat were seeking a final status resolution to the Israeli–Palestinian peace process (one year beyond the Oslo accord's deadline). The parties met at the US presidential retreat Camp David, where former Israeli Prime Minister Menachem Begin, Egyptian President Anwar Sadat and US President Jimmy Carter had for thirteen days fleshed out the first Israeli–Arab peace agreement between Israel and Egypt in late 1978, consummated in March 1979.

OUTBREAK OF THE SEPTEMBER 28, 2000 TOURISM CRISIS IN ISRAEL

The Camp David Summit of July 2000, in which Bill Clinton, Ehud Barak, Yasser Arafat and their aides were bunkered together for over two weeks, failed to reach an agreement. The Israeli government, supported by the Clinton adminstration, offered the most far-reaching concessions ever made by an Israeli goverment to the Palestinians, including an offer to withdraw from over 95 per cent of the West Bank and all of Gaza, and shared sovereignity in Jerusalem. This was rejected by Arafat on the grounds that Israel refused the Palestinian demand to grant all Palestinian refugees of 1948, and their descendents, the right to return to their former homes in Israel. The consequence of failing to achieve a United States-brokered Israeli–Palestinian political agreement was the underlying cause which eventually led to the outbreak of Palestinian–Israeli violence, commencing on September 28, 2000 and maintained into 2002. Simplistic and naïve media assertions that Ariel Sharon's visit to the Temple Mount days before the outbreak of the 'Al Aqsa Intifada' caused the violence, as opposed to its true position as a trigger event, do not stand the test of serious research.[6]

The critical point for this study is the indisputable fact that, from the time violence commenced and because it continued for an extended period, its considerable impact on tourism to Israel and extreme impact on tourism to the Palestinian Authority territories resulted in tourism becoming the principal economic casualty of this conflict for both sides. In the period October 1, 2000–December 31, 2001, Israel's Ministry of Tourism figures revealed that international tourism numbers were consistently down by 55 per cent on the corresponding months of the previous year. Tourism numbers from the PA's Tourism Ministry are less accessible. The combination of military blockades on crossing points between Israel and PA-administered territories, coupled with the fact that most of the violence occurred or originated in territories under PA administration, resulted in virtually all Western governments advising their citizens to defer travel to PA areas. It is estimated that foreign tourism to PA territories decreased (conservatively) at a rate of 90–95 per cent. The PA's Tourism Ministry website's press release of April 2001 revealed that the Palestinian tourism industry had lost US$150 million in revenue in the period October 2000–March 2001. In terms of the small Palestinian economy, losses in tourism revenues were catastrophic. Israel's losses in the corresponding period were estimated at US$1.5 billion, with a loss of over 20 000 jobs in tourism and tourism-dependent enterprises.[7]

The total of Israel's inbound tourism numbers in 2000 was an all-time record (2.675 million), but the downturn over the last three months of the year meant that Israel's tourism numbers fell short of its most conservative target for that year.

Israel has a well-developed contingency plan for the management of short-term crises impacting on its tourism industry. The two main Israel Ministry of Tourism websites, <www.infotour.co.il> and <www.goisrael.com>, provide the travel industry and travellers with a highly sophisticated guide to Israel and ready real-time information on developments. The IGTO offices in Israel and worldwide regularly update the travel industry and the media on developments during a crisis. This service has been upgraded since the 1990–91 Gulf War crisis. Israel government tourism offices have maintained contact with foreign ministries in the countries and regions in which they operate. The Israel Ministry of Tourism's head office in Jerusalem normally provides overseas IGTOs with immediate situation updates. Traditionally, there has been a post-crisis marketing strategy in place, which involved travel agents, media and key market segments (usually Christian ministers) with familiarisation visits. Since the 1991 Gulf War, most outbreaks of political violence in Israel and the PA territories have been of relatively short duration and recovery phases have tended to be relatively rapid. As tourists are rarely targeted deliberately or accidentally, Israel has normally been able to reassure tourists that there is minimal threat to their personal safety.

The major challenge for the Israel Ministry of Tourism is to deflect the impression of the country generated by the news media, which magnifies an outbreak of terrorism in a specific locality in Israel or the PA territories as either a 'Middle East' crisis or depicting all of Israel as a 'war zone' or a 'hot spot'. The main strategy in refuting this media imaging is the utilisation of an isolation strategy, in which consumers and industry are made aware of the specific trouble spots followed by a message that, overall, the country is safe. This approach is commonly used in destination crisis management worldwide.

There were several factors which made the 'Al Aqsa Intifada' a unique crisis in Israel's history:

- This was the first *long-term armed* conflict between Israel and the PA.
- There was no obvious timetable and any resolution appears to be open-ended.
- The extensive use by factions within the Palestinian community of suicide bombers who randomly target crowded areas where large

numbers of civilians gather has made it difficult to state with any degree of certainty that there are 'safe havens' for tourists.

- *Government Travel Advisories:* The US State Department, which impacts on Israel's largest single tourist source market, advised US citizens to defer travel to Israel from October 2000. By early 2002, The US advisory remained in force.

The US was alone among Western governments in advising their citizens to defer or avoid travelling to Israel. Virtually all major Western countries advised their citizens to avoid travel only to PA-controlled areas in the West Bank and Gaza. These advisories have been catastrophic for the Palestinian tourism industry, but have also negatively impacted on Israel. While most European and Asian countries fell short of advising their citizens to defer travel to Israel, many advised avoiding specific parts of the country (in many cases, Jerusalem) and all advised travellers to maintain a high level of security awareness. Travel advisories have an important influence on travel insurance coverage. If a government advises travellers to defer travel to a third country, then it is very difficult for travellers to obtain normal travel insurance coverage when visiting that country.[8]

- *Long-term closure of Bethlehem:* Many Christian pilgrims, who represented over a third of Israel's inbound market during 2000, either cancelled or postponed their travel to Israel after September 2000 on the grounds that they were unable to visit Bethlehem (the birthplace of Jesus), which is under PA jurisdiction. Most other major Christian holy sites were accessible to tourists during the crisis. The exclusion of Bethlehem (even though a visit there may involve only two to three hours of a one-week program) rendered a pilgrimage tour at best incomplete and at worst pointless for most Christians—especially Catholic and Orthodox pilgrims.

Some Israelis (including a small minority in the tourism industry) have little grasp of the significance of Bethlehem to most Christians. A minority of Israeli tourism industry professionals believe that Nazareth (City of the Annunciation), which is wholly in Israeli territory, is an acceptable substitute for Bethlehem. Important as Nazareth is to Christians, such opinions represent ignorance of, and insensitivity towards, Christians. During the 2000–02 political violence, Bethlehem and its environs were one of the most active flashpoints of the Israeli–Palestinian conflict. The most graphic image of the impact of the Bethlehem factor on tourism was depicted by the media on Christmas Day 2000. Usually the Christmas Eve/Christmas Midnight Mass in Bethlehem attracts between 10 000 and 15 000 pilgrims. Both Israeli and Palestinian tourist authorities were expecting a far larger than average influx of Christian pilgrims for Christianity's 2000th Christmas. In 2000, the Midnight Mass was cancelled and fewer than 100 foreigners attended Christmas services in Bethlehem. Bethlehem's anti-climactic Christmas was reflected in nearby Jerusalem, where hotels (which are usually overbooked) were almost empty. This scenario was repeated in 2001.

• *Media reporting:* International media reporting of the Israeli–Palestinian conflict has been intense and constant. From a tourism perspective the main problem raised by the coverage has been the reporting of events as a 'Middle East' crisis and the depiction of Israel as a 'hot spot' or 'war zone'. No tourism authority has the media resources at its disposal to effectively counter this level or extent of negative media coverage.

Media coverage of events in Israel resulted in neighbouring Jordan becoming a collateral destination victim of the Israeli-Palestinian conflict. Since the 1994 peace agreement between Israel and Jordan, the tourism industries of both countries have become increasingly intertwined. Israel and Jordan have been marketed since the mid-1990s as twin or complimentary destinations, especially in Europe, North America, Asia and Oceania. As the Israeli–Palestinian conflict continued, Jordan was forced to distance itself from its tourism ties with Israel.[9]

Marketing cooperation between Israel's tourism authorities and the private sector and their equivalents in Jordan and Egypt was downgraded.

As the conflict continued, a growing number of airlines and operators either downgraded, suspended or cancelled flights and tours to Israel. Even Israel's national carrier, El Al Airlines, reduced or cancelled services on certain routes.[10]

Many Mediterranean cruise services which included Israeli ports chose to exclude Israel from their itineraries. Many of their passengers were US citizens, whose government had advised them to defer travel to Israel.[11]

• *Travel insurance problems:* Travel insurance coverage is closely linked to government travel advisories. Consequently, some travel insurance companies either denied or restricted insurance cover or charged substantial premiums to travellers to Israel. An important fact made public to Israel's advantage was the passage in 1970 of legislation by the Israeli parliament (the Knesset) which provided that the Israeli government would extend free insurance cover to Israeli citizens and foreign visitors who suffered loss, injury or death due to acts of politically motivated terrorism on Israeli territory. Such coverage is rarely provided elsewhere in the world. The coverage overcame what the insurance industry defines as the 'general exemption'—a clause which entitles travel insurance companies to refuse claims for injuries or loss resulting from politically motivated violence anywhere in the world.[12]

- *MICE market (meetings, incentives, conferences, exhibitions) eroded:* Many organisations which had arranged conferences and incentives in Israel cancelled arrangements following the outbreak of Israeli–Palestinian violence. The rash of cancellations severely reduced occupancy rates of Israeli hotels and convention centres.[13]

The points outlined above represent some of the challenges faced by Israeli tourist authorities and their international representatives. The primary challenge, as the Israeli–Palestinian conflict became increasingly protracted, was to implement a marketing strategy for destination Israel *during* a crisis, rather than waiting for the problem to end. The majority of case studies in this work deal with developing and implementing a post-crisis marketing strategy. Israel realised (in common with Sri Lanka) that an economy of which tourism is an integral part was unable to wait indefinitely for the political crisis to be resolved.

While tourism represents 6 per cent[14] of Israel's GDP, it is a significant employer and plays an important role in the overall strength of the country's economy. Tourism contributes considerably to Israel's image in the outside world and its inclusion in the international community. For a country which has experienced a large part of its recent history as an international political pariah, the strength of the tourism industry is an important psychological barometer to Israel's international acceptability.

By the end of 2000, the Israel Ministry of Tourism internalised the reality that this particular crisis was protracted. By June 2001, some 50 000 jobs in Israel's tourism sector had been lost and many more tourism and hospitality employees were either employed only part time or placed on extended training schemes. The private sector had placed pressure on the Israel Ministry of Tourism to alleviate the economic impact of the crisis.[15]

ISRAEL'S TOURISM RECOVERY PROGRAM

In January 2001 the Ministry called all its PR specialists worldwide to a conference in Jerusalem to map a strategy for marketing Israel during and after the crisis. The Ministry hired international PR firm Ruder Finn to provide marketing consultancy services.[16]

Unlike many destinations which (apart from travellers visiting friends and relatives) rely predominantly on discretionary travellers, Israel is able to draw on specific market segments which travel to Israel out of a perceived connection or tie. The Diaspora Jewish community (irrespective of family links) is one such market which can be called upon to express solidarity with Israel through visiting. There is also a large group within the Christian world loosely defined as 'Christian Zionists', many of whom feel they have a special duty to express solidarity with Israel by visiting the country. In the United States, Christian Zionists are estimated to number 100 million people (compared with 6 million Jews in the United States). A smaller group of Christians who believe in an imminent Armageddon is attracted to travelling to Israel to witness the signs of the 'end of days'. A third market sector which tends to travel to Israel during politically difficult periods comprises business travellers involved in trade transactions in high-tech industries, diamonds, agricultural technology and exporting of raw materials to Israel. Although the tourism sector of Israel's economy was hit immediately by the Israeli–Palestinian conflict, commodities and commercial trade links between Israel and the rest of the world have eroded far more slowly. Israel's MICE market experienced a rapid and serious downturn (the non-MICE business travel sector took over a year to show an appreciable drop).

Israel's 'foul weather friends' have been a prime target market during the crisis period. Normally, IGTOs in countries with large Jewish communities (with the significant exception of the United States) have taken the Jewish market for granted or left the promotion of Israeli tourism to local Jewish organisations. As the Israeli–Palestinian conflict continued, Jewish communities and Christian Zionists shared many of the same concerns about security as other members of their community. IGTO offices in those countries with substantial Jewish communities or Christian Zionist organisations have added their weight and promotional resources to convince Jews and Christian supporters of Israel to keep visiting. No market segment could now be taken for granted.

It was also clear that the onset of a long-term political crisis would require a different strategy to maintain interest in Israel from the travel industry. The balance between push and pull marketing is a perpetual challenge to tourist authorities. However, a supportive travel industry is an essential element in destination marketing. Short-haul source markets to Israel adopted a strategy to focus attention on those parts of Israel least affected by political violence. This included active promotion of Israel's Red Sea resort Eilat and the Dead Sea area. Eilat has consistently been a popular winter sun destination for travellers from northern Europe, well serviced by direct charter flights from Germany, Scandinavia, the United Kingdom and the Benelux countries. The Northern European IGTOs intensively promoted Eilat following the outbreak of Israel's political problems. Eilat's location in Israel became an incidental fact. A similar approach was adopted for the Dead Sea, pitched at the European, US and Japanese markets where the Dead Sea was treated as a health and beauty resort attraction in its own right. In both cases, the resorts and activities were heavily emphasised while their location within Israel was de-emphasised.[17] Media and travel industry familiarisation tours were organised from these source markets to show that these parts of Israel were immune from the Israeli–Palestinian conflict, which was largely taking place in Gaza, the West Bank and the southern outskirts of Jerusalem.

One week after Israel's political crisis began, the Australian IGTO was the prime mover in establishing the Eastern Mediterranean Tourism Association (Australia) (EMTA). A committee representing 30 member companies was elected. Australia's position as a classic long-haul source market for Israel and the broader Eastern Mediterranean region provided practical motivation for the success of a regional tourism association within the Australian travel industry. For principals such as airlines, national tourist offices, wholesale tour operators and hotel chains, a regional marketing forum for a long-haul regional destination was a financially more viable means of marketing their range of products than involvement in single-destination promotions. For Israel and Jordan in particular, as destinations 'in trouble', EMTA was a 'trojan horse' to promote their respective destinations to a travel industry which would otherwise ignore destination-specific promotions.[18]

This principle would have been just as valid for Turkey in 1999 following the catastrophic earthquakes during that year or Egypt in the wake of the Luxor massacre of November 1997. Long-haul destination marketing tends to be regional, and most Australian and New Zealand-based wholesale tour operators, airlines and hotels market Israel within the broader context of the Eastern Mediterranean. EMTA included all Eastern Mediterranean countries between Italy in the west through to Jordan in the east. Its members are airlines, wholesalers and national tourist offices marketing Italy, Greece, Turkey, Israel and Jordan, although all countries were represented by member companies.

Shortly after its establishment in early 2001, EMTA ran a series of six well-attended travel industry product seminars throughout Australia. EMTA was an effective medium for pursuing a *push marketing* campaign to a large number of travel industry professionals. Serendipitously, EMTA also gave an equally useful forum to promote less well-known destinations such as Syria, Jordan, Lebanon, the Palestinian Authority, Libya and Cyprus and was a cost-effective means to promote well-established Eastern Mediterranean destinations such as Italy, Greece, Turkey and Egypt.

The relative success of the EMTA experiment in Australia was based on its credo to remain staunchly non-political. In late 2001, the Israel Government Tourism Office in the United States adopted the EMTA concept under the name of MEMTA (Middle East–Eastern Mediterranean Tourism Association), which followed the now Israeli-dominated organisation of the same name which was established originally as a regional marketing body for Israel, Jordan, Greece, Cyprus Turkey and Egypt in 1994 but was moribund outside Israel by the late 1990s.

The major challenge Israel encountered during the September 28, 2000 political crisis was finding a response to the overwhelming and largely negative media coverage. Israel has the dubious distinction of 'hosting' the third largest contingent of foreign correspondents in the world after Washington DC and London. The majority of these correspondents use Israel as their base to cover events in Israel and other parts of the Middle East. As the only democracy in the Middle East and the only country in the region committed to a free press, journalists in Israel face few restrictions compared with all other countries in the region. On rare occasions when restrictions are enforced, such as imposition of military censorship, Israel is the only country in which they can loudly voice their complaints without the fear of instant deportation. Israel offers Western journalists a standard of living comparable to Europe, ready access to all the communications technology necessary to work effectively and a large, literate population conversant in English and all European languages. As Israel is a country with many outspoken people given to expressing themselves on a wide range of issues, journalists readily inter-view Israeli citizens and politicians who advocate a wide range of contradictory opinions, including many critical of the Israeli government. In their coverage of the Israeli–Palestinian conflict, reporters have been granted access to areas of conflict which would be unthinkable in almost any other military conflict. The Pentagon's strictly controlled management of media coverage during the 1990–91 Gulf War and the 2001 war in Afghanistan stand in polar opposition to the relatively unfettered media access available to the Israeli–Palestinian conflict.

By contrast, the Palestinian Authority has carefully managed coverage of its side of the Israeli–Palestinian conflict. The PA's tightly controlled polity and press have resulted in a virtual uniformity of opinion from Palestinian spokespeople. Many of the demonstrations are conducted in a way which ensures that young people (especially young stone throwers) are almost guar-anteed to be the victims of Israel's 'military machine'. Journalists are tipped off as to the location and timing of demonstrations, most of which are sched-uled to fit in with prime-time news broadcasts on European and American television and with radio broadcasts and newspaper deadlines. Palestinian portrayal of victimhood tarnishes Israel's image politically and, by association, as a tourist destination.[19]

The media's ready daily access to graphic visuals of violence and conflict in which many of the victims on both sides are young has cultivated an image of Israel as a 'war zone'. Much of the media coverage has magnified the Israeli–Palestinian conflict into a regional conflict regardless of the fact that 90 per cent of violent acts occurred on the margins between Israeli-controlled and Palestinian-controlled territory. The Israel Ministry of Tourism devoted its limited resources to adopting a number of strategic approaches to chal-lenge much of the negative publicity.

- In Israel, the Ministry established a hotline for travellers which could advise them on the security situation applying to any region within the country that the traveller was planning to visit.
- In major source markets (the United States, the United Kingdom, Germany, Italy and France), the IGTOs placed paid advertisements in major newspapers, highlighting 'Israel Beyond the Headlines' and showing travellers on the day of publication experiencing Israel as a 'normal' destination. Through use of the Internet, photos of tourists

could be sent from Israel on the day of publication of the targeted newspaper. These images were a direct counterpoint to media coverage.

- Until the upsurge of suicide bombings in May and June 2001, IGTOs would focus much of their media promotion on those parts of the country which were either unaffected or least affected by political conflict.

- The Israel Ministry of Tourism continued to host selected media, particularly those involved in the specific promotion of tourism both to travellers and the travel industry. The Ministry also hosted large numbers of travel agents. In February 2001, several hundred travel agents were hosted on the Go Galilee program with the expectation that they would pass on details of their experiences to their industry colleagues.

- The Ministry's major websites were substantially upgraded and included regular updates explaining the security and safety situation. In real-time crisis management, the Internet is now an essential resource for destination marketers. Israel has made extensive use of the World Wide Web to communicate its position during the political crisis, in common with Britain's management of the foot-and-mouth disease crisis.

Israel Ministry of Tourism's PR directors from around the world visited Israel in January 2001, during the midst of the political crisis; this enabled them to utilise their own first-hand experience in addressing the issues of safety and normality in Israel.

Extensive use was made in press releases of testimonials from high-profile visitors who were either present in Israel or had recently returned, attesting that their experience in Israel was a positive contrast to the images they had witnessed in the media. There was also extensive promotion of specific events that would show Israel in a positive light. The most notable in the first half of 2001 was the opening of the Baha'i Gardens in the Israeli port city of Haifa on May 22, 2001. The Baha'i Gardens were a most impressive tourist attraction of tiered gardens ascending the slopes of Mount Carmel. The international Baha'i community organised several thousand adherents to attend the opening of the gardens, and Baha'i communities worked closely with IGTO's worldwide to inform the media of the event. As the Baha'is were neither Jews, Christian or Muslim, it gave Israel the opportunity to promote an impressive presence of a faith which contrasted with the stereotypical image of Israel. The lack of international media response to this positive story was partially due to its contradiction of the media's prevailing image of Israel as a land in crisis.

While the Jerusalem head office of the Israel Ministry of Tourism provided a large amount of material for media dissemination, each IGTO office was responsible for the distribution and presentation of those news items perceived to be relevant to each international source market.

One of the problems inherent in a tourism media campaign is that tourism-related publicity and material do not appear within the same section of a newspaper, television or radio broadcast as political material does. Tourism-related news, unless it involves a tragedy or disaster, is rarely considered newsworthy. During the crisis, the IGTO sought to highlight that tourists were still coming to Israel in large numbers. However, the media preferred to focus on the percentage drop in numbers from the previous year. While a skilled marketer can create a positive message from statistics, journalists seeking an angle for a news story will almost inevitably focus on the negative.

GOVERNMENT TRAVEL ADVISORIES

One of the most difficult challenges faced by destination marketers is to counter the impact of a negative government travel advisory. While media reporting can be challenged in the public domain, once a government has made a decision on a travel advisory it is extremely difficult for a national tourist office to convince a government to alter the advisory. During the Israeli–Palestinian political crisis, advisories have varied in their tenor from country to country. Government travel advisories, while not legally binding on travellers, are regarded as an authoritative analysis on the status of tourism safety for the citizens of that country when planning travel to the destinations to which the advisories refer. Consequently, they have a significant impact on tourism to countries cited and the decision by travel insurance companies to cover travel to that country. This in turn influences tour operator decisions to include the destination in their programs. Airlines also use advisories as a basis upon which to determine the operation and extent of air links to that destination. In June 2001, US airline Delta Airlines inaugurated a service from New York to Tel Aviv. The service was suspended after a very short period due to fears by cabin staff over their safety in Tel Aviv during a compulsory lay-over. Many travellers take advisories into account when choosing a destination to visit, and they are cited by travel writers in articles or guidebooks on destinations.

As discussed in Chapter 2, national tourist offices have minimal influence on government travel advisories. Foreign Affairs Department spokespeople, when justifying a negative advisory, usually state that they have to be especially cautious regarding the safety interests of their travelling citizens. Ultimately, the security of its citizens is the prime duty of a national government. The United States, as a 'superpower' and consequently a target for terrorists, is understandably sensitive about Americans being prime targets of politically motivated violence. While governments are not legally liable for the wording of advisories, in litigious Western countries—especially the United States—governments are concerned that they are still open to legal challenge.

In June 2001, the travel advisories of the United States, Canada, the United Kingdom, Australia and New Zealand represented a microcosm of travel advisories on Israel. There was considerable variation. The US State Department advised US citizens to defer all travel to Israel and the PA areas and detailed the main threats to safety. The Canadian, British, New Zealand and Australian governments advised their citizens to defer travel to Gaza and the West Bank but the advisories contained variations of places to avoid within Israel. The Australian government warned against visiting the Old City of Jerusalem on a Friday; New Zealand warned its citizens to avoid East Jerusalem and the Old City at all times. The British cautioned against Jerusalem, parts of Israel near the Lebanese border and areas adjacent to the Gaza Strip. Canada's advisory raised similar warnings to the British, adding the warning that some terrorist groups may attempt to purloin Canadian passports.[20]

Of the five advisories cited, the Australian government warning was the mildest in tenor. Consequently, the Israel Tourism Office (Australia), when communicating with media, tour operators and travel insurers, was able to endorse the advisory and use its wording as a counterpoint to the tougher language of neighbouring New Zealand when communicating with New Zealand travellers and tour operators. Canadian and British travel advisories included a number of restrictions on their view of the areas in Israel which travellers could visit, but they still left many options open for marketing.

The Israel Government Tourism Office in the United States was, and still is, faced with an advisory in which US citizens are told to defer travel to Israel along with all the implications, such as limited insurance coverage, and reductions in airline services and tour operators servicing Israel from the United States. While the American IGTO can suggest to travellers and the travel industry that the advisory overstates the situation, it clearly limits the market it can attract to Israel.

TARGETING STALWART MARKETS DURING ISRAEL'S CRISIS

During the January 2001 PR conference, the Israel Ministry of Tourism decided to assess the major market segments of travellers to Israel and rank them on a scale based on their propensity to visit Israel.

It was agreed that the market segments least likely to visit Israel during the political crisis would be broadly defined as the discretionary holiday traveller, especially those who would normally participate in a cruise or holiday package tour. The major exception to this group would be travellers whose primary destinations were the resorts of Eilat or the Dead Sea. Both areas are isolated from political violence and are primarily geared to tourism. The Israel Ministry of Tourism and the Israeli Hotels Association have revealed that hotel occupancy rates have maintained higher levels in Eilat and the Dead Sea than in any other parts of the country since October 2000, partly due to a growth in domestic tourism. Many Israelis chose to defer travel to Egypt and Jordan in favour of utilising domestic resorts.

The Israeli MICE market, especially the business conference and incentive element which draws much of its patronage from US groups, also experienced a significant downturn. The international travel organisation SKAL, which planned to hold its annual convention in Jerusalem in November 2000, cancelled at short notice, largely due to the fears of American and European delegates. The conference, which involved 2000 delegates, was one of many conferences cancelled following the outbreak of political violence from September 28, 2000.

There was a substantial impact on the Israel backpacker inbound market. While this market has access to a number of relatively safe options such as Kibbutz and Moshav volunteering experiences, and budget-priced adventure tours run by the Israeli Youth Hostels Association and the Society for the Protection of Nature in Israel, the backpacker market shared the same security concerns which reduced the demand from other discretionary travellers.

As discussed, the Christian pilgrimage market was the prime target for the year 2000. Until September 28 pilgrimage was the main source of tourism to Israel during that year. The outbreak of political violence demonstrated that the Christian pilgrimage market could not be treated as a solid block. The primary motivation for Christian pilgrims to visit Israel and the PA territories is to witness the holy sites of Christianity (some of which vary according to denomination). Many Christian pilgrims also take the opportunity to visit Jewish, Muslim and more secular attractions in Israel. There are some Christian groups who perceive a calling to express their identification with Israel. Certain streams of Christianity believe that the 'Second Coming' will only occur when all Jews are living in Israel and some groups are active supporters of Israel. A few Christian groups, such as the German-based Evangelical Sisters of Mary, believe support for Israel is an expression of their contrition for millennia of anti-Semitism.

The inter-denominational differences within the Christian world are manifested in many ways, including the degree of commitment to making a pilgrimage to Israel. During analysis of Christian pilgrimage group cancellations, the Israel Ministry of Tourism recognised that, when the political crisis broke out, most cancellations occurred within the Catholic and Orthodox denominations while the lowest proportion of cancellations occurred within the more 'non-conformist' Protestant streams. There are a number of groups within the fundamentalist Protestant denominations (especially in the Southern 'Bible Belt' states in the United States), which see themselves as 'Christian Zionists' and identify themselves with the more right-wing political elements within Israel. These groups especially retained a high propensity to travel to Israel at times when they perceived solidarity and support were required.[21] This group of Christians became a prime target market for the Israel Ministry of Tourism after September 28, 2000. (Following the events of September 11, 2001, fear of air travel undermined the commitment to visit Israel even of this dedicated group.)

The overall motivation of Christian pilgrimage tourism to visit Israel varies during a crisis. For denominations whose motivation is overwhelmingly religious, deferral of pilgrimage during an 'unsafe period' is an easy option. For Catholic and Orthodox Christians, access to Bethlehem is a far more compelling issue than for some fundamentalist Christians. This also applies to a lesser degree to most mainstream Protestant denominations, such as Anglicans, Episcopalians, Lutherans, Methodists, Presbyterians, Congregationalists and the Uniting Church (a Protestant amalgamation unique to Australia). Conversely, Christian denominations and sects which include an element of political identification with Israel retained a significant propensity to travel there, even against the advice of the US government. Israel's political crisis saw an immediate erosion of the Christian market to Israel.

One of the mainstay tourist markets to Israel is the Jewish market. Since 1990, Jewish tourism has averaged about 30 per cent[22] of Israel's total inbound tourists. In source markets with large Jewish communities of more than 75 000, including the United States, Canada, the United Kingdom, France, South Africa, Russia, Hungary, the Ukraine, Argentina, Brazil and Australia, the proportion of Jewish tourists from these countries was somewhat above the average.

In these countries, there is an active, organised Jewish community encouraging its members to visit Israel. Until late 2000, the role of the IGTO in these countries was primarily that of a supportive resource to the Jewish organisations rather than as the prime marketing mover—a role it adopts in its dealings with Christian communities. There are exceptions: in the United States, home to the world's largest Jewish community (numbering 6 million people), the IGTO has traditionally been more active within the Jewish community than in most other countries. Unlike many other countries with large Jewish communities, most US Jews have never visited Israel. Consequently, the IGTO in the United States has both a marketing and an educational role in encouraging US Jews to visit Israel. In countries with large Jewish communities, Israel's national carrier El Al Airlines actively promotes its flights to Israel to the Jewish community. El Al (at the time of writing) has yet to commence direct services from Australia, Brazil or Argentina, three of the top ten most populous Jewish communities in the world.

A portion of the Jewish market (approximately 40–50 per cent) are 'visiting friends and relatives' (VFR) travellers, but most of the remainder travel to Israel either as tourists or participants in a wide range of Jewish-orientated tour programs, many of which are organised by local Jewish communal organisations.

Since September 2000, IGTOs (especially those based in countries with large Jewish communities) adopted a more proactive approach to marketing Israel to the Jewish communities within their respective regions. Jews were exposed to the same negative media coverage of Israel and government advisories as everybody else in their countries of residence. Consequently, after

September 2000, many individual Jewish travellers and Jewish groups either postponed or cancelled their travel plans. Consequently, Israel could not take Jewish tourism for granted. The Israel Ministry of Tourism and IGTO offices worldwide, in association with Israeli diplomatic legations and Jewish communal organisations, began to more actively promote travel to Israel by Jewish groups. 'Solidarity missions' organised by Jewish communal bodies travelled to Israel as part of a campaign to encourage other members of the Jewish community to do so. In early 2000, the Israeli government organised a subsidised tour program for young Diaspora Jews who had never visited Israel known as the 'Birthright Program'.[23] The IGTOs intensified their promotional activities within their local Jewish communities and the local Jewish media.

The political violence between Israelis and Palestinians intensified during the second half of 2001. Suicide bombings were directed against clubs, restaurants, dance halls and discos frequented by young Israelis. Israeli retaliations against the PA escalated. The increasingly random nature of terrorist attacks against Israeli targets undermined the *isolation marketing strategy* of the Israel Ministry of Tourism (i.e. that violence was largely confined to the PA areas and not 'downtown Israel'). It became more difficult for the marketers of tourism to Israel to develop a strategy to promote safe tourism, even to more receptive markets such as Diaspora Jewish communities. This was reflected in the angst experienced by the organisers of the July 2001 Maccabiah Games (the quadrennial international Jewish sporting carnival) over the decision to proceed with the event. Although the games were held, the size of non-Israeli teams was far smaller then the games of 1997. The Maccabiah decision had particular poignancy in Australia (which sent a team in 2001) after members of its large 1997 contingent died as a result of the collapse of a pedestrian bridge during the opening ceremony of the games. The Australian contingent in 2001 was 15 per cent of the 1997 team. The US team's participation was contrary to the US government travel advisory. All Jewish and non-Jewish groups coming from the United States paid high insurance premiums when travelling to Israel contrary to the US government advisory. While all market segments to Israel have experienced a downturn since late September 2000, the Jewish market remained one of the most stable segments.

The political situation in Israel has led to a gradual decline in the number of business travellers on trade missions or as individual business travellers. The nature of most business trips, confined to hotels, offices, factories or farms, tends to cocoon business travellers from concerns about political violence (especially when they are not targeted, as has been the case in Israel). Provided they can conduct business activities in relative security, business travellers will continue to travel to destinations to do business and make foreign trade links. The IGTOs have worked closely with Israel Trade Commissioners and locally based bilateral chambers of commerce to maintain the momentum of business travellers and trade missions. However, the longer the political instability has continued, the greater the impact has been on business-related tourism and international trade.

THE STATISTICAL IMPACT OF ISRAEL'S TOURISM CRISIS ON INBOUND TOURISM

The statistical impact of Israel's political crisis was severe worldwide, and there were significant variances in different markets. The US market was handicapped by a government advisory which recommended US citizens defer travel to Israel. This impacted heavily on discretionary holidaymakers, the cruise market, the MICE market and Catholic pilgrimage. However, solidarity tourism from the Jewish, evangelical Protestant and Christian Zionist markets resulted in a relative firming of the US market.

By contrast, the Italian market, in which Jewish travel is a minor factor and Catholic pilgrimage a major sector of the market, plummeted. The closure of Bethlehem, as discussed, was a major disincentive to Catholic pilgrims and, of Israel's main source markets, the Italian market showed one of the largest decreases during late 2000 and 2001. With 2000 declared a holy year by the Vatican, Italian tourism to Israel showed unprecedented growth in the first nine months of 2000, which exaggerated the extent of the crisis collapse.

France and Britain, respectively home to the world's third and fifth largest Diaspora Jewish communities, showed a smaller decrease than the world average. Unlike the United States, government travel advisories of European countries, while cautious, did not recommend deferral of travel to Israel. A mixture of Jewish tourism and an aggressive marketing of 'sun tours' to Eilat and the Dead Sea contributed to the minimisation of crisis impact. Germany, a mixed Catholic/Protestant society with a small Jewish community, demonstrated an above-average decrease.

Figure 5.1: Israel inbound tourism numbers 1999–2001—world figures ('000s) by month[24]

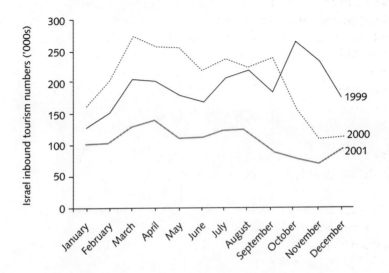

Figure 5.2: Israel inbound tourism numbers 1999–2001 ('000s)— USA, UK and Italy

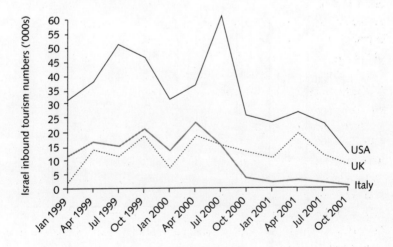

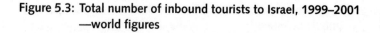

Figure 5.3: Total number of inbound tourists to Israel, 1999–2001 —world figures

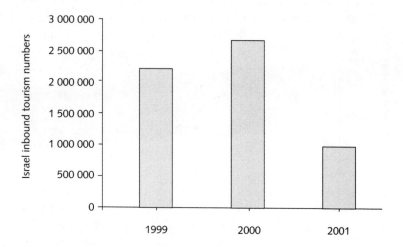

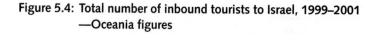

Figure 5.4: Total number of inbound tourists to Israel, 1999–2001 —Oceania figures

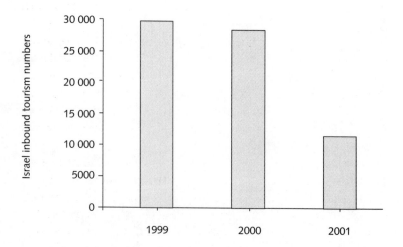

The Oceania market reflected a trend which closely corresponded with the world average. Australia and New Zealand have a combined Jewish community of 110 000 people. Distance and cost factors, especially considering Australia and New Zealand's poor exchange rates with the US dollar, contributed to make Israel a difficult destination to market, even to those predisposed to go. Christian pilgrimage—a very strong element in the Oceania market during the first three-quarters of 2000—dropped almost immediately from October 2000.

PUBLIC AND PRIVATE SECTOR COORDINATION IN ISRAEL'S TOURISM INDUSTRY

In most countries faced with tourism crisis, there is a high degree of response coordination between government-run tourism authorities and the private sector of the tourism industry (as demonstrated in many other case studies during this study). It has been a characteristic of Israel's response to the Israeli–Palestinian crisis that, while there has been a coordinated response in the government-owned sector of destination marketing, this has not been the case in the private enterprise sector. Public–private sector coordination in Israel's tourism response to its crisis has been limited.

Countries faced with a crisis which impacts on their tourism industry tend to apply strategies such as price reductions on accommodation, airfares and/or package tours as a means to entice the market. In Israel, the degree of private sector coordination has been minimal. Some hotels and operators reduced prices or marketed 'special deals', but many did not. The Israeli Hotels Association expressed concern about low occupancy rates, but there was no coordinated approach in marketing Israeli hotels. Many Israeli hoteliers adopted the attitude that it was better to charge a full commercial rate for the few guests they received than discount in the hope that volume may increase.[25]

The same problem applied to tour operators, where coordination is the exception rather than the rule. A number of packages promoted by Israel's national carrier, El Al, in conjunction with selected hoteliers and tour operators, discounted airfare/land packages to consumers in key markets such as the United States, the United Kingdom, France and Germany. The Israel Ministry of Tourism also increased the level of marketing and advertising subsidy support to Israeli and overseas-based tour operators as encouragement for them to promote Israel product. When the Israeli tourism industry is examined, attractions, tour operators, hoteliers, resort operators, restaurants, car rental firms, coach companies and airlines all faced a common problem in seeking to stimulate demand in a market affected by a common crisis. All experienced job losses, reduction in demand and, in some cases, closure of business. The Marriott Hotel in Nazareth was an early casualty of Israel's tourism crisis and closed its five-star doors at the end of 2000. It is clear that, while the crisis had a common impact on all sectors of the Israeli tourism industry, the lack of a coordinated response was a serious handicap to effectively countering the problem. There was a feeling within Israel's tourism industry that a coordinated response would be more effective as a post-crisis response approach than during the actual crisis. However, as the Israeli–Palestinian conflict grew increasingly prolonged, it became economically unsustainable for the Israeli tourism industry to wait until its denouement.

CONCLUSION

The Israeli case study reveals the problems associated with seeking to implement a destination marketing strategy during a crisis of indeterminate duration. One characteristic of the Israeli response has been the relatively high degree of coordination at the government tourism office level. In response to the crisis, the Israel Ministry of Tourism targeted those segments of the market with the maximum propensity to visit Israel during a period when global perception is negative. IGTOs appealed most strongly to those market sectors—namely the Jewish community and Christian Zionists—which have strong ideological/religious/emotional affinities with Israel. Few destinations can call on a large foreign group of solidarity tourists to help limit the extent of the damage to their tourism industry. Without minimising the severity of the impact of Israel's political crisis on its tourism industry, there are many examples in the world where similar problems have resulted in far greater damage to the tourism industry. As a counterpoint to Israel's loss of 55 per cent of inbound tourism since September 28, 2000, the negative impact on the Palestinian Authority's inbound tourism is far more severe than Israel's in percentage terms.[26]

The Israel Ministry of Tourism made effective use of the Internet as a means of communication to travellers and the travel industry, and continued an active campaign to maintain interest from the travel industry and the media. For most of the crisis period, Israeli tourism authorities adopted an isolation marketing strategy which has identified those relatively small parts of the country which are directly affected by the crisis and contrasted them with the bulk of the country, which is either completely or relatively free of problems. Israel has also pointed to the fact that, despite inter-communal violence between Israelis and Palestinians, tourists have not been specifically targeted. However, the random nature of the series of suicide bombings in central Israel since May and June 2001 has clearly undermined this approach. Two tourists killed in the Saborro pizza restaurant bombing in Jerusalem on August 8, 2001 were the first tourists to die from terrorism in Israel since 1972. The assassination of Israel's Minister of Tourism, Rechavim Za'evi, in November 2001 at the Hyatt Hotel in Jerusalem exacerbated the Israeli–Palestinian conflict and further complicated the security issue.

Nevertheless the *precision marketing* of resort areas in Israel, such as the Dead Sea and Eilat, as specific destinations with minimal reference to a broader Israeli context met with relative success in the Northern Europe and Japanese source markets. The Israel Ministry of Tourism has not attempted the financially unsustainable task of matching the extent of negative international media coverage with a full-blown counter-campaign. The Ministry chose to direct its response to specific segments of the media and the market with which it has the greatest affinity.

There were significant national and regional differences between government advisories on travel to Israel. Each Israel Government Tourism Office was obliged to either market with or against government advisories as circumstances demanded. A casualty of the political crisis in Israel has been the absence or downgrading of marketing cooperation between Israel, Jordan and the Palestinian Authority, a major feature in marketing Christianity's bi-millennial during 2000.

As the establishment of regional tourism associations in Australia and the United States have shown, it is still possible and viable to market Israel, especially to the travel industry, within a broader regional context from long-haul source markets.

Operationally, Israel's major problem in managing its tourism response to its political crisis has been the lack of coordination between the private and public sectors of the tourism industry. Inconsistent marketing and pricing strategies between hoteliers, airlines, inbound tour operators, resorts and attractions have handicapped Israel's ability to implement the fully co-ordinated marketing campaign which destinations need to conduct during and after a crisis to encourage a resurgence in the market. The greatest contradiction in Israel's tourism situation has been the perception versus the reality of security. Israel's security for tourists remains among the best in the world. After the events of September 11, 2001, airline and tourism security officials from all over the world visited Israel to emulate the methods of the national carrier El Al and to study tour operator security. Yet Israel's image, especially in the minds of the international travel industry and the media-led consumer market, remains dominated by fear.

6 | SRI LANKA: CIVIL WAR, 1995–2001

Marketing during a long-term crisis

RANKING: **DESTCON 2**

BACKGROUND

At the end of June 2001, Sri Lanka was on target for a record year of inbound tourism. Sri Lanka's tourism industry was showing every indication of achieving one of the great triumphs of crisis marketing. In June 2001, some 28 000 foreign tourists—a 30 per cent increase over June 2000—visited Sri Lanka. Sri Lanka Airlines was enjoying record passenger patronage.[1] In the midst of a prolonged civil war between the separatist guerrilla movement Liberation of Tigers of Tamil Eelam (LTTE)—commonly referred to as the Tamil Tigers—and the Sri Lankan government, the Sri Lankan tourism industry was experiencing a promising recovery with rising numbers of overseas visitors, a newly restructured national carrier and considerable success in attracting foreign investment.[2]

On July 24, 2001 the Tamil Tigers launched a destructive attack against Colombo International Airport, which resulted in the destruction of most of the Air Sri Lanka fleet of passenger aircraft. Many people were killed at the airport, including some tourists. The attack lasted three hours and severely damaged much of the international passenger terminal. The July 24 terrorist strike derailed a long-term tourism recovery process which was realising significant progress during the second half of the 1990s and the beginning of 2001.[3]

Jaffna

0 40
km

Trincomalee

SRI
LANKA

Tamil dominated
areas

Kandy

Colombo

The 2001 attacks were the most serious against tourism infrastructure since 1995 and 1996 when terrorist attacks in Colombo caused extensive damage to the five-star Hotel Ceylon Intercontinental and the Galadari Hotel.[4]

From the late 1990s to July 2001, the Sri Lankan tourism industry was a model of resilience in the face of a conflict which had effectively divided Sri Lanka into two separate political, social and ethnic entities. In early 2001, there appeared to be a tacit agreement between the government and Tamil separatists in which tourism would be excluded from the conflict. International tourists who had abandoned Sri Lanka for less troubled destinations were beginning to return in the late 1990s when the Sri Lankan government was in a position to give reliable guarantees that, provided the tourists avoided political friction points within the country, they would be safe.

The national carrier, formerly Air Lanka, relaunched itself in September 1999 as Sri Lankan Airlines, offering a range of new routes including direct

Buddhist Temple, Sri Lanka. Photo courtesy Sri Lanka Tourist Board.

flights to Sydney, Beirut and Stockholm, taking advantage of a growing interest from the Middle Eastern, Scandinavian and Australasian markets. In fact, 1999 was an all-time record year for inbound tourism numbers to Sri Lanka, with 436 000 arrivals in that year representing an almost 50 per cent bounce-back from the 1996 slump in which the civil war had involved well-publicised attacks on the capital city of Colombo.[5]

The success Sri Lanka achieved in rebuilding its tourism industry during the late 1990s and 2001 was due to a number of key factors. The Sri Lankan Ministry of Tourism engaged in a highly professional image-building campaign to depict the country as a safe and friendly destination for foreign tourists. The government enacted foreign investment policies which were attractive to private investors in hotels and tourist resorts. The changes to the national carrier, combined with an Open Skies Policy, made Sri Lanka an attractive and feasible stopover proposition for many long-haul carriers. Low labour costs ensured that quality tourist services could be offered to travellers at highly competitive prices.

Sri Lanka has much to offer tourists. Its image is one of an exotic and mysterious island, ethnically and culturally diverse. The beaches and coral reefs are world-renowned. Its mountainous interior, where the world-famous Ceylon Tea is grown, is also an area of national parks, rainforest and a host of protected indigenous wildlife species. Sri Lanka is home to a religiously and culturally diverse population of 19 million people, most of whom (69.3 per cent) are Buddhist. There are large minorities of Hindus (15.4 per cent), Muslims (7.6 per cent) and Christians (7.6 per cent). The inland mountain city of Kandy is regarded as a holy city to many Buddhists. Kandy's main attraction is the golden-roofed Dalada Maligawa where the sacred tooth of the Buddha is enshrined. One of the most popular natural attractions is Adam's Peak, situated on a 2243-metre high peak in the highlands and featuring a hollow resembling a human footprint; Hindus, Buddhists and Muslims venerate the site. Sri Lanka's cultural history is said to date back to 504 BC, when Hindu invaders conquered the island. Sri Lanka's cultural and ethnic diversity is dichotomously a major attraction and the main source of Sri Lanka's turbulent political history.[6]

Sri Lanka was known as Ceylon when it achieved independence from Britain in 1948. In 1972, the government of the day renamed the country the Socialist Republic of Sri Lanka. Almost three-quarters of Sri Lanka's people are Sinhalese; however, the minority Tamil, who dominate the northern and eastern regions of Sri Lanka, have sought to establish an independent political entity since 1960, when the national government passed a Bill making Sinhalese the only national language of the country. The Tamils protested violently against this Bill, and in 1996 the government relented by agreeing that Tamil was considered an official administrative language in northern and eastern Sri Lanka. Tensions between Sinhalese and Tamils have been a feature of Sri Lankan political life since independence. Since 1983, there has been a state of civil war between the Tamils and the central government which has resulted in the deaths of 40 000 people. During this period, there were cease-fires and lulls in the fighting; Indian troops acted as peacekeepers between 1988 and 1991. In 1995–96, central government forces recaptured the northern city of Jaffna, held by the Tamil Tigers for ten years. Despite some periods of relative calm, there has been no lasting resolution to the dispute between the

Tamils and the central government, although a Norwegian-brokered cease-fire was announced in February 2002.[7]

The challenge of marketing a country as a tourism destination during the midst of civil conflict is not unique to Sri Lanka, but it is a challenge which the Sri Lankan tourist authorities have faced for almost 20 years. Although the government's tourism authorities can claim some considerable success in isolating the country's political problems from its attractions as a tourism destination, there have been many instances in which tourism growth has been disrupted by acts of political violence, especially when hotels, the national airport and other elements of the national tourism infrastructure have been targeted by political dissidents. While the targeting of tourists and tourism infrastructure has been an uncommon feature of the civil conflict between Sri Lanka's central government and the Tamils, separatist attacks have caused considerable harm to the national tourism industry and directly affected Sri Lanka's economy.

The Sri Lankan economy is primarily agricultural. Tea, coconuts and rubber are the principal agricultural products produced and exported. The major processed items are garments and textiles, the country's single major export item. The tourism industry has not been traditionally regarded as a key industry, but it is one of Sri Lanka's most important sources of foreign exchange and is gradually becoming increasingly significant as a provider of employment.

The main sources of international tourism into Sri Lanka are Germany, Britain and India, although much of the Indian market comprises people visiting friends and relatives (VFR toursim) and work-related visits. Other major tourism markets, apart from Germany and the United Kingdom, are France, the Netherlands, Italy, Japan, the United States and Australia. In 1999, the year in which Sri Lanka effectively relaunched itself as a tourist destination, Sri Lankan tourism authorities sought to target a greater share of the Asian travel market and build up the European and, to a lesser extent, the Australian market.

The marketing of tourism in Sri Lanka is relatively centralised by world standards, with a high degree of government involvement. The Ceylon Tourist Board is the statutory body for tourism established by an Act of government in the mid-1960s. The CTB is responsible for implementation of the tourism policies of the Ministry of Tourism and Civil Aviation. The CTB's major responsibilities include destination marketing and promotion, market research, and the establishment and enforcement of trade standards for hotels, tour guides and attractions. The fourteen-member board of the CTB includes a chairman appointed by the Ministry, representatives of provincial ministries, professionals and corporate representatives selected by the Ministry. Each provincial council within Sri Lanka also has a tourism department with its own budget, marketing and promotional plan, which is presented to the central government and incorporated into the national tourism strategy. Due to the conflict between the Tamil Tigers and the central government, the northern and eastern provinces of Sri Lanka have been excluded from tourism planning and the promotional process.

Funding of the CTB comes from the national treasury. According to Neelam Matthews, there has been a long-running dispute between the Ministry of Tourism and Civil Aviation and the Ministry of Finance over the rights to utilise taxation income from the Commercial Enterprises Sales and Service Tax.

By the end of 1999, the CTB had been granted an annual budget of US$1.2 million, of which 60 per cent was devoted to marketing and promotion within Sri Lanka and worldwide. The small budget available to the CTB for marketing Sri Lanka internationally creates significant problems for Sri Lanka in competing with other Asian destinations. The government budget to market the destination has been augmented by private tour operators and Sri Lankan Airlines (formerly Air Lanka) but, when compared with regional destinations such as India, the Maldives and the Southeast Asian nations, Sri Lanka's marketing resources for key overseas markets, especially those of Europe, are minimal. Sri Lanka is in no position to conduct any media advertising campaigns, although it can and does participate in consumer and trade travel expositions in its key overseas markets. Over the past decade, Sri Lanka has promoted itself as a low-cost, high-value destination. The CTB has left the promotion of low-cost package tours to the private sector.[8]

The Ceylon Tourist Board has concentrated its overseas marketing efforts on its key source markets. There are four fully operational offices, located in Germany, the United Kingdom, India and France (Sri Lanka's four largest source markets). The CTB has appointed honorary directors (unpaid representatives) in strategic and growing source markets, including Japan, Thailand, Ireland, Dubai, Oman, the United States, Australia and New Zealand, all of whom have agreed to act as a conduit for promotional material. Sri Lankan Airlines offices and their General Sales Agents (GSAs), which are located in

50 countries around the world, distribute promotional material on Sri Lanka to travel agents and their clients.

The CTB website is a very useful information source on tourism to Sri Lanka. It provides comprehensive destination information and up-to-date statistical and contact information in Sri Lanka and overseas. However, its one major weakness (a weakness that is quite easily corrected) is that it fails to address the legitimate security concerns of tourists, travel agents and tour operators. As other case studies have demonstrated, destination websites are a cost-effective means to keep travellers and those who book travel updated on potential problems. The British Tourist Authority's site provides a prime example of a website used to monitor and inform travellers and travel professionals about the accessibility of tourism attractions during the foot-and-mouth scare. The Ceylon Tourist Board's website mentions nothing about security precautions for travellers, or even the security status applying to key destinations and attractions within the country. It could be argued that incorporating security-related material within a tourism promotion website may scare tourists away; however, the counter-argument is that the security problems of Sri Lanka are well-known, long-standing and have proven to be a disincentive to tourism. The adoption of a proactive approach providing reliable safety and security advice is helpful to tourists, establishes confidence in the CTB and assists travel professionals in planning viable itineraries within Sri Lanka for their clients. Although the CTB's chairman, Renton de Alvis, publicly committed his organisation to the development of a crisis management plan in October 2001, the CTB has not been forthcoming about its reasons for avoiding a public relations campaign on security concerns in the past.

The approach of the CTB to Sri Lanka's prevalent terrorist threat is typical of the attitude of many countries faced with a crisis. Sri Lanka's tourism authorities have often operated on the assumption that if you ignore the problem, either it will go away or nobody (especially the prospective tourist) will notice. The 'denial' strategy is sometimes successful. In fact, in the case of Sri Lanka, if the conflict with the Tamil Tigers could have been confined to the northeast of the country, the most appropriate approach would have been to quarantine this region as a no-go area for tourists in a similar fashion to Israel's periodic closures of the Palestinian Authority areas. However, Sri Lanka has been forced to confront the problem that the activities of the Tamil Tigers have not always been isolated and, as the attack of July 2001 graphically demonstrated, they can disrupt the national capital and the national tourism industry. The relative paucity of international media reports on the conflict in Sri Lanka during most of the 1990s gave travellers an opportunity to lose awareness of attacks after a period of time. Following a series of destructive Tamil Tigers strikes in Colombo in 1996, which attracted extensive media coverage—largely due to the fact that hotels were among the most frequent targets—the conflict after 1996 was once again confined to Tamil-dominated regions. Consequently, media interest rapidly waned and travellers began to resume visits to Sri Lanka.

In 1999, the Sri Lankan government established a Presidential Task Force on Tourism comprising an honorary body of private and government representatives who were commissioned to prepare a Tourism Promotional Plan for 2000 and beyond. The main strategic elements of the task force were:

- the prioritisation of markets based on their volume and their potential to be rapidly generated;
- a shift in marketing focus from the travel industry direct to the consumer;
- a decision that, due to the high cost of consumer marketing, activity without the cooperation of private tourism operators would only take place in primary markets.

The CTB recognised the primary markets as the United Kingdom, Germany, France, India and Japan, each of which was believed to have the potential to generate over 100 000 visitors per annum by 2004. By the end of 2001, only the United Kingdom and Germany markets were showing signs they may realistically achieve this target.[9]

Secondary markets were judged to have the potential to generate between 10 000 and 25 000 visitors by 2004; these included the Benelux countries, Italy, Spain, Scandinavia and Austria. By 2001, the Benelux countries were generating sufficient inbound tourism growth to be considered a primary source market.

Potential markets included Australia/New Zealand, South Africa, the former Soviet Union and Saudi Arabia. Of this group, Australia had already entered the secondary threshold by 1998.

The Sri Lankan government's commitments of 1999 to an Open Skies Policy for international carriers coupled with favourable tax arrangements for investors in tourism development was, until July 2001, facilitating a rebuilding of the tourism industry. Until the July 2001 attack against Colombo Airport, inbound tourism was steadily growing except for a slight downturn during 2000. Marketing focus was directed to special-interest, high-yield niche markets, including the wedding and honeymoon market, health market, eco-tourism and the soft adventure market, all of which achieved growth for the tourism sector of the Sri Lankan economy.

Table 6.1 tracks the development of tourism to Sri Lanka from 1995–2000. During the first half of 2001 (January 1–June 30) a total of 227 205 foreign tourists had arrived in Sri Lanka. On the basis of inbound tourism seasonality, which normally indicates that 40 per cent of tourists visit Sri Lanka from January to June, and 60 per cent visit from July to December, the figures for the first half of 2001 suggested that Sri Lanka was heading for a total approaching 500 000 tourists for the year, which would have been an all-time record. However, while statistics were not (at the time of writing) available for the second half of 2001, the devastating Tamil Tigers attack on Colombo International Airport would have impacted negatively on the July–December tourism figures. While the growth of tourism to Sri Lanka through to 2004 is likely to fall well short of the target of 1 million set by the Presidential Task Force, the growth during the second half of the 1990s demonstrated that tourism in Sri Lanka has vast growth potential which will be fully realised if and when the political conflict between the central government and the Tamil minority is resolved.

As Table 6.1 illustrates, there have been fluctuations in the growth of tourism to Sri Lanka during the late 1990s. A series of terrorist attacks in 1996 had a severe impact on tourism numbers during that year, but the period 1997–99 was a time of strong recovery. A combination of increased Tamil Tigers activity and millennial focus on other destinations during 2000 provides part of the explanation for the downturn in tourism to Sri Lanka in that year.

CRISIS MANAGEMENT ISSUES IN SRI LANKAN TOURISM

One of the major problems faced by the Ceylon Tourist Board and the Sri Lanka tourism industry has been communication of their awareness of the serious threat of terrorism to the national tourism industry. The CTB consistently failed to publicly counter consumer and industry concerns about

Table 6.1: International tourism arrivals to Sri Lanka showing regions and selected source markets, 1995–2000 ('000s)[10]

Country	1995	1996	1997	1998	1999	2000
North America	14.56	12.46	15.95	17.53	18.48	17.32
United States	9.10	7.77	9.47	9.99	10.57	9.82
Latin America	0.61	0.33	0.50	0.41	0.37	0.45
West Europe	250.15	167.34	212.05	238.96	275.80	260.82
Austria	6.93	5.15	5.82	6.80	6.11	6.29
Belgium	7.34	6.16	6.82	4.99	5.64	10.22
France	30.99	21.48	25.39	26.87	34.46	25.99
Germany	79.70	45.07	59.81	74.05	77.26	70.58
Italy	18.38	11.99	14.42	15.87	19.81	16.88
Netherlands	14.27	10.99	15.96	22.98	29.67	22.62
Switzerland	8.33	4.35	8.17	9.05	8.31	8.49
United Kingdom	63.58	52.09	63.00	66.43	80.92	84.69
Eastern Europe	4.58	4.54	6.43	7.24	6.20	6.84
Middle East	3.82	3.88	4.42	4.03	4.82	4.34
Africa	0.80	2.38	1.53	1.03	1.23	0.84
Asia	118.32	102.56	113.56	99.70	114.38	91.53
India	47.45	42.82	47.01	37.35	42.31	31.86
Japan	18.18	11.72	13.37	13.79	16.33	10.23
Australasia	10.25	8.73	11.71	12.16	15.16	18.22
Australia	9.07	7.63	10.39	10.33	13.22	16.44
Total	403.10	302.26	366.16	381.06	436.44	400.44

security. The July 2001 attack on the international airport and the Sri Lankan Airlines fleet was directed against the tourism industry. The strategy of denial no longer has currency: since the events of September 11, 2001 in New York City, security has become the pervasive concern of global tourism.

Mr Renton de Alvis, former chairman of the Sri Lankan Tourist Board (Ceylon Tourist Board) in an interview conducted by *Express Travel and Tourism* in October 2001, announced that Sri Lankan tourism was preparing a crisis management plan. The main thrust of the plan was to engender a total industry commitment, improve security and restore traveller confidence. However, de Alvis revealed no specific details.[11]

Between 1996 and 1999 specifically, the recovery of tourism to Sri Lanka was partially due to the reactivation of latent demand, but it was also a response to discounted pricing. While the Sri Lankan government did not increase the budget for the CTB, the new tax concessions for overseas-based tourism-related industries and the Open Skies Policy for international carriers made Sri Lanka a price-competitive destination. Tour operators which included Sri Lanka within their product portfolio and Air Lanka (relaunched as Sri Lankan Airlines in 1999) were more active in promoting the destination during the late 1990s to July 2000. The commercial imperative to market low-priced Sri Lanka as a safe destination rather than any initiative on the part of the Sri Lankan government had a great deal to do with the tourism resurgence in the final years of the 1990s. The strong growth of the outbound Indian travel market during the 1990s (especially the corporate market) for conventions and incentives provided a large prospective market for Sri Lanka.

The CTB reports on length of stay combined with actual numbers of tourists clearly demonstrate that Western European tourists—especially those from Germany, Britain, France, Belgium and the Netherlands—will be the key source market for the foreseeable future. Western European tourists have the longest stays of any source markets and have a high tendency to utilise up-market accommodation and take advantage of the availability of inexpensive villa accommodation with servants. However, tourists from Western countries have become increasingly safety-conscious and Sri Lanka's tourism authorities, to their detriment, have been reluctant to address these concerns directly.

Government advisories to Sri Lanka tend to urge caution for travellers. British, US and Australian advisories of December 2001 all referred to the Colombo Airport attack of July 24, 2001 and to varying degrees advised tourists to adopt a cautious approach to travel throughout Sri Lanka; they also advised avoiding travel to Tamil regions in the north and east of the country. The Australian advisory recommended avoidance of rail travel, while all three government advisories warned of terrorist threats throughout the country. While the three advisories pointed out that tourists were not specifically targeted by anti-government organisations, there was a strong message for tourists to minimise risk.[12]

The Sri Lankan tourist authorities need to address security concerns, especially as tourists have occasionally been victims—albeit unintended—of terrorist attacks. The Ceylon Tourist Board website would be an appropriate starting point, incorporating advice to travellers on where and how to maximise security and safety within Sri Lanka. CTB briefings to airlines and tour operators servicing Sri Lanka are vital. In turn, this information may be passed on to travel agents. Sri Lanka has a contingent of tourist police in the country, but it is not specified whether the tourist police are employed to heighten security or merely act as a source of general assistance and information. In common with most countries since September 11, 2001, advice on upgraded security measures on international aircraft servicing Sri Lanka, and on domestic transport, hotels and key tourist sites, needs to be undertaken and the key measures communicated to the international travel industry and prospective travellers.

Neither proactive nor even reactive to the security concerns of travellers, the Sri Lankan tourist authorities give every appearance of being in denial. The denial response is not uncommon among tourism authorities throughout the world when faced with a threat to the inbound tourism industry. In the medium to long term, this approach is counter-productive and erodes the credibility of all information provided by the tourist authority.

Linda K. Richter has been a long-time critic of the Sri Lankan government's approach to tourism marketing. She believes that Sri Lanka's focus on up-market tourism was reasonable in theory but unsustainable in practice, on the basis that the government had ignored the political realities of Sri Lanka. Consequently, tourism became a victim of the government's war with the Tamil minority. Richter doubted whether tourists would be seduced by the CTB's marketing pitch of Sri Lanka, 'Land of the Smiling People'. She proposed that, rather than focus tourism development on luxury resorts which are difficult to transform for other uses, Sri Lanka would have been better served by developing a somewhat more mid-range, culturally orientated and inclusive tourism infrastructure involving the Tamil minority rather than excluding them. Richter took the view that, by effectively excluding the Tamil northeast from the tourism equation, the social and economic divisions present in Sri Lanka were exacerbated, giving Tamil extremists a motive to attack the tourism industry. She believes that, because the Tamils had no stake in Sri Lanka's tourism infrastructure, they had nothing to lose by attacking it.[13]

Terrorism has been a long-term problem for Sri Lanka. The Sri Lankan tourism industry has undergone cycles of growth and decline. The attack of July 24, 2001 on Colombo International Airport exceeded security concerns. It destroyed most of the aircraft of the national carrier and reduced passenger capacity to Sri Lanka. The situation has been exacerbated by the fact that other carriers servicing Sri Lanka minimised their services to the country. Months after the attack, the Sri Lankan government's silence on preventative measures, and the CTB's apparent inability even to refer to the security issue, aggravated the Sri Lankan tourism crisis. Its prime source markets were increasingly nervous as a result of events in New York, the United States-backed war against Afghanistan's former Taliban regime, and the India–Pakistan conflict over Kashmir at the end of 2001 and early 2002. Sri Lankan tourism appeared set for a rapid and deep decline.

In addition to tackling the security issue head on, there were other possible remedies for the marketing difficulties which Sri Lanka faced at the end of 2001. In marketing to the long-haul source markets of Western Europe, North America and Australasia, the CTB had an option to join forces and market itself in association with India, subject to India's acceptance. India has a well-established chain of destination marketing representation in many parts of the world and, in common with Sri Lanka, has experienced its own regional security problems in Kashmir, forcing India to focus much of its marketing to the southern half of the country.

Marketing India in association with Sri Lanka and even the Maldives—most especially to long-haul source markets—offered synergies for all three countries, especially in their promotion to the travel industry in long-haul source markets. There are also sufficient differences between the destinations, which minimise competition but in fact complement one other. The growth of cooperative regional destination marketing, especially in long-haul source markets, has become common in the promotion of Europe, Southern Africa, the Eastern Mediterranean and South America. The paucity of Sri Lanka's tourism marketing budget makes the cooperative approach an attractive proposition. The main disadvantage would be Indian political or commercial opposition to such a proposal, which may be perceived as diluting its market. The other legitimate concern is based on the likelihood that India represents such a large and all-encompassing destination that Sri Lanka may be over-whelmed by comparison.

One reason why Sri Lanka's tourism authorities have avoided direct responses to the country's political situation is that they were awaiting the outcome of the national elections, held in early December 2001. It would appear that if the central government were able to accommodate some of the demands of the Tamil minority without losing face in the opinion of the majority Sinhalese, Sri Lanka's tourism industry would expand. However, in common with all long-running inter-communal disputes, including some discussed in this book, what appear to be rational solutions are not easily achievable between the parties, primarily because of the emotional dimension of the conflict. The cease-fire signed between the Sri Lankan government and the Tamil leadership, in February 2002, accompanied by a commitment to increased Tamil autonomy, represented a positive step towards the resolution of this conflict— a result from which the tourism industry would benefit significantly.

CONCLUSION

The long-running civil war between the majority Sinhalese and the Tamils of the north and east of Sri Lanka has constituted the biggest single constraint to tourism growth in Sri Lanka. Resolution of this conflict appeared possible following the February 22, 2002 cease fire between the Tamil Tigers and the central government brokered by the Norwegian government. Peace would give Sri Lanka the opportunity to realise its massive potential as an international tourism destination. Periods of relaxation or containment of the conflict have allowed for rapid recovery of inbound tourism. The Presidential Task Force on Tourism targeted international tourism numbers exceeding 1 million by 2005. However, even if the cease-fire extended to a peace agreement, the Presidential Task Force target appeared to be unrealistically optimistic. The damage to Sri Lanka's tourism image and its tourism infrastructure following the July 24, 2001 attack on Colombo Airport neccessitated a long-term marketing restoration project.

Following the 1995–96 Tamil Tigers' hotel bombings in Colombo, which caused considerable damage to hotels in the capital, some leaders of Sri Lanka's tourism industry blamed external factors for Sri Lanka's tourism problems. Mr Graham Hatch, manager of the Galadari Hotel in Colombo, was justifiably critical about Western government travel advisories, which cautioned their citizens about travelling to Sri Lanka but failed to warn them of similar terrorist threats in Europe.[14] While this line of criticism is justified (not only for Sri Lanka, but for many other countries), there was little evidence that the Sri Lankan tourist authorities were doing anything to engage the relevant decision-makers responsible for these advisories.

The greatest failing of Sri Lanka's tourism marketing authority has been an apparent policy of denying that a security problem exists. As the principal source markets are Western countries, all of which heightened their sense of security awareness post-September 11, 2001, the denial policy was damaging to Sri Lanka. The country has made considerable progress in establishing an economic environment favourable to the expansion of a high-quality, low-priced tourism infrastructure, readily accessible by international carriers. However, none of these measures will result in sustained tourism growth unless travellers are assured that their safety concerns are addressed. Sri Lanka has enjoyed success in recovering quickly from past episodes of terrorism, and the commitment of CTB former chairman Renton de Alvis to develop a crisis marketing strategy is a positive step. When implemented, such a strategy must address the security concerns of travellers to ensure that it is treated seriously by an increasingly safety-conscious global travel industry and consumer market.

7 | FIJI: POLITICAL COUPS, 1987 AND 2000

Post-crisis tourism recovery

CRISIS RANKING: **DESTCON 3**

INTRODUCTION

The Melanesian islands of Fiji are located in the Southwest Pacific, 1500 kilo-metres north-northeast of New Zealand. There are 300 tropical islands, of which 50 are inhabited. The Fijian islands incorporate the longest continuous stretch of coral reef outside Australia's Great Barrier Reef. These islands fulfil many idealised images of the South Seas, with their palm-fringed sandy beaches, dramatic forest-clad inland mountains, crystal clear waters and coral atolls. The Fijians are well known as friendly and hospitable people. Tourism marketers of Fiji seek to present the islands as encapsulating all the beauty and romance of the South Pacific. Brochures promoting holidays to Fiji are naturally filled with all these enticing images. For most tourists whose experi-ence of Fiji is confined to resorts on the main island of Viti Levu or on nearby islands, most of these idyllic images are fulfilled. Australian, New Zealand, American or Japanese package tourists to Fiji are welcomed by their genuinely friendly Fijian hosts with a hearty 'Bula' (hello and welcome) at Nadi Airport and transferred by air-conditioned coach to Fiji's magnificent coastal or island resorts.

Beneath the genuine beauty of Fiji and the hospitality shown by the Fijian people to its tourists, there is a society bitterly divided between two peoples of similar numbers competing for their political, social and economic place

in this sun-kissed Pacific island nation. The conflict which exists between Fiji's indigenous Melanesian majority and the large minority community of Fijians of Indian origin has been the main cause of political instability since Fiji achieved independence from British colonial rule in 1970.

Fiji's population, according to the 1996 census, was 772 655, of whom 51 per cent were indigenous Fijians, 44 per cent Indo-Fijians and 5 per cent of other ethnic and racial minorities.[1] Until 1987, the Fijian political system and constitution guaranteed political control to the indigenous majority. Fiji's influential military is subject to the government and to a lesser extent the Indigenous Council of Chiefs. However, the Indo-Fijian community has long sought to increase its influence within Fiji's political system, commensurate with its numbers. The demographic structure of Fiji reveals that the rapid growth of the Indo-Fijian population in relation to indigenous Fijians has the potential to exacerbate national, political and economic divisions. These tensions have posed the greatest threat to overall national stability and to Fiji's tourism industry. Tourism is Fiji's leading source of foreign exchange earnings and a major employer of Fijians. Fiji's tourism industry, in common with tourism

Tourists at a Fijian resort. Photo courtesy Fiji Visitors Bureau.

worldwide, flourishes in an atmosphere of peace and stability. Fiji's principal attraction as a tourist destination is its image of friendliness and the warmth of its people.[2]

However, this relaxed tourism image can easily be shattered in the event of civil disturbances. Since 1987, Fiji's reputation as a tourist destination has twice been compromised. The disturbances involved two very different coups against the government: two related coups in May and November 1987 and an abortive coup between May and September 2000. On both occasions, Fiji's tourism industry suffered major reversals from which it eventually recovered. This chapter deals with the coups and focuses on the impressive recovery made by the Fijian tourism industry following both crises.

TOURISM AND THE FIJIAN ECONOMY

The Fijian economy is far more diverse than most independent island nations of the Southwest Pacific, including Vanuatu, Samoa, Tonga and other smaller island nations, all of which are more economically dependent on tourism than Fiji. Yet, according to Berno and King, tourism directly and indirectly contributes 27 per cent of annual gross domestic product and employs 45 000 people—or close to 20 per cent of Fijians in the national workforce.[3] Fiji's other major industries include sugar, manufactured products (dominated by garments and textiles), fish and other food products. King and McVey point out that, in the period 1988–91, tourism earnings represented just over 50 per cent of merchandise export incomes; by 1996, this had come down to 40 per cent.[4]

Low tourism figures for 1988 illustrate the after-effects of the political problems of 1987 on Fiji's tourism industry. Overall, the above figures—subject as they have been to variations over the years—are indicative of the significance of tourism to the Fijian economy. Additionally, a large portion of foreign investment into Fiji is tourism-related. Multinational hotel chains and, in more recent years, Japanese investment has played a significant role in the funding and development of resorts and other tourism-related projects. Investment policy is coordinated by the Fiji Trade and Investment Board. The economic significance of tourism clearly indicates that any crisis which impacts on the tourism industry has major implications for the overall economic viability of Fiji.

Table 7.1: Fijian tourism earnings and the balance of payments, 1988–96 (F$ millions)[5]

F$ millions	1988	1989	1990	1991	1996
Total merchandise exports	449.3	552.4	607.4	562.7	1200.5
Sugar	198.3	228.3	230.0	220.4	301.7
Garments	30.1	99.3	115.8	134.2	189.9
Fish	48.2	44.8	49.3	51.4	60.4
Total merchandise imports	658.8	860.5	1192.9	961.7	1266.4
Trade balance	−209.5	−308.1	−505.5	−399.0	65.9
Tourism earnings	186.5	295.1	329.0	309.9	430.9
Tourism share of merch. exports (%)	41.5	53.4	54.2	55.1	40.0

The Fijian government legislated a comprehensive range of investment concessions and incentives for tourism infrastructure investment for hotel development. Paresh Narayan cited a detailed list of these incentives, including the following for five-star hotels:

- 100 per cent write-off on all capital expenditure in any one year of eight years;
- carry-forward of losses for up to six years;
- duty-free import of all capital equipment;
- no corporate tax on profits for 20 years;
- permission for the tourist plant to generate its own electricity and sell any excess to the Fiji electricity authority.

The incentives for five-star property investment are the most generous of a large number of tax and duty concessions available to investors in the Fijian tourism industry. While the above may appear to be almost excessively generous to an outsider, the large cost of establishing premium accommodation in Fiji is accompanied by considerable risks arising from political problems and from natural disasters, especially cyclones. For Fiji, the overwhelming benefits of resort development for the creation of employment and tourism income make the concessions and incentives a long-term investment.[6]

THE FIJIAN TOURISM INDUSTRY AND ITS INFRASTRUCTURE

The Fijian tourism industry has developed a sophisticated and professional infrastructure since Independence. It is based mostly on resort tourism, and there are many resorts throughout the country. The greatest concentration of resorts is near Nadi, within easy reach of the international airport. Most other main resorts are dotted along the southern (Coral Coast) of the main island of Viti Levu and in the Mamanuca Islands. Suva, the national capital, has relatively little tourist accommodation and, while it is an attractive city and an interesting and popular place to visit, it is primarily an administrative capital. During the late 1990s, the Fijian tourist industry sought to encourage the diversification of the country's tourist infrastructure by marketing to the needs of eco-tourists, backpackers, adventure tourists and visitors who wanted to explore the scenic and cultural diversity of Fiji. However, the largest segment of Fiji's inbound tourism market comprises visitors (of whom Australians and New Zealanders form the largest source markets) who want a resort holiday.

The other element of the market which remains strong is cruise traffic. Many Pacific island cruises include a port stop at Lautoka, located on the west coast of the main island of Viti Levu.

The Fiji Visitors Bureau (FVB) has sought to open up more remote parts of Fiji to low-key eco-tourism, requiring a campaign of stimulating the market to change its image of Fiji (presenting itself as more than a resort holiday playground). Within Fiji, there is an extensive network of inter-island transport links by air and sea. The coast of Viti Levu can be circumnavigated by road, although road access to the interior is limited. Tourists can either use the inexpensive public bus services or hire a vehicle for a self-drive experience.

One of the problems which has restricted Fiji from reaching its full potential as a tourist destination has been the lack of international airlines servicing the country. The main international airport in Nadi is well-equipped to handle the largest jumbo jets, yet relatively few international carriers have used Nadi as a mid-Pacific stopover point, especially following the 1987 coup. Since 1990, the major trans-Pacific air routes between North America, Australasia and Southeast Asia have been serviced by 747 400 jets, which are capable of travelling across the Pacific non-stop. With the exception of Fiji's national carrier, Air Pacific, no other carriers have given air travellers the option of Fiji as a mid-Pacific stopover point. In the 1980s, Air New Zealand, Qantas and Canadian Pacific offered Nadi as a stopover option on their trans-Pacific routes. Many of these services between Nadi and the West Coast USA were terminated after the 1987 coups in favour of either non-stop flights or alternative stopover points, including Honolulu or Papeete (Tahiti).

International carriers treat Fiji as a final destination rather than an *en route* trans-pacific stopover especially when it come to its principal source markets: Australia, New Zealand, Japan, the United States, the United Kingdom, other Pacific islands and Canada. The main carriers servicing Fiji included Fiji's national carrier, Air Pacific (partially owned by Qantas), Qantas, Air New Zealand, Ansett (which collapsed in September 2001) and some of the regional Pacific carriers such as Samoan-based Polynesian Airlines and Royal Tongan Airways.[7]

Fiji's national carrier, Air Pacific, has an extensive network of services throughout the Pacific islands, and flies to Australia, New Zealand, Japan and West Coast USA.

The marketing arm of Fijian tourism, the Fiji Visitors Bureau, is a highly professional national tourist office. The bureau has overseas branches in Australia, New Zealand, the United States, Canada, Japan, Britain, Germany,

France, Belgium and South Korea, and is represented by Fijian diplomatic missions in several other countries. The Bureau's website, <www.bulafiji.com>, is of international standard, providing a comprehensive range of tourist information for travellers and the travel industry.[8]

Until the late 1990s, a large portion of the Fiji Visitors Bureau's promotional budget was sourced from the European Union-funded Tourism Council of the South Pacific (TCSP), which provided financial support for the tourism promotion of thirteen South Pacific island states. Since the suspension of EC funding in 1997, the Fiji Visitors Bureau and the national tourist authorities of all the Tourism Council of the South Pacific countries have had to rely on their own funding.

Overall tourism policy for Fiji is coordinated by the Ministry for Tourism, Culture, Heritage and Civil Aviation. Air Pacific is largely government-owned. The Native Land Trust Board controls 83 per cent of Fiji's land area, all of which is indigenous land; it determines which areas may be set aside for tourism use. The private sector of the Fijian tourism industry has its own umbrella organisations, including the Fiji Hotel Association and the Society of Fiji Travel Associates, which represents travel agents, inbound tour operators, car rental firms, tour boats, bus operators and attractions.

The highly organised structure of Fiji's tourism industry was a crucial factor in Fiji's rapid recovery from its 1987 and 2000 crises. In both cases, government and private organisations, including Air Pacific, coalesced under a super roof body, the Tourism Action Group (TAG), which mobilised the Fijian tourism industry and marketing agencies to respond unilaterally and rapidly to the threat which the two crises posed to the tourism industry and to the Fijian economy.[9]

FIJI'S COUPS OF 1987 AND 2000: THEIR IMPACT ON TOURISM

The Fijian coups of 1987 and 2000 both arose out of a concern among indigenous Fijians that political, social and economic control was falling outside their grasp. Both were responses to governments in which Indo-Fijians held high positions following recent elections. Consequently, there was fear within elements of the indigenous Fijian majority that the control of their landholdings faced a potential challenge.

There were also important differences. The two coups of May and September 1987 were directed by elements within the Fijian Army, ultimately resulting in the elevation of coup leader Colonel Sitiveni Rabuka to the post of Prime Minister. The coups led to amendments to the Fijian constitution, guaranteeing indigenous rights to land ownership. The 1987 coups were essentially a bloodless military-dominated takeover.

The 2000 attempted coup, which commenced on May 19, 2000, was a response by elements within Fiji's indigenous community to the May 1999 election of a multi-ethnic government led by Fiji's first Indo-Fijian Prime Minister, Mahendra Choudry. A group of political dissidents under the command of a civilian, George Speight, and supported by armed rebel elements within the Fijian military, occupied parliament and held virtually all members of the Cabinet, indigenous and Indo-Fijians, hostage for over two months. The coup lacked support from the bulk of the Fijian Army and the Council of Chiefs, who demurred from supporting the coup but sought to act as mediators between the coup leaders and the military to peacefully end the coup.

Sitiveni Rabuka, who led the 1987 coup and was in 2000 head of the Council of Chiefs, led attempts to end this coup. This abortive coup resulted in over ten deaths and involved attacks against Indo-Fijians, primarily in Suva but also in other parts of the country. It was not until September 2000, when the rebels finally surrendered to the Fijian military, that George Speight and his accomplices were arrested and charged with treason.

International media coverage of the 1987 coup was extensive but heavily censored and television coverage was limited. International publicity about the events of 2000 was transmitted instantaneously by a technologically sophisticated international media accompanied by live updates of events on the Internet. In 1987, the military suppressed media coverage, while in 2000 George Speight sought, with limited success, to use the media as his messenger to the world. Subsequently, the 2000 coup attempt became a global media event.

Both coups were widely condemned by the international community, especially by the Australian and New Zealand governments. As a consequence of the 1987 coup, Fiji was suspended from the Commonwealth of Nations and subjected to sporting boycotts for several years. Fijian membership of the Commonwealth was not an issue in 2000, although Commonwealth nations led by Australia and New Zealand imposed intense diplomatic and economic pressure on the Fijian military and indigenous leadership to crush the Speight rebellion.

Both coups had an extremely negative impact on the Fijian tourism industry. Inbound tourism numbers plummeted during the years of each coup, especially from Fiji's two principal source markets of Australia and New Zealand. The recovery process following the 1987 coup was more protracted than the recovery after the political resolution of the 2000 coup attempt. The impact of cancelled airline services was especially severe in 1987, when Air New Zealand and Canadian Pacific cancelled services linking Fiji to Honolulu and West Coast USA and Canada—services which were never fully resumed by either carrier. Air Pacific finally had to include those routes within its own network.

The marketing program Fiji developed in response to the 1987 coup was implemented (with revisions) in 2000. As a result of the 1987 coup, the Fiji Visitors Bureau developed an effective contingency plan, which it rapidly deployed in 2000.

Both coups severely disrupted the Fijian economy and the long-term plans of the country's tourism industry. However, it was a feature of the market recovery phase after both coups that the nation's centralised tourism infrastructure, accompanied by a high degree of cooperation between the government and private sector, achieved a relatively rapid recovery from the two crises. The success of Fiji's marketing recovery program was predicated on the assumption that the twin weapons of intense and well-targeted media and travel industry promotion and price-driven consumer inducements could be employed across the full range of tourism services: air fares, accommodation prices, internal transport deals and the full range of land arrangements and restaurants. The only relative failure of Fiji's recovery program was in the management of government travel advisories in key source markets. During both coups Tourism Action Groups (TAGs) were formed, comprising representatives from the Fiji Visitors Bureau, Fiji Hotel Association, the national carrier (Air Fiji in 1987 and Air Pacific in 2000), Fiji Travel Associates, and the Fijian Tourism Ministry and Ministry of Transport. The TAGs' prime role was to formulate and coordinate a national crisis response and a tourism recovery strategy.

THE STATISTICAL PERSPECTIVE

Tourism to Fiji during the 1980s was subject to substantial growth. Total numbers of inbound tourists grew from 189 996 in 1980 to over 250 000 by 1986, a growth of 35 per cent over the six years. The coups of 1987 resulted in a 35 per cent drop in total tourism during a single year. The drop in the Japanese inbound market was far greater than average, while the Pacific market, primarily comprising visitis to friends and relatives (VFR tourism), was the least affected. The Australian, New Zealand and US markets reflected an average drop, while the cessation of Canadian Pacific services in 1987 had an above-average impact on the Canadian source market.

Overall, the recovery period took between eighteen months and three years. Only in 1990 did inbound tourism numbers indicate real growth from the 1986 figures. This growth had some interesting features, indicating that Fiji's post-coup marketing strategy achieved some success. By 1989, the Australian and New Zealand markets had fully recovered, but of greater significance was the very strong growth in the United Kingdom/Europe markets and the quantum growth in the Japanese and Asia source markets which had been achieved by 1990. The only negative had been lack of recovery of the US and Canadian markets. Much of this could be attributed to the lack

Table 7.2: Fijian inbound tourism in selected years before, during and after the 1987 crisis period (includes main markets)[10]

	1985	1986	1987	1988	1989	1990
Australia	89 459	86 297	65 382	75 264	96 992	103 595
New Zealand	19 450	22 720	16 197	21 507	28 128	29 432
United States	49 557	69 732	47 037	42 144	34 425	36 928
Canada	18 908	23 651	16 819	16 883	16 536	18 438
United Kingdom	7707	9972	8511	8464	11 404	16 775
Europe	12 667	15 088	14 726	20 498	23 916	27 211
Pacific	11 936	12 815	11 217	14 219	18 064	17 528
Japan	12 610	11 801	5487	3425	13 840	21 619
Taiwan	na	na	na	na	na	na
S. Korea	na	na	na	na	373	1783
Asia	na	na	na	na	1802	4470
Other	5800	5748	4490	5751	5085	1277
Total	228 184	257 824	189 866	208 155	250 565	278 996

of direct airline links between West Coast USA, Canada and Fiji, which had been severed during 1987 and only partially compensated for by Air Pacific. American and Canadian travellers took advantage of other, more easily accessible Pacific destinations such as Honolulu, Saipan, Guam and Tahiti. Even ten years after the 1987 coup, Fiji had yet to recover its losses in its North American source markets.

Paresh Kumar Narayan correctly observed that one of the key strengths of Fiji's tourism marketing was its strategic approach to diversifying its source markets. Although Fiji was heavily dependent on the Australian and New Zealand source markets during the 1990s and in the early years of the twenty-first century, it had made considerable progress in attracting a growing market of Japanese, Korean, North American, European and Southeast Asian tourists to augment its dependence on and vulnerability to changes in sentiment from the Australasian market. The growth of high-quality accommodation had also aided in attracting the new markets.[11]

The Fiji Visitors Bureau increased its attention to the Asian market after 1987 and this was clearly reaping dividends. For European travellers, Fiji was still deemed an attractive, exotic and distant option easily incorporated in certain round-the-world fare options which gained popularity in the late 1980s and early 1990s.

The coups of 1987 and 2000 exposed the major threats to Fiji's tourism development. The perception and manifestation of political instability threatens the desirability of a destination to tourists and tourism investors alike. For tourism investors, the risks—even if cushioned by incentives and tax concessions—are unacceptable. Fiji's high level of dependence on tourism as a source of foreign exchange was undermined by the coups, and the potential of future political instability remains a threat to foreign exchange earnings and overall economic viability. In turn, this impacts on Fiji's capacity to improve infrastructure. The coups failed to resolve the uncertainty on the matter of land and fishing rights.[12] During the 2000 coup, a group of indigenous Fijians occupied Turtle Island, claiming ownership of the resort. This led to concern from tourism investors that ownership of tourism property might be subject to challenge.

The figures related to the 2000 coup show that tourism to Fiji prior to the outbreak of the coup rose steadily. The trend for the first five months of 2000 indicated that, had there been no coup, tourism numbers to Fiji would have achieved an all-time record of close to 440 000 for the year. The Japanese

Table 7.3: Inbound tourism numbers to Fiji before, during and after the 2000 coup attempt (1999, 2000 and 2001)[13]

Year	Total	Australia	NZ	USA	Canada	UK	Europe	Pacific	Japan	Taiwan	S. Korea	Asia	Other
1999													
Year	400 955	118 272	72 156	62 131	13 552	40 316	28 371	26 090	37 930	259	1489	7538	1851
JAN	28 950	7851	3617	3654	1182	3823	2516	2599	2863	34	127	483	201
FEB	25 263	4947	2382	4395	1132	4191	2531	2221	2601	42	94	566	161
MAR	31 589	7945	3698	5637	1597	4074	2314	1668	3719	30	172	571	164
APR	29 082	8562	5174	4074	964	2827	1996	1909	2478	0	149	811	138
MAY	34 203	11 733	6324	5001	742	2871	2016	2272	2426	0	135	492	165
JUN	38 445	11 262	10 932	5261	1227	2601	1612	2082	1612	0	123	486	96
JUL	41 031	12 504	8949	6529	1284	3293	2244	2119	3187	0	147	666	141
AUG	40 680	12 292	7397	5224	1284	3413	2967	2267	na	0	139	723	116
SEP	36 806	12 621	8274	3766	696	2355	1793	2034	4113	0	90	968	96
OCT	36 800	9680	7417	6047	1155	3618	2651	2229	3126	0	62	607	208
NOV	35 180	8828	4258	6691	1613	4396	3088	2820	2619	0	120	571	176
DEC	31 926	10 047	3734	5852	1219	2854	2643	2071	2519	87	131	580	189
2000													
Year	294 070	76 883	49 470	52 534	10 532	29 215	22 506	21 534	19 674	610	3386	6140	1586
JAN	30 321	8877	3051	4542	1320	3426	3133	2204	2738	61	167	539	263
FEB	30 558	5987	2528	5322	1367	5167	2678	2593	3507	54	81	553	221
MAR	34 840	8236	3578	6583	1727	4591	3046	1757	4402	43	82	642	153
APR	38 069	11 857	6797	6546	1381	3778	2497	1916	2251	81	82	769	114
MAY	29 352	7838	5862	5402	787	3002	2065	1730	1834	54	79	545	154
JUN	12 066	2743	2129	3590	317	909	807	1029	173	11	85	230	48
JUL	12 804	2217	2202	3862	450	909	1033	1188	255	44	125	344	85
AUG	12 265	1524	1500	3282	431	881	1127	1768	448	71	533	648	85
SEP	19 867	5550	5946	2615	273	1056	825	1451	901	75	448	642	52
OCT	24 275	6203	7061	3184	684	1469	1534	1903	102	57	535	495	85
NOV	25 724	8201	5473	3358	783	1975	2218	2056	936	41	690	397	130
DEC	24 429	8201	3343	4248	1012	1962	1543	1939	1209	18	479	331	137
2001													
Year	348 014	98 213	66 472	57 711	10 752	30 508	20 917	23 606	20 411	776	8143	8263	1936

Note: Asia statistics issued by the FVB have a separate section for Malaysia, but in these figures the small Malaysian numbers are incorporated into Asia.

market and the fledgling South Korean source market indicated considerable promise. The traditional key source markets of Australia, New Zealand, the United States and the United Kingdom were all growing. The coup resulted in an immediate downturn in the market. While tourism numbers began to recover immediately after the coup, it is clear that in 2001 inbound tourism numbers to Fiji were well below the pre-coup level figures of 1999. It is always difficult to predict the length of time it takes for any destination to show a statistical recovery after a crisis but according to Josaia Rayawa, manager of the Fiji Visitors Bureau in Australia,[14] Fiji was confident that by 2002 tourism numbers would achieve real growth.

All markets were hit hard by the coup. The Japanese market, traditionally a security-sensitive market, was the major source market most severely harmed by the coup and its aftermath. During the 2000 coup attempt, the Australian and New Zealand governments imposed trade sanctions and issued particularly harsh travel advisories, which recommeded that their citizens defer travel to Fiji. The timing of Speight's coup attempt was particularly damaging from a tourism perspective, as it occurred during Fiji's peak tourism season (the Southern Hemisphere winter) and exacerbated the economic impact of the tourism slump. It was noticeable that the Australian and New Zealand markets made a rapid recovery immediately after the attempted coup was crushed. During 2001, Australian and New Zealand figures remained below 1999 levels. With the notable exception of the Korean figures, which achieved staggering growth, all main source markets recovered gradually.

FIJI'S MARKETING ACTIVITIES FOLLOWING THE COUPS OF 1987 AND 2000

The 1987 coups

The Fijian tourist industry's marketing recovery program following the 1987 coups was significant in establishing the benchmarks for recovery programs, following other problems which can impact on Fiji's tourism industry. These include acts of nature, especially typhoons and cyclones, which are a periodical threat to Fiji.

In 1987, the Fijian tourism industry established the precedent of forming the first Tourism Action Group which, as described earlier in this chapter, comprised representatives of leaders of government tourism organisations and the Ministry of Tourism and major private industry bodies. The Fiji Visitors Bureau quickly axed the original 1987 campaign slogan, 'Fiji the Way the World Should Be', as 'inappropriate' (a perfect target for amateur and professional satirists). The new slogan released in 1991 was 'Visit the Fiji You Don't Know'. In the meantime, TAG undertook a number of special tasks. These included:

- approaches to governments of key source markets to modify travel advisories which had advised citizens to defer travel to Fiji.
- reduction to prices on tours, air fares, accommodation and other land arrangements in a concerted campaign to lure key source markets to return;
- conducting market research to build up new potential market sources. These included Germany, South Korea, the Benelux nations and Taiwan;
- diversifying Fiji's tourism image through the promotion of eco-tourism and outer island destinations;
- promoting Fiji to the MICE markets, especially as an incentive and conference destination for Australian, New Zealand, US, Japanese and Canadian business;
- organising an intensive program of marketing promotion to the travel industry and travel media in key source markets, especially Australia, New Zealand and the United States. This was to include familiarisation tours for travel agents, and media hostings;
- doubling the Fijian government's budget for tourism promotion.

As Table 7.2 (on p. 141) demonstrates, the Fijian inbound tourism industry took two years to recover sufficiently to approach its 1986 levels. By 1989, key markets such as Australia, New Zealand and Japan had fully recovered and returned to growth, but the United States and Canada slumped severely. Even by 1990, when the Fijian inbound market had returned to overall growth, the reduction of airline services linking North America and Fiji had greatly retarded recovery from this source market. In the meantime, Hawaii, the Marshall Islands, Tahiti and American Samoa had vied to fill the vacuum created by the complications Americans and Canadians encountered to reach Fiji, in addition to their concerns about Fiji's political situation following the 1987 coups.

Fiji's tourist authorities sought to cultivate alternative markets to compensate for the drop in US and Canadian inbound tourism. A special focus was placed on the emerging 'Asian Tiger' economies of South Korea and Taiwan, whilst developing the British and continental European markets. Particular emphasis was directed towards the lucrative German and Benelux outbound markets. Fiji's tourism marketing ties with the EC, principle sponsor of South Pacific tourism marketing from the late 1980s until 1997, provided a dual opportunity for Fiji to promote EC investment into its tourism infrastructure and attract tourists from EC countries. The dual-track approach of cultivating investors and a market from the same source was an effective means for realising capital gain from European investment in resorts and hotels.

During the 1990s, Fiji's tourism industry continued to grow strongly as the country returned to political stability. By 1999, inbound tourism numbers reached a long-held goal of the Fiji Visitors Bureau when they exceeded 400 000 for the first time in the country's history. During the 1990s, the Fijian tourist authorities refined their marketing strategies. Berno and King[15] claimed that total focus on sun, sea and sand had become outdated, especially for the Australian source market where resorts in Queensland and in Southeast Asia (e.g. Bali) were frequently price-competitive and of superior quality to those available in Fiji. There was a concern in Fiji that, despite efforts to market a more diverse image of destination Fiji, other countries in the Pacific and in Southeast Asia were actively promoting themselves and eroding Fiji's market share from traditional sources. In the Southwest Pacific, Fiji could no longer ignore increasingly strong competition from Vanuatu, Western Samoa, Tonga, the Cook Islands and New Caledonia, all of which vied for a share of Fiji's traditional source tourist markets.

In 1997, the Fijian government published its *Fijian Tourism Development Plan 1998–2005.* The master plan was devised to build inbound tourism numbers to Fiji to 600 000 by 2005. The plan included a number of specific tasks:

- Implement a series of tourism development areas as a mechanism for encouraging investment.
- Adopt a proactive approach to securing additional investment in hotels and resorts.
- Simplify investment procedures for domestic and international investors and abolish withholding tax.
- Initiate investment with Nauru to rehabilitate the Grand Hotel in Suva.
- Insist that Fijian architectural themes are incorporated into the design of new resorts.

- Increase the staffing and budget of the Ministry of Tourism and Transport.
- Increase the budget of the Fiji Visitors Bureau to be funded by an increase in airport departure tax.
- Prepare for designation of World Heritage sites for the islands of Ovalau and Taveuni.
- Legislate and enforce minimum standards for the diving industry and regulate the operation of duty-free stores.

The plan was ambitious and heavily dependent on an expectation of economic stability in major source markets to achieve both a growth in tourism numbers and a commensurate growth in investment. Their strategy would be derailed by three major events:

- The economic downturn in several of Asia's tiger economies—most notably South Korea and Taiwan, which were prime targets of Fiji's promotional strategy.
- A rapid decline in the Australian and New Zealand currencies in relation to the US dollar.
- George Speight's abortive coup, the biggest factor in upsetting Fiji's tourism plans.

Marketing Fiji after the 2000 coup attempt

The TAG, originally mobilised in response to the 1987 coups, was reactivated in mid-2000. TAG sought to lobby the Australian and New Zealand governments to revoke the very harsh travel advisories which had called on Australians and New Zealanders to defer all travel to Fiji during the coup. The failure of the Fijian government to maintain a consultative relationship with the Foreign Affairs Ministries in Australia and New Zealand, especially on tourism matters, resulted in the lack of success of these approaches. During the coup and its immediate after-effects, the Fiji Visitors Bureau involved itself in an intense media campaign to isolate the actual problem of the coup (largely confined to Suva's parliamentary precinct) from the relative peace which dominated the remainder of Fiji.[16] However, it must be pointed out that during the coup attempt there was an attack on Fiji's main power station, a takeover of two tourist resorts by coup supporters, and attacks on two small airports, including the taking hostage of two New Zealand pilots employed by the domestic carrier, Air Fiji. Josaia Rayawa recalled that the Australian and New Zealand media's coverage of the Speight coup attempt made it clear that most political violence was restricted to a small part of Fiji confined mainly to the capital of Suva.[18] The Fiji Visitors Bureau kept prospective travellers and the travel trade informed through press releases and regular updates on the actual extent of the political problem on its website, stressing that the rest of Fiji remained a safe destination for tourists. Most media coverage reinforced the fact that the coup was largely confined to Suva.

Nevertheless, as is the case for any destination deemed unsafe by government advisories, travel insurance companies either restricted or refused to provide travel insurance coverage for travellers to Fiji until the advisory was either revised or revoked. Between August 8–18, 2001, travel bans on Fiji announced by the British, Japanese, Australian and New Zealand governments were revoked.[18]

Following the surrender and arrest of George Speight and his supporters, the FVB and Fijian travel industry rapidly implemented a market recovery program. The strategies employed in 1987 were largely emulated in 2000–01. The main point of difference was the extensive utilisation of the Internet as a marketing tool to the tourism trade and travellers alike. Travel writers, travel industry media and travel agents from key source markets were invited to visit Fiji on familiarisations. The Fijian travel industry introduced a range of discounted package deals to lure tourists to return. The FVB also advertised heavily in journals pitched at the MICE market.[19] In Australia and New Zealand, a highly professional TV campaign was used showing a peaceful beach scene depicting Fiji as it was before and after the coup. The message was that nothing had changed.

By March 2001, in a political sense, the coup made no difference. The Council of Chiefs agreed that the 1997 constitution, which Speight supporters had opposed, should be upheld. It cannot be stated with any certainty that the defeat of the Speight coup attempt has resolved Fiji's political divisions, but it is clear that the coups of 1987 and 2000 demonstrated that Fiji's economy and its travel industry are vulnerable to outbreaks of political instability. The election of George Speight as an MP in the 2001 national elections was evidence that Speight retained a modicum of support from a minority of Fijians.

CONCLUSION

Fiji's tourism industry was still in recovery mode by the end of 2001. If the FVB statistics are a guide, Fiji was well on target to surpass its record 1999 inbound tourism during 2002. However, the 2000 coup may prove to be a major obstruction to achieving the master plan target of 600 000 tourists by 2005. The Fijian tourism industry and its tourism authorities revealed an outstanding level of professionalism and coordination in their response to the crises of 1987 and 2000. Fiji's tourism prospects for future growth will be heavily dependent on the prevention of violent manifestations of political conflict. Due to the importance of tourism to the national economy, the Fijian tourism industry must play a leading consultative role in resolving the underlying political causes which led to the coups of 1987 and 2000.

The coordination between the government and the private sector of Fiji's tourism industry during and after both the 1987 and 2000 coup crises represents one of the world's most outstanding examples of post-crisis tourism marketing management. Fiji's approach to post-crisis marketing is a role model which many other national tourism authorities would do well to emulate.

Part III | NATURAL DISASTER

8 | TURKEY: IZMIT EARTHQUAKE, 1999

Rebuilding the tourist industry

CRISIS RANKING: **DESTCON 3**

BACKGROUND

During the 1990s, Turkey's inbound tourism industry underwent massive growth, catapaulting the country from a middle range tourist destination to one of the top 20 most popular tourist destinations in the world. Statistically, inbound tourism grew from 5.389 million in 1990 to 10.428 million in 2000.[1] There has been considerable speculation about the reasons for Turkey's sudden burst of popularity at the end of the twentieth century. The most credible explanation is that, during the 1990s, Turkey mounted an aggressive and professional promotional campaign to showcase the country's many compelling tourist attractions to its key source markets.

Geographically and culturally, Turkey straddles the two continents of Europe and Asia. Its largest city, Istanbul, bridges both continents. Turkey is a country of many paradoxes. Almost 99 per cent of Turkey's 66 million people[2] are Muslim, but its political orientation is democratic, secular and Western-orientated. Turkey is a member of NATO and—unusually for a predominantly Muslim nation—enjoys cordial relations with Israel and has actively sought membership of the European Community. Conversely, Turkey has often maintained tense relations with its neighbouring Arab states of Syria and Iraq to its south, problematic relations with Iran to its east, and there has been traditional tension in Greek–Turkish relations to Turkey's west. Historically,

in the days of the Ottoman Empire (1500–1917), Turkey dominated much of what is referred to today as the Middle East, including Syria, Iraq, Lebanon, Israel and Egypt. The Ottoman Empire also dominated Bulgaria, Greece and parts of the former Yugoslavia to the west. In a region where political memories are long, there is lingering resentment between many Arab countries and their former Turkish overlords.

To its northeast, Turkey borders the two newly independent states of Armenia and Georgia, formed as a result of the collapse of the former Soviet Union. Relations with Armenia in particular are coloured by Armenian claims of genocide which allege that between 1 million and 1.5 million Armenians were killed by the Turkish army during World War I. The Turks hotly deny claims of genocide and state that the numbers involved were far smaller and most Armenian deaths resulted from a military response to Armenian insurgency during that war. The establishment of an independent Armenian state in 1990, bordering on Turkey, has led to the first tentative attempts to resolve this historic chasm between the two countries. The collapse of the former Soviet Union enabled Turkey to establish diplomatic and economic relations

Sultanahmet Mosque (Blue Mosque), Instanbul. Photo courtesy Turkish Ministry of Tourism.

with many of the predominantly Muslim republics in what was the southern part of the Soviet Union.

The major source of recent and contemporary political conflict in the eastern and southern frontier regions of Turkey has been the challenge of Kurdish separatism. The Kurds are a stateless ethnic group numbering 25 million, most of whom live at the confluence of Turkey, Syria, Iraq and Iran. The Kurdish plight has rarely been reported in the Western media and only came to prominence during the 1991 Gulf War when the United States-led coalition established a 'safe haven' for them in Northern Iraq, an area which has been variously attacked by Iraqi and Turkish forces. Both countries accuse the Kurds of undermining their sovereignty. US government foreign policy towards the Kurds has at best been confusing: Kurdish nationalism is viewed positively by the US as a source of opposition to Saddam Hussein's regime in Iraq and viewed negatively when it is in conflict with its ally, Turkey.

Kurdish nationalist and territorial claims have long been consistently vague and subject to internal debate among the various Kurdish factions. Some Kurdish factions seek statehood, while others want autonomy in the countries in which they live or simply seek rights as a minority. Kurdish separatists have been in conflict with the governments of all the countries in which they reside. The confrontation between Kurdish nationalists and Turkey, home to half the Kurdish population, has been especially bitter. Between 1991 and 2001 there were many instances of Kurdish orchestrated terrorism in Turkey aimed at attracting international attention to Kurdish nationalist claims.[3] Some terrorist acts were targeted at tourists, which has presented a continuing problem for the Turkish government and Turkey's image as a safe and desirable tourist destination. Although this chapter will focus on the impact of the 1999 earthquake on tourism to Turkey, Turkish tourism authorities have regarded Kurdish terrorism as an impediment to the uninterrupted growth of its tourism industry, though a lesser threat than natural disasters.[4]

One of the compelling attractions of Turkey as a tourist destination has been the impact the cross-currents of human history have wrought upon the country's cultural landscape. Modern Istanbul is one of the great urban chameleons of history: it was known as Byzantium during the days of Roman dominance, and was a bulwark of emerging Christian power; after the fall of Rome and the rise of Islam, the city was named Constantinople, the capital of an empire which encompassed Egypt, the Levant and spread into Greece, Bulgaria and the Balkans. From the rise of the Ottoman Empire, it became known as Istanbul. The city was the setting for the rise of secular nationalism led by Kemal Ataturk at the end of World War I.

All over Turkey, there is evidence of indigenous societies and the influence of empires ranging through Greek, Hittite, Assyrian, Roman, Persian, Babylonian and Sumerian. St Paul (born the Jewish Saul of Tarsus in Southern Turkey) traversed Turkey during his journey throughout the Roman Empire to spread Christianity. It is said by some New Testament scholars that Jesus's mother Mary died in Ephesus. The Turkish town Catalhoyuk is claimed by

Turks to be the oldest known human urban settlement on earth, dating back 9500 years—a title traditionally challenged by Jericho. Since the September 2001 discovery of a town in Israel on the shores of the Sea of Galilee dating back 23 000 years, both claims are now redundant. However, there is no dispute that the history of human civilisation in Turkey is long, varied and fascinating. The city of Troy, one of the world's most famous archaeological treasures, is located in western Turkey. Capadoccia, curious rock formations of conical peaks, were hollowed out as homes to thousands of people 4000 years ago in southern central Turkey. Nearby Pamukkale is a series of calcium-rich bleached thermal springs millions of years old, which have formed a series of terraced pools along the slopes of a mountain.

Geographically and scenically, Turkey is a country of immense contrasts and beauty. The mountainous east is dominated by the country's highest peak, Mt Ararat, fabled resting place of the biblical Noah's Ark. Turkey is girded by 8000 kilometres of coastline on the Black Sea, Sea of Mamara, Aegean Sea and the Eastern Mediterranean. Turkey's 775 000 square kilometres range from deserts to lush and fertile lands. In recent years, the Turkish Ministry of Tourism has become increasingly effective in communicating the variety and quality of the country's scenic, historical and cultural attractions.

The curse of Turkey's geographical location is that it is situated at the epicentre of a series of fault lines caused by the pressure exerted by three major plates of the Earth's crust. The Arabian, African and Eurasian plates literally squeeze Turkey from north, south and east. The convergence of these tectonic forces on Turkey has caused frequent earthquakes over the centuries, some of which have been highly destructive and inflicted many thousands of casualties. During the twentieth century alone 96 major earthquakes in Turkey caused 100 000 deaths. The two most destructive earthquakes in Turkey during the twentieth century were the Erzinkan earthquake of 1939, which caused 32 000 deaths, and the Izmit earthquake of August 17, 1999, which resulted in 17 000 deaths. The Izmit earthquake is the focal point of this case study.[5]

THE GROWTH OF TURKEY'S INBOUND TOURISM INDUSTRY, 1990–2000

Turkey's tourism industry was one of the few success stories of Turkey's troubled economy during the 1990s. As described at the beginning of this chapter, inbound tourism numbers almost doubled between 1990 and 2000. Tourism receipts increased from US$2.705 billion in 1990 to US$7.636 billion in 2000. In 2000, the Turkish tourism industry employed at least 2.5 million people in Turkey, although unofficial estimates are double this figure when taking into account Turkey's large black economy (business conducted without records and in cash only to avoid taxes) and the many merchants who derive much of their living from selling goods and services to tourists. The tourism industry was estimated to contribute 2.1 per cent of Turkey's GNP in 1988. By 1997, tourism's contribution to GNP had more than doubled to 4.5 per cent, or 25 per cent of export earnings.

During the decade 1990–2000, tourism matured to become a significant and strategically vital element in Turkey's economy. The major source market was Europe. Turkey successfully marketed the destination worldwide and attracted a growing diversity of source markets. In 2000, the total inbound tourism numbers reached 10.428 million. Turkey's leading source markets are shown in Table 8.1.

The largest single source market was Germany, primarily driven by the 'visiting friends and relatives' (VFR) market drawn from the 3 million Turks living in Germany at that time.

Turkey's ease of access from Europe by road, rail, air and sea, coupled with the modest prices (by European standards) of its accommodation, shopping and internal transport, made it an increasingly popular destination for tourists of all types, ranging from backpackers to luxury travellers.

Table 8.1: Top ten source markets to Turkey, 2000[6]

Source market	% of total
Germany	21.8
United Kingdom	9.3
Russian Federation	6.6
United States	4.9
Netherlands	4.4
France	4.4
Iran	3.6
Bulgaria	3.3
Austria	3.2
Israel	3.1
Total % of top ten source markets	64.6

The growth of Turkish tourism during the 1980s was driven by government-funded developments and marketing initiatives based on a series of five-year plans. These included infrastructure development projects exemplified by the establishment of the Turkish Riviera based on the southern Mediterranean port of Antalya. In the city of Antalya, the opening of a series of casinos (the only legal casinos in the Muslim world) attracted large numbers of tourists from the former Soviet Union and Israel especially, who took advantage of low-priced package tours to the Antalya area. The casinos were closed in the late 1990s due to religious opposition, but by that time the region was well established as a sun-and-fun resort area with or without the dubious attractions of legal gambling. As prices in Greece began to steadily increase, the high-quality, low-priced Mediterranean resorts of southern Turkey were marketed as an attractive alternative. Turkish tour operators and developers established ski resorts and a well-defined series of tour programs, which included many of Turkey's historical, scenic and cultural attractions. The industry diversified to promote eco-tourism and adventure tourism; Christian, Jewish and Muslim pilgrimage tourism; and educational, archaeological and historically-oriented tours. The international marketing of destination Turkey was coordinated by the Turkish Ministry of Tourism, based in the capital of Ankara. Turkish information offices were located in 23 countries by 2000. The activities of Turkish tourism offices were actively supported by the national carrier, Turkish Airlines, and a growing number of Turkish and internationally based tour operators, all of which were able to take advantage of marketing subsidies available from the Turkish Ministry of Tourism. During the 1990s, the Turkish Ministry of Tourism was utilising the marketing consultancy services of international PR consultants PPK.[7] The strategic and high-quality advertising of Turkey in leading publications and television stations in key source markets was improving destination awareness. The advertisements featured diverse images of Turkey to reinforce the message that Turkey was a destination that appealed to many market segments. Certain niche marketing programs were also developed, ranging from promotions to Christian pilgrims in the years leading to 2000 (Christianity's bi-millennial); business travellers from Russia and the Arab world; war veterans and their descendants, packages which had strong appeal to sections of the British and Australasian markets; golfing for the Japanese; and sporting and adventure travel options which appealed to the European and North American markets. A special campaign was conducted to appeal to the large UK and European academic and schools tour markets, promoting Turkey's many price-competitive and well-preserved historical, cultural and archaeological sites. Turkey was increasingly incorporated into multi-destination European package tours.

At the luxury end of the market, Istanbul was featured as the true end of the line on the fabled Orient Express, which until the 1990s only went as far as Venice. Overall, the prime marketing message was the promotion of the diversification of Turkey's appeal as a destination and the capacity of its tourism infrastructure to meet varied tastes and budgets. During the 1990s, the Turkish government upgraded and expanded the main international gateway airports of Istanbul, Ankara and Antalya to more efficiently manage increased demand and also to improve the image of these gateway points. Turkish Airlines services 113 destinations worldwide and plays an important role in Turkey's destination marketing. Its recent opening of a route from Istanbul to Shanghai is indicative of increasing awareness of the potential importance of a rapidly growing outbound market from China (PRC) which also has a government policy of 'approved destinations' based in part on a proviso that the approved destination must have a direct air link with China.[8]

The Turkish Ministry of Tourism and Turkish tourism offices worldwide actively sponsored familiarisation trips and hostings for travel agents and travel journalists to assist in spreading the marketing message. The Ministry also sought to overcome the powerful negative images portrayed in the highly successful 1978 Hollywood film *Midnight Express*, which depicted two American tourists incarcerated on charges of drug smuggling in Turkey, and that affected a large segment of young American and Western European markets. The film, which depicted cruelty and corruption in Turkey, coloured negative Western—and especially American—images of Turkey for many years, a stereotype that the Turkish tourism industry was anxious to alter. The growth of high-quality hotel and resort accommodation in Turkey's major cities, resort areas and tourist attractions was beginning to lure the big-spending but fickle markets of the United States and Japan, where travellers sought new and different destinations which offered high-quality accommodation and service. By 2001, Istanbul alone had 5000 five-star hotel rooms operated by most leading international hotel chains.[9] In their tourism marketing, Turkey's tourism authorities were careful, almost to the point of paranoia, to depict Turkey as a European destination and anxious to avoid being labelled or depicted as a Middle Eastern destination.[10] Turkey did, however, accept being defined in certain markets—such as Eastern Asia and Australasia—as an Eastern Mediterranean destination, provided it was promoted in conjunction with primarily European countries in that region. This attitude was a marketing position and reflected Turkey's geopolitical alignments.

The overall picture of Turkish tourism during the decade 1990–2000 was one of considerable growth. The diversification of Turkey's tourism infrastructure and its weak currency meant that Turkey was a relatively inexpensive destination for foreign visitors, irrespective of the standard of travel, tourist services and accommodation required. The key interruptions to Turkey's inbound tourism growth in 1991 were attributable to the Gulf War (Operation Desert Storm) and Turkey's actual and perceived proximity to the war zone. Although the war between the coalition and Iraq was officially over by early March 1991, there was an extended period of Turkish involvement in the Kurdish dominated region in northern Iraq.

In 1993, Turkey experienced internal political instability and there was an upsurge in Turkish–Kurdish conflict which impacted on tourism during that year. However, the largest downturn in Turkish tourism numbers during the decade was directly linked to the August 1999 earthquake, which occurred during the height of the summer tourism season and led to a substantial reduction in inbound tourism numbers in late 1999.

The August 1999 Izmit earthquake was one of the most destructive and costly natural disasters afflicting Turkey during the twentieth century, both in terms of human casualties and destruction of residential and industrial

Table 8.2: Number of visitors to Turkey ('000s) and tourism receipts, 1990–2000[11]

Year	Visitor numbers	% change	Receipts US$	% change
1990	5 389	20.9	2705	5.8
1991	5 517	2.4	2654	−1.9
1992	7 076	28.3	3639	37.1
1993	6 500	−8.1	3959	8.8
1994	6 670	2.6	4321	9.1
1995	7 726	15.8	4957	14.7
1996	8 614	11.5	5650	13.9
1997	9 689	13.0	7080	23.9
1998	9 752	0.7	7177	2.0
1999	7 464	−23.5	5193	−27.6
2000	10 428	28.4	7636	32.0[1]

property. The exceedingly rapid recovery of tourism to Turkey after this well-publicised disaster was partly because most of Turkey's major tourist attractions were spared damage from the quake but due mainly to the highly effective campaign to restore the tourism market after the disaster.

THE IZMIT EARTHQUAKE, AUGUST 17, 1999

On August 17 at 3.00 a.m. local time, an earthquake measuring 7.4 on the Richter scale with an epicentre near the Turkish city of Izmit, 100 kilometres east of Istanbul in the Marmara region of northern Turkey, devastated a large area.[12] Seismologists defined the earthquake as a *shallow quake*. This maximised the destruction to buildings. Casualties were estimated to be 20 000 dead and 50 000 injured. The region in which the earthquake struck was a heavily populated and highly industrialised region of the country. According to a UN report, 350 000 housing units and business premises were damaged or destroyed. Many of the dead and injured were buried in the rubble of their homes while they were sleeping.[13]

The earthquake met with a massive international response of sympathy and support. In addition to the mobilisation of thousands of local rescue workers and medical professionals, rescue and medical aid teams from Israel, the United Kingdom, the United States, Greece, Kuwait, Germany and nineteen other countries arrived at the scene within 72 hours. There was an international effort involving 64 countries to provide food, medical assistance, temporary shelter and clothing aid to the victims. Rescue and aid teams were hampered by the extensive damage to roads and bridges and the on-site difficulty of access to victims trapped among the rubble of collapsed multi-storey buildings. While the rescue efforts were both heroic and extensive, the reactive nature of response to the Izmit earthquake revealed an ongoing problem of disaster management in Turkey.

Turkey's vulnerability to earthquakes and floods has been a fact of life for thousands of years, yet there appears to have been little done to develop contingency plans and measures which could have assisted in casualty and damage minimisation. A common observation of rescue and relief teams, engineers, financial planners and others involved in assessing the impact of the Izmit earthquake was that there was little or no indication of readiness for earthquakes. There was little evidence of legislation or enforcement of building regulations to protect structures against the impact of earthquakes. Most private residences and business premises were uninsured. Emergency facilities were poorly equipped or non-existent. There were few if any procedural guidelines to facilitate rescue or evacuation from danger zones. In fact, only since the 1980s had the Turkish government devoted resources to establish seismic stations and it was only as recently as 1998 that early warning systems for floods and other natural disasters were developed.[14]

In November 1997, the Turkish government, in association with the United Nations Disaster Relief Program, established the Disaster Management Implementation and Research Centre.[15] The DMIRC was established concurrently with the foundation of the General Directorate of Disaster Affairs as a Branch of the Turkish Ministry of Public Works and Settlement.[16] The two organisations were empowered to research and develop contingency plans to deal with disasters and establish early warning systems. The General Directorate of Disaster Affairs had in fact proposed a series of building codes in early 1999, but by August 1999 they were not subject to legislation—and even if they had been, it would have been unlikely that more than a small fraction of existing structures could have been altered to meet the technical requirements. Turkey's rapidly growing population and residential and industrial building requirements were met by rapidly and poorly built, cheap and usually flimsy buildings.

The Izmit disaster and the criticism levelled at the Turkish government's lack of preparedness by the United Nations, the World Bank, the media and some of the rescue teams led to Turkey upgrading its disaster management infrastructure. In fact, the global effort to assist Turkey led to Ankara hosting the Global Disaster Information Network Conference in April 2000, which resolved to implement global cooperation in the prevention, contingency management, information-sharing, financing, and rescue and recovery procedures for major natural disasters.[17]

The human cost of the Izmit earthquake was massive. However, the financial cost all but crippled the Turkish economy, which had been burdened by 50 per cent per annum inflation, poor balance of payments, massive external debt and a government hampered by ongoing deficit budgeting. The Izmit earthquake ruined much of Turkey's productive industrial heartland. The World Bank's assessment of the Izmit disaster suggested that the net cost of the earthquake would be in the region of US$3.6–6.5 billion, or between 1.5 and 3.3 per cent of GDP in 1999–2000. The assessment was based on increased output in unaffected regions and external financial support. The report was critical of Turkey's lack of preparedness for the disaster in relation to the paucity of enforceable building codes, poor insurance cover and a shortage of contingency measures. It did, however, praise the Turkish government's preparedness to increase tax to finance social welfare measures to assist the 500 000 homeless and to provide social security, educational and medical services and housing to the families of the 20 000 killed and 50 000 injured. The report called on the Turkish government to establish a centralised fund for disaster relief.[18]

The Center for Strategic International Studies in Washington DC published a detailed paper by Rusdu Saracoglu, a former Governor of the Turkish Central Bank and Minister of State for the Economy. Saracoglu observed that, during the 1990s, Turkey had experienced high GNP growth coupled with high inflation and a large number of outstanding government and private-sector loans. He described the Turkish financial system as small and weak by world standards. Saracoglu believed that Turkey needed to operate under tighter controls such as those enforced by the International Monetary Fund. A more disciplined fiscal system would lead to control of interest rates and reduction in inflation and government deficits. In his view, the Izmit earthquake was evidence that these measures needed urgently to be implemented by the government.[19]

The Izmit earthquake generated a vast amount of media coverage, much of it sympathetic to Turkey and especially the plight of the victims. The rescue and recovery effort did a great deal to build bridges between Turkey and the nations involved in providing assistance. The Izmit earthquake was a scene of cooperation of rescue teams from Israel and Arab states and the extensive involvement of US military rescue teams reinforced the Turkey–United States alliance. The political dividend from the US perspective was Turkey's vocal and strategic support for the US 'war against terrorism' following the September 11, 2001 attacks against New York and Washington DC. Turkish support was politically valuable for the United States in seeking to galvanise support from predominantly Muslim countries.[20] A positive outcome was a thawing in relations between Turkey and Greece. The Greek government provided considerable assistance to Turkey and sent rescue teams. Turkish rescue teams reciprocated when Greece experienced a severe earthquake in 2000. Cultural links and other bilateral contacts increased between Greece and Turkey following the earthquake.[21]

THE IMPACT OF THE IZMIT EARTHQUAKE ON THE TURKISH INBOUND TOURISM INDUSTRY

The initial impact of the Izmit earthquake was devastating and immediate. From all key source markets, there were cancellations and a reduction of forward bookings to Turkey. The media coverage at the time of the earthquake painted a picture of Turkish devastation. The normally sober BBC reported that even central Istanbul was badly hit—though these reports were eventually revised when the actual extent of damage was realised.[22] The eastern outskirts of Istanbul were indeed affected by the quake, but not the central part of the city. The UK Foreign Office established an update line. On August 18, 1999, the Association of British Travel agents warned British travellers to 'reconsider' visits to Istanbul in the days immediately after the earthquake.

John Cunningham, reporting in *The Guardian* (London), summed up the response of many would-be tourists to the Turkish earthquake: 'after empathising with the victims . . . is to wonder whether it is safe to go or holiday there'. His article went on to discuss the impact of disasters, be they terrorism, war or natural disaster, on all destinations.[23] The blanket coverage of global media TV services including BBC, CNN and Deutsche Welle had a particularly profound and negative impact on tourism from Turkey's three largest source markets: Germany, the United Kingdom and the United States. The impact was magnified when the largest Kurdish resistance movement PKK (Kurdistan Workers Party) issued statements in October 1999 warning tourists to avoid Turkey and threatened attacks on tourists who visited the country.[24]

Although there was intense media interest in the Izmit earthquake at the time of the event, media coverage ran its course and waned within one month. Unlike some other countries discussed in this book, Turkey does not have a large permanent contingent of foreign correspondents and media coverage is subject to far stricter controls than in Western European countries or North America. Other stories such as the onset of the millennium and the great scare of the 'Y2K Bug' rapidly replaced the Izmit earthquake in Western media headlines. Even the PKK's genuine threats against tourists, which were tactically timed to gain media coverage while world attention was focused on Turkey, failed to stir a great deal of media interest—much to the relief of the Turkish government and the chagrin of the Kurds.

In the months between August and December 1999, inbound tourism figures were 30 per cent down on comparable months of 1998.[25] Within a month of the earthquake, Turkish tourism authorities began the task of restoring the market. The main tasks were:

- highlighting the minimal earthquake damage to most visited tourist sites in the country and the tourist attractions of Istanbul;
- encouraging the travel industry to demonstrate support for Turkey by urging their clients to visit;
- stressing the overall safety of Turkey as a destination;
- organising familiarisation visits by travel industry and tourism journalists to see Turkey first-hand and pass the message on to their clients/readers/listeners/viewers;
- cooperate with allied tour operators in the various source markets to help disseminate a positive message about Turkey.

The success story of the restoration of Turkey's tourism market in 2000 had a great deal to do with the professionalism of the Turkish Ministry of Tourism's marketing management and the onset of 2000, so frequently and incorrectly described as the 'New Millennium'.

TURKEY'S TOURISM RECOVERY PROGRAM, 1999–2000

The Turkish Ministry of Tourism was provided with strong moral and financial support by the Turkish government, enabling it to embark on a marketing restoration program after the Izmit earthquake. The Turkish government recognised that tourism was a strategically important source of foreign exchange and goodwill. Turkish ethnic communities worldwide were encouraged to support the country during the emergency period and to assist in encouraging foreigners to visit.

The first priority for Turkish tourism offices was the mobilisation of media and travel agency hostings to Turkey facilitated by the Turkish Ministry of Tourism with the cooperation of Turkish Airlines and the major tour operators servicing Turkey. Television crews, journalists and travel agents were invited to see the extent of earthquake damage and then visit the main tourist areas to reinforce the message that they were largely untouched by the quake.

This strategy sought to convey a dual message of support for the victims of the quake by spending tourism dollars in Turkey. The Ministry also increased marketing subsidies to operators promoting Turkish tourism product.

The Turkish Ministry of Tourism established a crisis management team immediately after the earthquake to control press releases and messages tailored to the travel industry, the public and the media. The excellent Turkish Tourism website, <www.tourism.turkey.org>, was utilised to reinforce the prime messages that tourism infrastructure was undamaged, access to the country and popular sites was unaffected and that tourists were safe if they visited. While it is impossible to give a statistical measure of the success of these PR activities, there is no doubt that by January 2000 inbound tourism to Turkey had reached and surpassed the levels of the pre-earthquake period of 1999.

Turkey also actively promoted itself, sometimes in conjunction with Israel and Italy, as a key destination for Christian pilgrims during Christianity's bi-millennial in 2000. During Pope John Paul II's series of visits to Christianity's holiest sites during the 2000 Holy Year declared by the Roman Catholic Church, Turkey was an integral part of the Pope's eastern Mediterranean itinerary.

Mr Erdal Aktan was appointed in 2001 to manage the Turkish Tourism Office in Australia. He had served in London during the early 1990s and was involved in the PR campaign to thank rescue teams in Turkey during 2000. As a gesture of the Turkish government's appreciation for their efforts Mr Aktan organised the hosting in Turkey of members of rescue teams from the 24 countries that provided rescue and medical teams during the earthquake crisis. According to Mr Aktan, these hostings were warmly welcomed by the invitees and generated considerable positive publicity about Turkey in the countries which had provided the teams. The hostings also included reunions between rescuers and the people and communities they had assisted and helped publicise the recovery of devastated areas.[26]

The Turkish Ministry of Tourism, with the assistance of its marketing consultants DDB Dreamworks, designed a new logo for Turkish tourism and released a new advertising campaign in 2000. The campaign focused on traditional themes of the diverse attractions of destination Turkey, but it also emphasised spirituality, 'green' and environmentally sensitive themes. The campaigns of 2001 were ethereal compared with the simple message of the 1990s, which was that Turkey was a jigsaw of attractions.

Considerable emphasis was placed on finding testimonials from people who had visited after the earthquake and whose opinions would carry weight in source markets. Concerts were staged in Turkey featuring European and American celebrities who could show their concern for the victims of the earthquake and then see Turkey and pass on the message to their audiences that it was safe to visit—a popular, mutually beneficial and effective public relations strategy.

The combination of creating a new marketing image, reassuring travellers and travel agents, and promoting a new millennial interest in Turkey all contributed to the acceleration of Turkey's tourism restoration. Overall, the combination of strategies was highly successful. The other element which helped to achieve rapid recovery was the working alliance between the national tourism authority, airlines servicing Turkey (especially Turkish Airlines), and the Turkish and overseas tour operators marketing Turkey. Turkey's phenomenal growth as a destination during the 1990s provided considerable business for many private companies, hoteliers, charter carriers, and transport and tour operators servicing Turkey. Apart from a genuine concern about speeding the recovery of Turkish tourism for all these businesses, there was a powerful element of enlightened self-interest to facilitate and accelerate the recovery.

CONCLUSION

Of the case studies in this book, the recovery of Turkey's tourism industry from the devastating Izmit earthquake was one of the most rapid and complete marketing restoration campaigns. While the Izmit earthquake represented a single incident, it was one of a series of earthquakes which Turkey, due to its geological structure, will regrettably continue to experience.

Turkey's strength, in common with that of Fiji, involved a well coordinated marketing campaign combining the resources of the government and private sector. A distinguishing factor of the Turkish recovery was the well-targeted and effective PR campaign directed at the travel industry from major source markets and the media.

In the future, Turkey's position in a geologically and politically volatile part of the world will almost certainly require Turkey's tourist authorities to maintain their crisis management contingency plans in good working order.

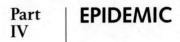

Part
IV | **EPIDEMIC**

| # BRITAIN: FOOT-AND-MOUTH DISEASE, 2001

Restoring confidence through information dissemination

CRISIS RANKING: **DESTCON 3**

BACKGROUND

Great Britain is one of the world's leading tourist destinations. In 2000, some 25.2 million people visited the United Kingdom from all over the world, spending a total of £12.5 billion or US$19 billion.[1] Britain is ranked fifth in the world for tourist earnings after the United States, Italy, France and Spain. Britain's proximity to Continental Europe makes it ideal for many long-haul travellers to combine a visit to Britain with travel to European countries.

The United Kingdom's rich cultural history is a major attraction: the Kings and Queens of Britain, representing 1000 years of monarchy; pomp and circumstance; Buckingham Palace; the Last Night of the Proms at the Royal Albert Hall; the land of Shakespeare and the enduring tradition of British theatre; pop music; fashion; fish and chips. The outstanding universities Oxford and Cambridge, the British Museum and the National Art Gallery represent a small selection of Britain's cultural icons. In the field of sport, Britain is home to the world football code of soccer as well as rugby, football and cricket. Tourists are attracted to British institutions ranging from the pub—social centre for working-class Britons—to the clubs and societies of the professional, academic and social elites. Whereas trappings of the British class system often give rise to domestic discord, they fascinate foreign visitors. The brief

life of Princess Diana reawakened a sense of glamour, controversy and mystery in the British royal family and attracted millions of tourists to England.

The scenic attractions of the British Isles include magnificent tracts of green countryside, the splendid Highlands, the lochs and islands of Scotland, the brooding landscape of Wales, the beauty of the English Lake District and Devon's 'English Riviera', Cornwall's picturesque fishing villages, the pre-historic mystery of Stonehenge (at least 5000 years old), Boadicea, the Romans, tales of King Arthur and the knights of the Round Table. Britain's tourist attractions draw 25 million visitors annually, with London remaining Britain's premier attraction.

The sun may have set on the British Empire as a world-dominant power, but millions of people in North America and the countries of the former British Empire retain a special attachment to Britain. Britain resists pressures

Tourists at Big Ben, London. Photo courtesy British Tourist Authority, Sydney.

to conform to the rest of Europe: cars are driven on the left-hand side of the road and the British maintain their pound sterling, rejecting the introduction in 2002 of the Euro as common currency over much of Western Europe. Britain provides an air of familiarity for millions of Britons and their descendants who live abroad, and for hundreds of millions more who are part of the English-speaking world.

The United Kingdom reflects its people: resilient, indomitable with a strong sense of national identity. Incidents which would spark a crisis for other tourist destinations—for instance, the Irish Republican Army (IRA)'s terrorist attacks and other acts of violent crime—rarely cause a ripple in Britain's appeal to tourists. The 1986 meltdown of the Chernobyl nuclear power station in the Ukraine resulted in massive environmental damage to Britain and its livestock and crops, yet it had virtually no impact on tourism. In Britain's southwest port city and tourist centre of Plymouth, the Campaign Against Nuclear Storage and Radiation (CANSAR) has identified that operations carried out at the United States-owned Devonport Royal Dockyards have resulted in massive increases (700 per cent) of discharges of nuclear waste into the River Tamar. In bunkers near Plymouth city centre, nuclear fuel rods and reactors from decommissioned British and former Eastern bloc submarines are stored, posing what CANSAR Chairman Ian Avent describes as a serious nuclear threat to Plymouth and southwest Britain.[2] Yet, despite the nuclear threat which Mr Avent describes in Plymouth—a potential cataclysm which could occur in a number of locations throughout the United Kingdom— this has had a negligible impact on tourism.

Since the late 1970s, Britain has experienced many destructive outbreaks of IRA terrorism. Terrorist groups and political activists espousing a variety of international causes have used London as a world stage to conduct acts of political violence. Acts of terrorism related to a variety of Middle East and African conflicts, and even outbreaks of local inter-ethnic violence and riots have occurred on the streets of London and in many other British cities with minimal impact on the overall appeal of destination Britain.

FOOT-AND-MOUTH DISEASE

In recent years, the biggest single threat to Britain's tourist industry has resulted not from the traditional crises generated by war, terrorism, crime, natural cataclysm or even human epidemics. Perversely, the 2001 foot-and-mouth crisis was caused by the outbreak of a disease contracted by farm animals. Normally, foot-and-mouth has little more effect on animals than the human version of influenza, but it makes stock unsaleable on world markets.

From an economic perspective, foot-and-mouth disease is the equivalent of the Black Death. Although it is a mild affliction for animals, from which they recover and is not known to affect human beings,[3] it is highly contagious and feared by farmers, rendering their stock virtually unsaleable on the meat, dairy and wool markets. It is contracted by cloven-hoofed animals including sheep, cattle, pigs and goats.

The first confirmed case of foot-and-mouth disease occurred in February 2001, followed by a growing number of outbreaks on British farms. Outbreaks were reported by the Ministry of Agriculture, Fisheries and Food (MAFF) to have quickly spread to many parts of Britain. The British agricultural authorities sought to quarantine affected areas and ordered farmers to kill stock on farms with infections and on adjacent properties. People who visited quarantined zones were required to disinfect their footwear and vehicles. The sickening media images of burning pyres of animals, people in rural areas undergoing disinfection procedures and the news of parks, gardens and rural attractions quarantined off limits to tourists rapidly transformed a rural problem into a tourism crisis (a word disavowed by British tourist authorities) and rapidly resulted in a significant drop in tourist arrivals to Britain during 2001. The crisis placed the rural tourism sector of the inbound tourism industry under severe hardship and threat. Restricted access to parts of rural Britain undermined the promotion of popular rural tourism programs, including the 'Gardens of Britain'.

The British tourism infrastructure is highly developed and offers tourists a myriad of choices. By world standards, Britain is an expensive destination, especially for land arrangements. However, many aspects of its wide range of tourist choices are popular with and affordable for travellers on a moderate or low budget. Two segments which became increasingly popular and heavily promoted by the British tourism industry were Farm Stay holidays and rural and provincial Bed and Breakfast establishments. As an overall policy, the British Tourist Authority, in conjunction with the private sector and county tourist authorities, sought to encourage tourists visiting Britain to travel beyond London and other key cities and experience as much of the country as possible. Facilitated by excellent air, road, sea, ferry and rail links throughout Britain, tourists can easily reach almost any location in England, Wales, Scotland and Northern Ireland. A consistent policy of British national, regional and local tourist authorities has been to spread the benefits of tourism income as widely through the nation as possible.

The United Kingdom has more international gateway airports for its geographical size than almost any country in the world. London's two largest airports, Heathrow and Gatwick, rank among the busiest airports on earth. With the exception of the Channel Tunnel rail link, foreign visitors must enter Britain by air or sea. The vast majority of long-haul travellers to Britain arrive at either Heathrow or Gatwick as their initial point of entry, although there are a growing number of direct long- and medium-haul air services to the major cities of Manchester, Edinburgh, Glasgow, Liverpool, Leeds, Birmingham and Belfast. The spread of global multi-airline conglomerates, such as the Star Alliance and the One World group, has enabled travellers on a single international carrier's ticket to travel from almost any point in the world to any sizeable town or city in the United Kingdom.

One element of the foot-and-mouth problem which impacted on British and international travellers was the growing concern with ensuring disinfection procedures were carried out for travellers departing Britain and arriving from Britain in third countries. Many nations required travellers arriving from Britain to undergo disinfection procedures for certain items of luggage, such as footwear and camping equipment, if it was deemed they had visited farming areas. The UK Ministry of Agriculture, Fisheries and Food issued bulletins advising Britons and foreign visitors about restrictions relating to infected areas. People were refused the right to enter or exit certain properties within infected areas, and as a further precaution travellers by road were also required to disinfect vehicles, especially when departing British territory.[4] These measures deterred many travellers from visiting rural Britain during the first half of 2001.

As an integral part of the marketing decentralisation of destination Britain, activities and tourism services within rural Britain had been extensively marketed since the early 1990s. In fact, as British rural production has declined over the years, rural tourism has grown commensurately. The international growth in demand for eco-tourism options aided the popularity of Britain's easily accessible rural tourism attractions and accommodation services. During the 1980s and 1990s, many walking tracks, bicycle paths and canals were reopened or established as tourist attractions. The National Parks and National Trust also assumed control of an increasing number of properties and land-holdings.

Since 1980, and prior to the 2001 foot-and-mouth outbreak, the international marketing of destination Britain by both government-linked marketing arms of the British tourism industry—the British Tourist Authority and the tourism private sector—devoted an increasing portion of its budget to promoting rural tourism. BTA brochures on Britain and the majority of tour wholesaler packages gave considerable prominence to rural tourism. It is indicative of the changing nature of tourism packaging since the mid-1980s that tourists have demanded an increasing range of tour module options affording them far more flexibility and choice. Self-drive holidays with vouchers for farmhouse or Bed and Breakfast stays became a popular option for visitors to Britain.

By mid-March 2001, the raw statistics of the foot-and-mouth problem were very disturbing. On March 22, 2001, the BBC reported that MAFF had described the impact as follows:

- cases confirmed: 435;
- animals slaughtered: 272 824;
- animals awaiting slaughter: 130 634;
- carcasses destroyed: 190 284.

Professor Roy Anderson, head of forecasting the epidemic for MAFF, was quoted as predicting that the foot-and-mouth crisis would peak by May but could continue into early August and that two new cases were being reported every day.[5]

By the end of April 2001, the figures had greatly surpassed Professor Anderson's predictions. By April 24 there had been 1465 cases reported, resulting in the slaughter of almost 2 million animals with another 232 000 awaiting slaughter.[6] The same report also suggested that two people had been infected with foot-and-mouth disease, though neither case was verified. Remains of slaughtered animals polluted watercourses and the water table in several regions, and the burning of carcasses was creating a fear that this would spread the disease through the air. Many people in Britain expressed concern that MAFF's policy of mass slaughter was creating more problems than it solved and was an inhumane and extreme method of dealing with the foot-and-mouth problem. The daily images depicting burning pyres of slaughtered animals which were transmitted through both the British and international media between February and June 2001 seriously harmed Britain's overall image and especially its image as a tourist destination.

The British government, through MAFF, restricted visitors' access to increasingly large tracts of land. Between March and August 2001, the British Tourist Authority issued regular updated bulletins on its website, advising on cancelled events, closed tourist attractions, parks, gardens, zoos and national parks. The National Trust closed most of its rural properties to the public. Many country walking trails and roads were closed to foot, cycle and vehicular traffic. While some of these closures were due to the presence of the disease, many more were enacted as a preventive measure. There were restrictions, predominantly self-imposed by local authorities and private organisations, on hunting, fishing, horse racing, car rallies and even sporting events including the Six Nations Rugby Union competition. The general elections in Britain were postponed, partly because many Britons living in restricted areas would be unable to leave their properties to attend polling booths. The government believed that it was inappropriate to hold elections under such circumstances.

In addition to the information on closures and cancellations disseminated through the BTA's website, various national, county and regional tourist authorities, including the Scottish, Welsh and Northern Ireland tourist authorities, sought to promote their own websites, which stressed that their regions were largely unaffected by foot-and-mouth disease. A number of private rural tourism enterprises which saw their own viability endangered by the BTA website developed their own websites to counter what they saw as the BTA's alarmist approach.[7]

A typical bulletin issued by the BTA in March 2001 contained a comprehensive list of events and activities cancelled, postponed or curtailed.[8] The temporary closure of large areas of rural Britain forced the BTA, government and privately owned marketers of tourism to Britain to radically alter their marketing approach. The overall approach was to promote Britain's urban and cultural attractions and wait out the rural crisis. This resulted in a massive slump in rural and provincial tourism during the period February–May. Britain's Tourism Minister, Mr Chris Smith, was quoted on April 16 as stating that the government had 'overreacted'. He stated: 'Six weeks ago [early March] we thought the best possible thing to do was to keep tourists away from the countryside. The devastating impact this has had on the rural economy shows we got it all wrong. Now the government and government funded tourist agencies are trying to reverse the situation.'[9]

It is, of course, possible to respond to Mr Smith by suggesting that the government, facing an imminent election, was more concerned about shoring up potential rural votes than about responding with due candour to the actual position. During March and April, the closures enacted by MAFF in rural areas, national parks and National Trust properties would have restricted the movement of all travellers to large tracts of rural Britain. Blaming British tourist authorities for their alleged 'over-reaction' to the foot-and-mouth crisis was a *politique* means to distance an optimistic minister from his department.

The BTA's approach to explaining the foot-and-mouth situation to the international travel industry and travellers worldwide was conducted in accordance with the policy outlined by Burson-Marsteller in its handling of Egypt's crisis (as discussed in Chapter 4) and in accordance with the World Travel and Tourism Council's guidelines for responding to natural disasters. The BTA fulfilled its prime obligation during a crisis to honestly and accurately depict the situation to the best of its ability. The BTA's approach minimised the overall damage to Britain's tourism industry despite the fact that the rural sector clearly suffered, not as a result of action by the BTA but from the restrictions on access to tourism sites enacted by MAFF, the National Trust, English Heritage and other local and government authorities. One of the major problems the British tourism industry faced in responding to the foot-and-mouth crisis was the uncertainty of its duration. By July 2001 it appeared to have waned, but a series of outbreaks in August 2001—especially in Wales—meant that a re-emergence was possible. By September 2001, the disease ceased to be a major issue for tourism and media coverage of foot-and-mouth was overshadowed by the events of September 11 and Britain's involvement in the 'war against terrorism'. In February 2002, the BTA officially announced the end of foot-and-mouth outbreaks. Immediately following the BTA's announcement, a suspected outbreak was investigated in Yorkshire.

The uncertainties of the foot-and-mouth emergency led Britain's national and regional tourism authorities, together with the inbound tourism industry, to adopt a twin-track crisis management response. One track was directed to damage control and the marketing of activities in parts of Britain either unaffected or minimally affected by the disease. The second track involved devising and implementing a recovery policy when the crisis was deemed to have passed.

THE BTA'S RECOVERY PLAN

Although most BTA officials were reluctant to publicly refer to the foot-and-mouth epidemic as a crisis, the BTA established a special unit under the management of the Tourism Recovery Unit, headed by Deirdre Livingstone, to devise a recovery program. BTA Chairman David Quarmby wrote an article entitled 'Fighting Fit', which outlined the BTA's overall approach to what he described as managing the foot-and-mouth 'crisis'. In terms of damage control, the BTA (which has offices in 27 countries worldwide), in association with British carriers and leading tour operators, sponsored numerous familiarisation trips for local and foreign travel journalists and leading travel agents to visit Britain and assess the situation at first hand. The BTA's website, in common with those of all national and local government tourist authority units in the United Kingdom, was utilised to maintain a real-time situation update dealing with access to tourist sites and the status of events, both in the United Kingdom overall and in specific regions. The British employment of the World Wide Web has been one of the most sophisticated and effective examples of using the Internet as a marketing and media tool during a tourism crisis. BTA offices worldwide prepared and delivered bulletins updating prospective travellers and travel industry professionals who lacked access to the Internet.

STATISTICAL IMPACT OF FOOT-AND-MOUTH ON BRITISH TOURISM

The British Tourist Authority's Internet site contains a wealth of statistical information on inbound tourism to Britain. For the purposes of this study, the prime focus will be on the specific impact of the foot-and-mouth crisis on inbound tourism. During 2000, the United Kingdom attracted a total of 25.19 million visitors, who spent a total of £12.8 billion (US$19 billion). The main markets in terms of numbers of visitors were:

1. United States: 3.939 million;
2. France: 3.223 million;
3. Germany: 2.794 million;
4. Irish Republic: 2.075 million;
5. Netherlands: 1.617 million.[10]

Apart from the United States, which is a long-haul source market and spends more time and twice as much money per capita than any other market, Britain's principal source markets are its nearest neighbours geographically. Long-haul source markets such as Japan, Canada, Australia and New Zealand, while numerically smaller than those listed above, feature longer stays and far higher per capita spending than most European source markets.

Some markets were more affected by the foot-and-mouth crisis than others. The principal impact was on source markets showing the highest propensity to be influenced by media coverage. As many travellers from neighbouring countries were visiting Britain for short-term business or holiday visits to London or other major cities, the foot-and-mouth problem would have had little impact. In major VFR source markets such as the Commonwealth countries, the impact of foot-and-mouth was minor.

Japan was the major international source market which demonstrated the greatest downturn during the height of the foot-and-mouth epidemic. The Japanese outbound travel market is often regarded as one of the most fickle tourism markets in the world, and the large-scale culling of farm animals (especially cattle), regarded in Japan as a prized source of meat, would have offended many Japanese as it would have engendered fear that many other British food items may have been inedible. The BTA pointed out that the downturn of the Japanese economy resulted in a decline in Japanese tourism to Britain, but Japan's economic problems failed to explain a sudden slump of 24 per cent between March and May 2001 and an overall downturn in the Japanese market of 37 per cent during 2001.

The one source market for rural tourism most affected by the closure of parks and rural attraction was the domestic tourism market. Britons, to a far higher degree than international visitors, are drawn to the British countryside for holiday visits to farms, caravan parks, campsites and country rambling.

Table 9.1 represents the statistical changes between January and May 2001 and the corresponding period during 2000. The table also shows the variations for key source markets during the entire year 2001 compared with 2000.

As the figures indicate, the overall global impact of the foot-and-mouth crisis on raw tourism numbers to Britain could hardly be described as catastrophic during the first five months of 2001. However, BTA Chairman David Quarmby has indicated that the impact of foot-and-mouth is greater than the raw data suggest. He claimed that in April 2001 the number of international tourists fell 22 per cent compared with April 2000 and that tourist spending fell by 16 per cent compared with April 2000.[12] The downturn in Britain's largest single source market, the United States, had a significant impact on tourism expenditure, as did the more substantial downturn in the big-spending Japanese market. There are indications that the foot-and-mouth crisis impacted negatively on qualitative features in the market, such as length of stay in the United Kingdom, spending per tourist and the actual distribution of tourists through the United Kingdom. The foot-and-mouth problem reduced the number of tourists visiting London and other key cities, but its impact in rural Britain was far greater. Rural Britain's high degree of dependence on domestic tourism magnified the impact of foot-and-mouth during the summer season June–September, although it is notable that restrictions related to foot-and-mouth eased during the second half of the 2001 summer season.

Table 9.1: Percentage change in tourist numbers to Britain, January–May 2000 vs January–May 2001, and full year 2000 vs 2001 (key source markets)[11]

Country	Jan–May 2000 vs 2001	Full year 2000 vs 2001
France	–10%	–6 %
Germany	–16%	–12%
Irish Republic	+ 5%	+5%
Netherlands	+ 4%	+1%
Belgium/Luxembourg	+19%	–2%
Italy	–20%	–5%
Eastern Europe	–7%	–5%
Spain	–3%	–4%
Sweden/Finland	–6%	–15%
Switzerland	+ 2%	–7%
Austria	–18%	–15%
Denmark	+ 6%	–3%
Norway	–17%	–18%
Portugal	+10%	0%
Rest of Europe	–14%	–9%
Europe	–5%	–6%
United States	–7%	–10%
Canada	–13%	–12%
Central and South America	–6%	–7%
Middle East	–3%	–6%
South Africa	+36%	+11%
Rest of Africa	+15%	+1%
Japan	–24%	–37%
Australia/New Zealand	–3%	–9%
Southeast Asia	+ 5%	–14%
Rest of Asia/Pacific	0%	–8%
Long haul West	–5%	–10%
Long haul East	0%	–10%
World total	–5%	–7%

The figures in Table 9.2 quantify the numerical differences over each of the five months January–May 2000 and 2001 from the key market regions. They also demonstrate that by April and May 2001 the real impact of the foot-and-mouth problem was statistically demonstrable. The impact of foot-and-mouth on inbound tourism in Britain was gradual, unlike the sudden impact of war, terrorism or natural cataclysm in other countries. While the British Tourist Authority was hopeful that the recovery process would be relatively rapid,[13] the gradual process of the foot-and-mouth-induced erosion of Britain's inbound tourism was matched by a gradual recovery, slowed by the international implications of the post-September 11, 2001 tourism slowdown. The critical period for gauging the full impact of foot-and-mouth, as BTA Chairman David Quarmby stated, was revealed during the peak summer tourist months of June–September 2001. The fading of the epidemic occurred during that period and was reflected in a recovery of inbound tourism numbers from September 2001. By November 2001, European tourism to Britain surpassed 2000 levels for that month.

It cannot be said with complete certainty that the decline in tourist numbers during April and May 2001 was solely due to the impact of the foot-and-mouth problem. However, it is likely that it was the dominant factor. Other influences, such as the decline of exchange rate values against the British currency in countries that include Japan, Australia, New Zealand and Canada, may have been contributing factors, but this is contradicted by growth from South Africa where the South African rand had depreciated more rapidly than the currencies of the countries mentioned above. An important factor which ameliorated the impact of the foot-and-mouth crisis on British tourism was the fact that rural tourism represented one of many niche markets within the British tourism industry's infrastructure. It was possible for government and private-sector marketers of destination Britain to isolate the problems that afflicted the rural sectors from other attractions in Britain. BTA Chairman David Quarmby stated that Britain's historical sites were the prime attraction for 65 per cent of visitors to Britain, and while some of these heritage sites were closed during the crisis period (especially National Trust properties in rural areas), most were unaffected.[14]

Table 9.2: Overseas visitors to the United Kingdom by month, January–May 2000 and 2001 ('000s)

Month	January		February		March		April		May	
Year	2000	2001	2000	2001	2000	2001	2000	2001	2000	2001
Source										
Europe	1030	1009	1129	1028	1175	1200	1537	1439	1480	1337
Long-haul West	323	303	251	263	442	417	417	369	500	434
Long-haul East	267	297	171	181	206	227	237	228	327	270
World total	1621	1610	1553	1470	1819	1840	2187	2040	2304	2040

THE BTA'S VIEW OF MARKETING BRITAIN DURING AND BEYOND FOOT-AND-MOUTH

British Tourist Authority Chairman David Quarmby, in his July 2001 paper 'Fighting Fit', effectively outlined the BTA's view of the foot-and-mouth crisis. Quarmby observed that foot-and-mouth clearly had a detrimental effect on inbound tourism to Britain. He also pointed out the loss of tourism, especially to rural Britain, was obvious from both international and domestic source markets. He claimed that forward bookings had dropped appreciably and the full impact would be reached in mid-summer. Mr Quarmby outlined the recovery program, which would operate in several stages. In the short term, he saw the BTA's key role as providing reassurance and factual information and, as already discussed, the BTA's website and those of other tourist authorities achieved this aim. He also saw it as necessary to build on partnerships with carriers and the local travel industry to rebuild Britain's tourist industry. Quarmby saw these partnerships as vital to restoring the British tourism industry on a long-term basis. He also saw it as necessary to encourage marketing support for rural tourism enterprises which had been hardest hit in what he described as 'the worst crisis ever to hit British tourism'. The major marketing stages are outlined below:

Stage 1: Facts, information and rebuttal

The BTA's website was the key tool for presenting facts about places which were open and operating or closed and non-operational. The information was meticulously gathered from attractions, Bed and Breakfasts and regional authorities all over the United Kingdom.

Global PR company GCI was appointed to target rebuttals (where necessary) to the media and to fully brief the travel media and the travel industry of all source markets.

The BTA invited 40 key travel industry leaders from around the world for a 'summit' meeting with British travel industry chiefs and Prime Minister Tony Blair, plus an inspection of major areas of Britain. The invitees included senior executives of major travel associations, major wholesalers, travel editors of leading publications and other opinion-shapers. Mr Quarmby claimed these leaders returned to their home countries as 'ambassadors of Britain'.

There were some special events which provided a focus for positive publicity. In April 2001, the Eden Project was opened in Cornwall in southwest England. This massive venture involved the planting and display of over 85 000 species of plants from all over the world under a series of massive transparent domes. The Eden Project, conceived by Tim Smit, was an instant tourist attraction for Cornwall and captured the imagination of environmentalists all over the world. Mr Smit who had led another famous Cornish garden project cum tourism attraction, the 'Lost Gardens of Heligan', was a significant pioneer in British eco-tourism. Ironically, the Eden Project was so popular that visitors created traffic jams 20 kilometres long, creating exhaust pollution over a huge area. Nevertheless, amidst the gloom of foot-and-mouth, the Eden Project provided a very positive impetus for tourists to visit at least one part of rural Britain.

Stage 2: Medium-term plans

This strategy involved tactical marketing blitzes on specific markets in association with airlines, tour operators and hoteliers to draw tourists back to Britain, especially from the worst-affected markets of the United States and Canada. The tactic centred on the promotion of a range of special deals for limited periods. The campaign included a mail-out and the promotion of Britain by popular celebrities from sport, show business and the arts.

The BTA made a strategic decision to support broadcasts of the FA Premier League (soccer), which it sponsors in association with Barclaycard. The FA is widely broadcast all over the world. The sponsorship included opportunities to utilise football broadcasts to include positive images of destination Britain.

Stage 3: Long-term plans

The third stage dealt with relaunching and re-presenting Britain under a number of umbrella themes, including heritage, culture and the Golden Jubilee of the reign of Queen Elizabeth II, which was the dominant celebration in Britain during 2002. The 2002 Commonwealth Games in Manchester was promoted as a major attraction to Britain for Commonwealth source markets. The BTA worked closely with British government ministries. It sought the cooperation of the Ministries of Tourism, Sport, Media and Culture, and the Foreign and Commonwealth Office (Foreign Ministry) to disseminate positive stories on Britain. The BTA was granted an increased marketing budget and, not surprisingly, the BTA chairman directed the obligatory accolades to Tourism Minister Janet Anderson.

Mr Quarmby indicated in his article that the foot-and-mouth crisis had the one key silver lining of placing the British tourism industry on the map as a vital part of the British economy, valued at £64 billion (US$100 billion) or six times the value of agriculture.[15] Mr Quarmby's article presented the broad strategy. At local levels in each source market, the BTA (in common with all national tourist offices) implemented the overall marketing plan in accordance with the state of the market in which they operated. The foot-and-mouth crisis only marginally affected the Australian and New Zealand markets. Most tourists visiting friends and relatives in Britain, and the majority of working holidaymakers continued with their plans. There was less urgency in these source markets to 'lure' consumers back to Britain than was the case in the United States, Canada and Western Europe, where a far more aggressive marketing campaign was required to reassure visitors that they would not be inconvenienced by foot-and-mouth. The markets most severely affected were countries with a preponderance of short-term discretionary visitors.

The BTA works on a range of partnership arrangements with airlines and tour operators worldwide. The partnership relationships were mobilised during the foot-and-mouth crisis to encourage airlines and operators to cut tariffs during the height of the crisis and what appeared to be its immediate aftermath in June 2001. This was especially apparent in the United States, Western European and Japanese markets, which experienced the most appreciable decline. Overall, the partnership between the private and government sectors in Britain is strong but by no means universal. Few rural operators and accommodation providers sought to increase prices during the northern summer to compensate for the appreciable loss of business they experienced in the February–May period. This was especially evident in Devon and Cornwall. While airlines and the larger operators were keen to cooperate with the BTA, especially at the global level, this was not always reflected at the local level. National, county and local government authorities did provide marketing subsidies to the private sector of the tourist industry in Britain, but this did not necessarily maintain the viability of private tourist business in rural Britain. Without being able to accurately quantify the situation, there were many jobs lost and a number of tourism-related businesses collapsed in rural areas.

The only silver lining on the horizon for rural tourism in Britain was that the worst of the foot-and-mouth crisis had passed by the beginning of the peak summer tourist season.

THE MEDIA AND FOOT-AND-MOUTH

The international media found the foot-and-mouth crisis irresistible. The disease was rapidly dubbed a 'rural crisis' and an 'economic cataclysm'. The dramatic and sickening images of thousands of animals being slaughtered and their carcasses burning in vast pyres across the green and pleasant land of Britain made compelling television. Bereft farmers, angry environmentalists, police closures, tourists and locals forced to have footwear and vehicles disinfected, traditional events cancelled—this was all daily fare on the international media between February and June 2001. The tabloid media magnified the issues into a national catastrophe, with Britain depicted as the 'sick man of Europe' and 'the pariah of Europe'. Many BTA offices and tour operators were bombarded with questions such as 'Can I eat the food there?' and 'Will I need to be quarantined when I return?'

The media images contributed to an atmosphere of fear about travelling to Britain. There was concern over possible conflict between British farmers and the government. Many farmers believed that the Ministry of Agriculture, Fisheries and Food had overreacted to the foot-and-mouth problem, especially when orders were issued to many farmers for what was termed 'preventative' slaughter of flocks which were not in themselves diseased but were in a 'danger zone'. These issues were intensely debated in the British media. The British media cast a giant international shadow. British-based worldwide networks BBC, B Sky B and major newspapers including *The Times* and the *News of the World*, owned by international media conglomerates, result in British news rapidly becoming international news. London, with Washington DC and Jerusalem, is one of the world's three principal international 'nesting places' for foreign correspondents. Consequently, foot-and-mouth was big global news—all of it negative. The British tourism industry, to its credit, tuned its messages to the technology favoured by modern news-gatherers. The BTA made extensive use of its website and email for press releases, information and rebuttals of the more outlandish media claims.

As mentioned earlier, the BTA attempted to counter the media agenda by providing updated information on the closure of sites, status of events, and so on. By positioning itself as a reliable news source, the BTA sought to work with the media rather than adopt the adversarial position of some tourist authorities during a crisis. The British tourism industry encouraged local and international journalists to view the situation first hand, and it also impressed upon them the need to consider the impact their reporting had on rural British businesses, jobs and communities affected by the loss of tourism. This relatively subtle approach gradually led sections of the local media to launch a campaign to encourage Britons to holiday in Britain, enabling domestic tourism to cushion the impact of the loss of international visitors to Britain. Tourist authorities and rural tour principals heavily supported these campaigns.

As the extent and frequency of the foot-and-mouth outbreaks declined during and after June 2001, media reports became less frequent. It is characteristic of media reportage worldwide that the onset of a crisis is subject to heavy coverage but the resolution or diminution of a crisis is normally subject to perfunctory reporting, at best. While exceptions to this rule most certainly exist, the diminution of foot-and-mouth in Britain was not one of them.

CONCLUSION

The British foot-and-mouth crisis represents one of the most unusual crises dealt with in this book. The damage to the image of destination Britain arose from fear of the effects of a disease which impacts directly on animals, not humans.

The most specific impact on Britain's tourist infrastructure was on rural and regional tourism, a segment on the British tourist infrastructure targeted as one of the major growth areas. The impact on overseas source markets was uneven. Key markets demonstrating the greatest decline were Western Europe, North America and Japan. Conversely, some major source markets were relatively unaffected, including Australasia, Africa, Southeast Asia, Eastern Europe and the Middle East.

The government-funded British Tourist Authority adopted a highly responsible approach to managing the crisis and avoided the trap of understating the problem and running a slick disinformation campaign in response to negative media coverage. The BTA coordinated a professionally managed campaign of keeping travel retailers and travel consumers informed of developments. It was overwhelmingly an open and transparent campaign using the Internet as the key tool of information dissemination, especially to the media and the travel industry. The key strength of the BTA campaign was its flexibility. It ran parallel campaigns featuring elements of in-crisis management, coupled with a post-crisis marketing strategy. In this particular case, the duration of the problem could not be predicted. The main failure of the campaign was the lack of compensation and support of private enterprises in rural Britain, which felt betrayed and neglected by what they perceived as a lack of support from government in general, and the BTA specifically.

While the overall marketing approach isolated the rural tourism crisis from other aspects of destination Britain, the travel industry and the government sector in particular saw it as a major priority to assist in the recovery of the rural and regional tourism sector.

There was a high level of coordination between the government and private sector in both crisis management and post-crisis marketing. However, the complexity, diversity and the sheer size of Britain's tourism industry infrastructure were insurmountable barriers to achieving the unity of purpose in post-crisis marketing which could be achieved in a small state such as Fiji, as outlined in Chapter 7. Certainly, with large operators, airlines and government authorities and enterprises, the degree of coordination was far more extensive than most cases examined in this book.

The British tourism industry's marketing management of the foot-and-mouth crisis appears to have been successful. Provided there are no future outbreaks, recovery—which was already well advanced by the end of 2001—looked set to be complete during 2002. The British tourism industry's response to a very difficult crisis has been professionally managed and, overall, provides a good role model to other large democratic countries.[16]

Part
V | CRIME

10 | SOUTH AFRICA: CRIME WAVE, 1994–2000

Pre-emptive response to a potential tourism crisis

CRISIS RANKING: **DESTCON 4**

BACKGROUND

South Africa is a land of contrasts and contradictions which often verge on the extreme. The country's land mass of over 1 million square kilometres would easily encompass France, Germany and the Benelux countries. Within its borders are deserts, dramatic mountain scenery and verdant plains intersected by mighty rivers. This vast land is surrounded by dramatic coastal scenery on both the Atlantic and Indian Oceans. South Africa is famous for its wildlife. The largest of its many national parks, Kruger National Park, is the size of Israel and home to the 'big five wild animals' (elephants, rhinoceros, lions, leopards, buffalo) and many other species of African wildlife including antelope, giraffe, wildebeest and zebras. Its natural attractions are augmented by a number of magnificent cities, among them the southern port of Cape Town, the stylish capital of Pretoria, and the nation's largest city, Johannesburg.

Until the 1990s, South Africa's tourism industry was hampered by its political status as an international pariah nation resulting from the constitutional entrenchment of minority white government which operated under a system known as Apartheid.

Apartheid is an Afrikaans word literally translated as 'separate development'. Its supporters claimed that the three main racial groupings—Whites, Blacks and Coloureds—would receive separate but equal government

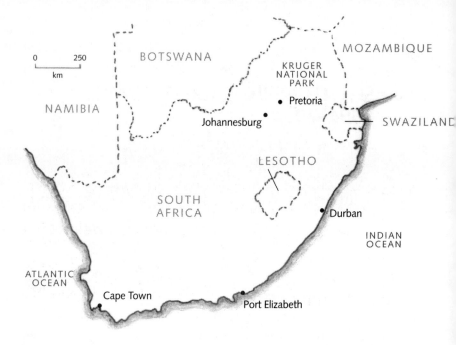

support. In practice, Apartheid was widely viewed as institutionalised racial discrimination in which South Africa's 5 million-strong White minority held most of the political and economic power and received the bulk of government benefits at the expense of the 40 million non-White majority. The most overt manifestations of Apartheid—including segregated beaches, public transport, hotels, toilet facilities, theatre and restaurant seating—were compared at worst with Nazi Germany or at best with the crude excesses of segregation in the pre-civil rights period in the Deep South of the United States. Non-Whites were long denied the opportunity of selection in national sporting teams, a practice which resulted in wide-scale international sporting boycotts against South Africa, including the banning of South African team participation in a succession of Olympiads. A combination of growing internal opposition and external condemnation, boycotts and isolation led to the gradual erosion of the Apartheid system and its ultimate abolition by the government of F.W. De Klerk in 1994. Nelson Mandela spent almost 27 years imprisoned by the regime from 1963 for his role as leader of the opposition

Leopard in Kruger National Park, South Africa. Photo courtesy of Abercrombie & Kent.

African National Congress (ANC). Mandela was released at the beginning of 1990: within four years of his release, the Apartheid regime had collapsed. In South Africa's first multi-racial democratic elections, held in 1994, the ANC won an overwhelming majority (65 per cent of primary votes) and former prisoner Mandela was installed as President Mandela, South Africa's first Black African President.

President Mandela's release from imprisonment was the culmination of a long-running campaign conducted by anti-Apartheid activists within South Africa and internationally. He embodied the struggle against a political system which was widely condemned as racist and unjust. Mandela's personal dignity throughout his political career and during his imprisonment, and his refusal to engage in vengeance upon attaining power were the qualities which made him a charismatic leader in South Africa and an iconic figure amongst international leaders. Mandela was without doubt—albeit unintentionally—a tourism symbol of the 'new South Africa'.

Contrary to the fears of many South African Whites, majority rule did not manifest itself in anarchy and vengeful massacres against Whites. Nelson Mandela sought to institute a government pledged to reconciliation and renewal. The vast political changes resulted in the removal of political and economic barriers between South Africa and the international community. The beginning of the 1990s created expectations of a golden new era for South Africa. As frequently occurs in the wake of an epochal political transformation, there were over-optimistic expectations that long-term problems would be rapidly solved. However, even with the best will in the world, the massive extent of poverty, health problems, poor housing and educational inequalities between Blacks and Whites would require a long-term and expensive program for the new South African government.

The relaxation and ultimate demise of Apartheid hastened the easing of visa restrictions for outbound South African travellers. Restrictions, including denial of entry into third countries, were abolished for international travellers with South African visas stamped in their passports. During the Apartheid era, South Africa operated a loose-leaf visa policy similar to Israel. It was among a number of inconveniences deterring some travellers from visiting South Africa during the Apartheid era. Restrictions against citizens of neighbouring African countries visiting South Africa were repealed during the early 1990s.[1]

The introduction of a majority rule democratic political system in South Africa created a vast new potential for a 1990s tourism boom. The collapse of Apartheid erased the moral dilemma which had inhibited many international tourists from visiting and removed the politically motivated restrictions imposed by many governments on their national flag carriers against flights to and from South Africa. South Africa's national carrier, South African Airways, was freed from restrictions against overfly rights across the air space above many African nations and landing rights in countries which had previously denied it access. South Africa was in a position to promote itself as a tourist destination to source markets in many countries which hitherto had been off-limits. The resumption of sporting ties between South Africa and the rest of the world enabled South Africa to host international sporting events especially in popular games such as cricket, Rugby Union, soccer and athletics—all of which were to prove popular drawcards for overseas visitors. In 1995, South Africa hosted the Rugby Union World Cup which attracted record inbound tourism arrivals during that year from Rugby supporter countries such as Australia, New Zealand, France, the United Kingdom, Argentina and Ireland.[2]

From an economic perspective, the 1990s was a decade in which South Africa's reliance on mineral and commodity exports created an economic downturn. The price of gold, South Africa's principal export, declined significantly during the 1990s. Coupled with the vast infrastructure costs involved in attempting to improve the conditions of South Africa's impoverished majority, the national currency—the rand—dropped in value against most foreign currencies. From a tourism industry perspective, the devaluation of the rand made South Africa a relatively inexpensive destination. International visitors were able to enjoy a wide range of fine accommodation, tourism attractions and even upmarket rail services, such as The Blue Train and Rovos Rail, at affordable rates.[3]

While the end of Apartheid opened up many opportunities for a massive growth in tourism, one major problem restricted what was otherwise a spectacular growth: crime. In the days of Apartheid, repressive legislation confined many poor Blacks and Coloureds to separate residential areas. Many Black South Africans lived in fetid, poverty-ridden districts in which the poor preyed on the poor. Wealthy Whites lived in well-guarded luxury ghettos. Black and Coloured South Africans had limited access to these districts through imposition of the 'pass laws'. Draconian laws meant that many non-White South Africans could be imprisoned for long periods of time without trial on suspicion of an offence. The abolition of Apartheid, its excessive police powers and the pass laws meant that the institutionalised separation of rich and poor South Africans was abolished. In common with the collapse of most repressive regimes, criminal acts by the have-nots against the haves grew. There was considerable growth in attacks by a minority of impoverished South Africans against their more wealthy fellow citizens. Incidents of crimes such as assault, carjacking, theft, rape and murder grew. Wealthy South Africans responded by hiring bodyguards and arming themselves to deter such attacks. Tourists, usually deemed as wealthy, almost invariably unarmed and relatively naïve about the local situation, were often seen as easy targets for acts of theft, assault and occasionally more serious crimes. However, while the rate of crimes of violence in South Africa grew alarmingly during the first years of the post-Apartheid era, by 2000 the crime rate was either stabilising or dropping in various categories.

The above remarks do not infer that crime was not a problem during the Apartheid years. Jonathan Bloom observed that crime was a long-term background issue for tourists travelling to South Africa in the late 1980s.[4] However, for the reasons mentioned above, the crime rate in urban centres such as Johannesburg, Durban and Cape Town began to rise and crime became a growing concern for tourists from Western countries visiting South Africa during the transition period from White rule to majority rule between 1990 and 1994.

The dark side of the new South Africa eventually received unwelcome attention from the international media. The beginning of majority rule and the presidency of Nelson Mandela attracted intense media attention from all over the world. While there was much positive coverage about the new South Africa, the easing of the old regime's restrictions on the media meant that the same reporters who may have idolised Mandela were also witnessing the problems of the new South Africa. The intertwined problems of poverty, unemployment and crime would dominate the political and social agenda of post-Apartheid South Africa.

In addition to the problem of post-Apartheid crime, the marketing of South Africa had to overcome another hangover of the Apartheid era. Tourism has long been regarded as a minor economic activity in South Africa. Domestically, commercial tourism was largely the preserve of wealthy Whites and, until the early 1990s, commercially viable long-haul tourism to South Africa (apart from the large number of inbound visitors from neighbouring African countries who were mainly short-term drive-in visitors or job-seekers) was a minor constituent of the national economy representing less than 3 per cent of GNP. Neither the Apartheid governments of South Africa nor the post-Apartheid governments have treated tourism as an industry worthy of the resources necessary to pursue a fully effective international marketing campaign. Worldwide, the South African Tourism Board, later to be named South African Tourism (SATOUR) has consistently experienced budgetary constraints from the 1990s through to the present day. According to John Seekings, tourism's poor contribution to the South African economy proved to be a serious hindrance to efforts to persuade government officials and politicians that tourism should be taken seriously, especially as a significant growth sector for employment. The political and economic decision-makers in South Africa have not realised the very real potential that the tourism industry has as a growth sector in the broader South African economy.[5]

Despite this, tourism continued to grow strongly in South Africa following the establishment of majority rule. Between 1993 and 1995, inbound tourism numbers increased by an impressive 73 per cent. Apart from the opening of South Africa to the world engendered by majority rule, the fall in value of the South African currency in relation to other Western currencies was rapidly transforming South Africa from an expensive destination into a relatively affordable destination. Tourism numbers continued to grow substantially up until 2000.[6]

The distinguishing mark of this case study is that, despite a serious social crisis and negative coverage by sections of the international media, South Africa has experienced substantial growth in the number of inbound tourists during the second half of the 1990s. While it may be argued that tourism growth may have been somewhat inhibited by crime, growth continued nevertheless. SATOUR's overall approach to dealing with the crime problem has been to underplay it.[7]

ANALYSING THE CRIME PROBLEM OF SOUTH AFRICA, 1994–2000

The South African Police Service's Crime Information Analysis Centre has a highly informative website containing a wealth of statistical information on crime trends recorded nationally and according to regions or policing areas. However, in a statement made in May 2001, the Minister for Safety and Security, Mr S. V. Tshwete, called into question the reliability of South Africa's crime statistics based largely on what he saw were inaccuracies of recording, registration, classification, procedures and analysis. Mr Tshwete's statement pointed out that the South African police force was seeking to streamline its organisational infrastructure to more effectively monitor and prioritise police action against crime.[8]

The raw statistics of crime in South Africa (even allowing for inaccuracies) reveal extremely high rates of violent crime by world standards. In 1994 there were 26 832 murders and, even though this figure had been reduced to 21 683 in 2000, there were 27 300 attempted murders in 1994 and 28 023 attempted murders in 2000. Assault with intent to inflict grievous bodily harm rose from 210 250 reported cases in 1994 to 274 622 in 2000. Rape and attempted rapes rose from 42 429 reported cases in 1994 to 52 860 in 2000. The crime of carjacking, which until 1996 was statistically incorporated into the category of robbery with aggravated circumstances, became a separate category in 1996, with 12 860 incidents reported; this peaked in 1999 to 15 447 incidents, but had stabilised in 2000 to 14 999 incidents.[9]

The figures mentioned above are literally the tip of the iceberg of South Africa's massive crime problems. As a point of comparison, in 1999 there were 313 murders in Australia out of a population of 19 million people. In South Africa, out of an estimated population of 43 million in 1999, there were 23 823 murders. Taking population differences into account, the murder rate in South Africa was over 30 times that of Australia and over ten times that of the United States.[10]

Table 10.1 examines selected categories of violent crime between 1994 and 2000 in South Africa as a whole and the occurrence rate of that crime per 100 000 of population. Most crime is local and few non-South Africans were victims.

The statistics in Table 10.1 relate to a small proportion of crimes committed in South Africa and, with the exception of carjacking (which in some cases results in injury or even death to people), the categories cited are primarily crimes against persons. The occurrence rates of such crimes in South Africa are well in excess of rates in Western countries, although there are countries in the Third World with far higher rates of crime in these categories than South Africa.

As in most countries in the world, the highest concentration of crimes of violence tends to be in cities. The rate of murder and aggravated robbery in Johannesburg is more than twice as high as for any other part of South Africa. The incidence of rape in Port Elizabeth is double the national average. There is a higher incidence of assault in cities than the rural areas. Taking into account 20 categories of major crime against persons and property, by 2000 there was statistically a 5 per cent chance that in any given year a South African could be a victim of a serious crime. The statistical likelihood was doubled in urban areas.

The implications of crime for the South African tourism industry and its infrastructure are actually more significant than tourist authorities are prepared to openly admit. The South African tourist infrastructure is quite decentralised by world standards. Although Jan Smuts Airport near Johannesburg is the principal international gateway airport, most tourists spend relatively little time in Johannesburg itself. Cape Town is a preferred destination city, while Kwa Zulu Natal which includes the eastern and southern seaboards is the most popular tourism region, along with the national parks.

Table 10.1: Crime in selected categories, 1994–2000, South Africa: actual reported incidents and rates of occurrence per 100 000 of population

Year	1994		1995		1996		1997		1998		1999		2000	
	No.	Rate	No.	Rate	No.	Rate	No.	Rate	No.	Rate	No.	Rate	No.	Rate
Crime category														
Murder	26 832	69.5	26 637	67.5	25 782	63.9	24 558	59.6	24 875	59	23 823	55.4	21 683	49.3
Attempted murder	27 300	70.7	26 512	67.2	28 516	70.7	28 158	68.3	29 418	69.8	28 662	66.8	28 023	63.7
Robbery	84 900	220	80 071	203	67 249	167	69 691	169	88 319	210	97 173	226	110 590	251
Aggravated rape and attempted rape	42 429	110	47 506	120	50 481	120	52 159	127	49 280	117	51 249	120	52 860	119
Assault with intent to inflict grievous bodily harm	210 250	544	220 990	560	230 425	571	234 554	569	234 056	556	256 434	597	274 622	624
Common assault	193 764	502	205 101	520	205 333	509	201 863	490	199 313	473	221 927	518	250 476	569
Carjacking*					12 860	32	13 011	32	15 111	36	15 447	36	14 999	34

Notes: The above figures come from the South African Police Service.
　　*Carjacking was treated as a separate crime category from 1996.

As a rule, tourists are encouraged to experience the countryside of South Africa rather than the cities, and consequently are less likely to be exposed to crime than South African residents. Tourists on organised package tours in South Africa (in common with package tourists worldwide) are especially shielded from the more unattractive aspects of daily life.

There is no doubt that the primary attraction for many tourists to South Africa from Western countries is the unique wildlife of the country. Elephants, lions, leopards, rhinos and buffalo take precedence over the urban attractions of South Africa's cities, with the major exception of Cape Town.

Virginia Haddon, former public relations and marketing manager of South African Tourism (Australia), points out that, while many Australian travellers are aware of South Africa's crime problem, it is rarely seen as a reason to defer travel to the country. While SATOUR does advise travellers on how to maximise safety, this is rarely an issue that SATOUR has needed to address in its dealings with the media or the travel industry. The Australian government's travel advisory, in common with those of other Western countries, warns travellers to take extra precautions to minimise their exposure to crime in South Africa and it highlights areas of greatest risk.[12]

The South African case is indicative of what can best be described as a tolerable background problem. This can be defined as a problem that travellers should take account of and take precautions against and is not seen as a serious enough disincentive to avoid visiting a destination. Some examples include high crime rates in certain districts of major American cities, the risk of political terrorism and violence in British and European cities, and natural threats such as being a main course meal for a crocodile or a shark or a victim of venomous bites on land or water in Australia. While all the above are tangible risks which tourists need to take into account, they are not usually deemed to be reasons for avoiding travel to these destinations. The South African crime problem is more borderline than the examples mentioned above, but while it may deter some tourists from visiting, it certainly hasn't prevented substantial tourism growth during the 1990s and the beginning of the twenty-first century. While crime in South Africa does attract media attention, it is not the blanket media coverage which has so severely impacted on many of the other case studies dealt with in this book. Ed O'Loughlin's report on South Africa's crime problem in the *Sydney Morning Herald* travel section on September 1, 2001 is the exception to most tourism-orientated coverage of South Africa. O'Loughlin's report focuses primarily on Johannesburg. The same newspaper, the week before, contained a tourism article twice as long focusing on the wildlife wonders of South Africa.[13] The issue of crime in South Africa has also frequently been raised on tourism-orientated programs on the BBC and CNN.

TRACKING SOUTH AFRICAN TOURISM SINCE THE MID-1990s

In his 1999 analysis of South Africa's tourism industry, John Seekings observed that the marketing of South Africa had been hampered by a government perception that tourism was a minor element in South Africa's gross domestic product. This may have been true during the Apartheid years, when inbound tourism arrivals were low. According to the World Travel and Tourism Council, tourism (narrowly defined) represented 2.6 per cent of South Africa's gross domestic product in 1998. The figures do not take into account infrastructure development associated with tourism development.[14]

On the basis of the perception of tourism being a minor element in the South African economy, tourism marketing—and especially SATOUR—is often starved of funding and ancillary services such as the maintenance of reliable and up-to-date tourism statistics and support for tourism research. South African consultancy firm Grant Thorton Kessel Feinstein was highly critical of the deterioration in the quality and reliability of tourism-related statistics and research. The low rate of government funding for marketing activities requires South African Tourism to depend heavily on private-sector support to develop any meaningful destination promotional material. According to Virginia Haddon, the low level of funding of her office's operation and its marketing activities was an ongoing problem for all SATOUR offices worldwide for most of the 1990s.[15]

Since 1992, South African Tourism has placed more emphasis on encouraging South Africans to visit their own country than on promoting tourism to overseas markets. Research conducted by South African Tourism certainly demonstrates that the domestic tourism sector is strong and has considerable growth potential but is highly seasonal, with 43 per cent of all South African leisure trips taking place in December.

Several key points have emerged from even the limited amount of research which has been conducted in tourism in South Africa. They are:

- International tourism is undergoing massive growth.
- International tourism is surpassing domestic tourism as an income source.
- The depreciation of the rand makes South Africa a relatively cheaper destination for overseas tourists (especially from Western countries) than for domestic tourists.
- The tourism and hospitality industry in South Africa needs international tourism to make the operations of its businesses a viable year-round enterprise.

Table 10.2 demonstrates the enormous growth in the inbound tourism market to South Africa during the 1990s.[16]

As discussed earlier in the chapter, the South African currency, the rand, has fallen in value against most 'hard currencies' during the 1990s. To give three examples:

- Rands to the US dollar: (1993) 3.3; (2000) 6.8;
- Rands to the British pound: (1993) 4.9; (2000) 11.1;
- Rands to the German deutschmark: (1993) 2.0; (2000) 4.2.

The devaluation of the rand has been an important factor in making South Africa a significantly more affordable destination during the past decade for travellers from long-haul source markets including Europe, North America, Australia and New Zealand, Japan, Argentina and India. As the figures illustrate, tourism numbers to South Africa have undergone massive growth during the 1990s. The South African tourist authorities treat tourism from the neighbouring African states and intercontinental tourists as separate entities. As a rule, tourists from neighbouring countries tend to stay for a relatively

Table 10.2: Trends in tourist arrivals, South Africa, 1993–98 ('000s)

Year	1993	1994	1995	1996	1997	1998
Market						
Africa	2474	2964	3816	3771	4050	4100
Total overseas	619	705	1072	1173	1480	1600
Europe	411	445	698	771	950	1000
Other	208	260	374	402	530	600
Total	3093	3669	4888	4944	5530	5700

Table 10.3: Leading source markets for South Africa, 1997

Overseas		Regional Africa	
United Kingdom	310 000	Lesotho	1 266 000
Germany	215 000	Swaziland	810 000
United States	143 000	Zimbabwe	627 000
Netherlands	71 000	Botswana	474 000
France	69 000	Mozambique	379 000
Australia	57 000	Namibia	210 000
Switzerland	37 000	Zambia	56 000
Italy	35 000	Malawi	49 000
Belgium	32 000		
Canada	26 000		
Total overseas	1 173 000	Regional Africa	4 050 000

short period (unless they are arriving to seek employment) for a shopping visit. Most arrive and depart by vehicle and tend to spend relatively small sums on accommodation. However, within the African market, just over 6 per cent arrive by air, stay longer and are moderate to big spenders. By 1997, this represented a market of 250 000 people.

The overwhelming majority of overseas visitors tend to have a reasonably long stay (fourteen days) and will visit large areas of the country, spending over US$100 per day. Some do arrive by road as part of a broader Southern African travel experience. The bulk of overseas visitors to South Africa state that they are on holiday. To date, the South African tourist authorities do not have a separate category for travellers visting friends and relatives (VFR). As many former South Africans have settled in Australia, Britain, Canada, the United States and Israel, and many South African citizens have family links in Britain, Germany, the Netherlands and Israel, it is likely that many visitors to South Africa from these countries will be visiting friends and relatives. The VFR factor has been a significant factor for some of South Africa's leading overseas source markets.

Business travel is a significant element in a number of source markets, notably the Middle East, Asia and North America, where business- or work-related travel accounted for between 20 and 25 per cent of visitors in 1997.

Unlike the domestic market, there is a relatively balanced distribution of overseas visitors throughout the year with the large British and German markets displaying a preference for the warmer months from October to March.

According to research conducted by SATOUR, the prime concern expressed by tourists is the high crime rate and the response to this has been manifested in several ways. Cape Town is preferred to Johannesburg as the key destination. This is largely due to the wealth of tourist attractions centred on Cape Town and also due to a far higher crime rate in Johannesburg than in Cape Town. Hotel occupancy rates in Johannesburg by 1998 had fallen to below 40 per cent, while in Cape Town they are close to 80 per cent. In Durban, which has been a growth centre for crime, hotel occupancy rates declined rapidly during the 1990s.

Tourists spend at least 50 per cent of their stay outside the three main cities of Johannesburg, Cape Town and Durban. The proportion of tourists on organised package tours has risen from 10 per cent in 1993 to 25 per cent in 1999.[17] The major attractions for overseas visitors are Table Mountain and Cape Point in the Cape Town area, the wine route near Cape Town, Kruger National Park and Kwa Zulu Natal coastline north and south of Durban. This spread of preferences involves considerable travel in South Africa and, conse- quently, a number of small towns on or near the Cape Town–Kruger Park crescent route have sought to develop alternative tourist services such as Bed and Breakfast establishments and resorts.[18]

South Africa's tourism infrastructure offers a wide range of choices for visitors and, while escorted package tours remain very popular with overseas tourists, many tourists from English-speaking countries, the Netherlands and Germany find South Africa a country which lends itself to independent self- driving travel arrangements, which in many cases can incorporate land arrangement modules purchased from wholesale tour operators at the country of origin. SATOUR's well-produced travel manuals provide a wealth of options for independent travellers to South Africa.

THE MARKETING OF SOUTH AFRICA INTERNATIONALLY

South African Tourism has offices in most of its prime international source markets. There are eleven SATOUR offices outside South Africa located in Australia, Austria, France, Germany, Italy, Japan, the Netherlands, Switzerland, the United Kingdom, the United States and Zimbabwe. It is notable that the only SATOUR office on the African continent outside South Africa is located in Zimbabwe. South African Tourism also boasts a website which acts as a useful guide and tour planner. In order to compensate for restricted budgeting, SATOUR offices have been active in developing promotional partnership ties with carriers and wholesale tour operators which service South Africa and neighbouring countries.

In Australia and New Zealand, SATOUR has played a prime mover role in marketing Southern Africa to both the travel industry and consumers since the early 1990s. As South Africa is a long-haul destination for most of its non-African source markets, there is a mutuality of benefit for all the southern African nations and the operators and carriers which service them to engage in regional marketing to European, American, Asian and Australasian source markets at both trade and consumer levels. The greatest benefit of the post-Apartheid era for South Africa has been that it assumed a regional leadership role in tourism marketing, free of the threats of political ostracism and economic boycotts which greatly restricted marketing opportunities during the Apartheid years. The collective marketing strategy has also spread the cost of trade and consumer marketing among many groups and has enabled SATOUR offices to effectively and professionally promote the destination to both the travel industry and the travelling public.[19]

South African Airways (SAA), previously government-owned, was privatised in April 1999. Nevertheless, it continues to play an important role in promoting South Africa as a destination in Europe, Asia, South America and the Middle East, and works in concert with SATOUR in countries where both SAA and SATOUR have offices. Despite the loss of value of the rand, the relatively small number of carriers which service South Africa has enabled routes servicing South Africa from most source markets to operate at relatively profitable yields compared with many other international air routes.[20]

The marketing of South Africa in Western countries has tended to be pitched to a relatively upmarket clientele. Even though South Africa's tourism infrastructure is well able to cater for tourists on all budgets, the relatively limited choice of airfare options, especially on globally respected carriers, tends to filter out much of the price-sensitive Western backpacker market. In order to get the most out of visiting the prime tourist attractions of South Africa, especially its nature reserves, tourists need to be prepared to spend money. For tour operators either specialising in or featuring South Africa as a major destination for Western clients, it is considered a relatively lucrative high-yield destination. Although some Western backpackers have discovered that South

Africa can be a relatively inexpensive tourist destination on arrival, the lack of cheap airfares to reach it have deterred this market, which is not actively cultivated by South African tourist authorities and operators.

Virginia Haddon indicated that there was a strong element of client loyalty for South Africa from all major source markets. Repeat visits are common. An organisation known as the Circle of Sunshine comprises tourists who have visited and revisited South Africa and seek to promote the destination wherever possible. They have active chapters in India, Australia, Canada, the United States and the United Kingdom, and are a valuable source of genuinely enthusiastic testimonials for South Africa and valuable allies for SATOUR offices in all these countries.[21]

Sporting links, especially in the field of cricket and Rugby Union, between South Africa, the United Kingdom, France, Australasia and the Indian sub-continent, have provided a useful niche market to promote South Africa to these source markets. The Rugby Union World Cup, which was held in South Africa in 1995, was a particularly auspicious opportunity to open post-Apartheid South Africa as a sporting destination to the rest of the world.

CONCLUSION

Unlike most of the other case studies examined in this work, post-Apartheid South Africa is not a destination which is experiencing a marketing crisis. It is a destination which enjoyed substantial growth during the 1990s—growth which has continued into the first years of the twenty-first century.

The natural attractions of the country, coupled with the ending of the oppressive racial strictures of Apartheid, have combined to attract a spurt of tourism growth both from neighbouring African countries and from the rest of the world. The devaluation of the South African currency has made South Africa a far more affordable destination for Western travellers than was the case in the past.

South Africa's high crime rate has been treated as a background risk to visiting the country, but it has not noticeably deterred tourists from visiting. Violent crime is acknowledged by South African tourism authorities. Tourists are not especially targeted and singled out by local criminal elements and the main tourist attractions in South Africa are not subject to especially high rates of crime. This national social problem, especially had it been targeted to any significant extent at foreign tourists, could have triggered a crisis of confidence in the safety of South Africa as a destination, as was the case in Florida during the early 1990s. Fortunately for the South African tourism industry, this has not been the case to date; however, it is a potential problem for the tourism industry—one which, at the time of writing, certainly requires a strong contingency marketing management plan.

11 | AUSTRALIA: PORT ARTHUR MASSACRE, 1996

Tourism Tasmania's response to an aberrant crisis

CRISIS RANKING: **DESTCON 3**

BACKGROUND

Two-thirds of mainland Australia is desert or semi-desert, but located due south of the continent lies the verdant island state of Tasmania. The visually dramatic, wild and almost uninhabited, mountainous southwest region is an important World Heritage site and one of the largest temperate wilderness areas on Earth. The alpine areas in central Tasmania boast some of the most spectacular scenery in Australia, with high ramparts, glacial lakes, massive waterfalls and rushing rivers not unlike the highlands of Scotland. Tasmania has flora and fauna which are unique to the state, including the Huon Pine and a carnivorous marsupial, the famous Tasmanian Devil. Adventurers still seek the Tasmanian Tiger (Thylacine), officially declared extinct since 1937. The capital city of Hobart, located on the Derwent River, is Australia's second oldest city and its oldest buildings are of English Georgian style. The eastern half of Tasmania is a land of cultivated rolling hills with many small villages, rich farmland and a scenic coastline. By Australian standards, Tasmania is small, easy to traverse and unusually varied. It is well suited to a driving holiday and the most popular tourism packages are car hire/accommodation combinations or campervan holidays. Unlike most mainland Australian states, which require travelling long distances between points of interest, the scenic highlights of Tasmania can be experienced within a week.

Tasmania appeals to many different market segments, and is a sought-after destination for eco-tourists and adventure travellers. The World Heritage national parks comprise 40 per cent of the state's land area and Tasmania's mountains are renowned for their challenging and scenic hikes and unique flora and fauna. Tasmania is also very popular as an Australian family holiday destination. Annually Tasmania becomes a focal point for the Australian and international yachting fraternity. The world-famous Sydney to Hobart and the Melbourne to Hobart Yacht Races finish in Hobart at the end of each calendar year. Tasmania has a reputation for excellent wines and fresh produce and for many years traded on its reputation as the 'Apple Isle'. Australia's first legal casino was opened in Hobart in 1973. Although bigger and gaudier gambling establishments in Australia have long surpassed Wrest Point Casino, it remains Hobart's leading international convention centre.

From a tourism perspective, Tasmania is primarily a popular domestic short-break destination for mainland Australians, but is appealing to a

Convict church, Port Arthur Historic Site, Tasmania. Photo courtesy of Tourism Tasmania.

relatively small but growing number of overseas travellers. According to Tourism Tasmania, during 2000 Tasmania received 510 700 visitors (over the age of fourteen) of whom 82.2 per cent were Australians and 17.8 per cent were from overseas.[1] It is notable that the portion of non-Australian tourists increased from 14.1 per cent in 1996 to 17.8 per cent in 2000. The 90 000 overseas tourists who visited Tasmania in 2000 represented 2 per cent of the total inbound market to Australia.

Port Arthur is the most visited site in Tasmania outside the capital, Hobart. A former prison settlement about 100 kilometres southeast of Hobart, the site is accessible by a dramatic coastal drive along the Tasman Peninsula. According to Tourism Tasmania, an average of 40 per cent of visitors to Tasmania include Port Arthur during their stay.[2] Tasmania can only be reached by air or sea connections; therefore visitors make a considered choice to travel there. For this reason, Tasmanian tourism trends are more accurately monitored than for any other part of Australia.

Tasmania was the second convict colony established by the British in Australian territory. Hobart was established in 1804 and the Port Arthur prison was built in 1830 to incarcerate the men and women branded as the most hardened criminals in the Australian convict colony. The nineteenth-century history of Port Arthur is infamous, containing much pain, blood, toil and torture. The prison came to symbolise the dark side of Tasmania's history. Britain's colonisation of Tasmania also led to the genocide of Tasmania's indigenous people, most of whom perished from diseases introduced by European settlers or because they were hunted down and killed by the colonists.

Port Arthur, as tourists experience it today, comprises the gloomy remnants of the prison settlement and the convict church. The prison complex ceased operation in 1887 and is the largest and one of the best-preserved convict-era prison complexes in Australia. For Australians and overseas visitors, Port Arthur remains one of the most potent symbols of Australia's convict past. Until 1996, Port Arthur represented a well-documented part of Australia's past in which the pain and torment experienced by human beings was beyond living memory. However, that was to change.

THE PORT ARTHUR MASSACRE AND ITS IMMEDIATE IMPACT

On April 28, 1996, a new chapter of Port Arthur's violent history was enacted. That day, 35 people—many of whom were interstate Australian tourists, as well as four overseas tourists (two Malaysians and two Singaporeans)—were shot to death with many more injured. A young, intellectually impaired man, Martin Bryant, was ultimately charged with and convicted of the crime, which is Australia's worst recorded incident of mass murder.

The Port Arthur mass murder shocked Australian society and was the catalyst for an intense and bitter national debate regarding firearm laws. Prime Minister John Howard used the incident as an integral element in his campaign to legislate the banning of private ownership of a large range of automatic guns and rifles. The incident contrasted with the long-held image of Tasmania as a quiet, tourist-friendly, crime-free state. Tasmanian tourist authorities could justifiably claim that this incident was completely out of character with the norms of the state, but many prospective tourists instantly cancelled their travel plans as a reaction to the incident. Martin Bryant was arrested at the scene of the crime. The fact that the majority of Port Arthur massacre victims were tourists generated massive Australian and overseas media coverage of the incident. Mourning for victims in many parts of Australia and in Malaysia and Singapore, the funerals and the subsequent trial of Martin Bryant resulted in media coverage extending into weeks and months.

The Port Arthur massacre was a stark contrast to the clean, green and peaceful image successfully promoted by Tasmania's state and regional tourism authorities. Although logic dictated that the massacre was an aberrant singular event, highly unlikely to be repeated in Port Arthur specifically or Tasmania generally, and thus not a deterrent to tourism, logic is not a key determinant in a tourist's decision to visit a destination. The extensive media coverage of the massacre; the funerals and their impact on the Port Arthur community and Tasmania, the families of victims and survivors of the event; the national debate over firearm laws and the subsequent trial of Martin Bryant ensured that, in Australia, the Port Arthur massacre would become ingrained as a primary image of Tasmania. The extensive and overwhelming coverage of the massacre and its impact presented a staggering challenge to the Tasmanian tourism industry. In the months immediately after the massacre, tourism to Tasmania declined. However, the decline was brief and largely confined to Port Arthur and the Tasman Peninsula. Tourism numbers to Tasmania for 1996 were almost identical to those of 1995.

Malcolm Wells was (at the time of writing) Deputy CEO of Tourism Tasmania. His official title in Tourism Tasmania in 1996 was Director Strategic Projects and he was acting CEO of Tourism Tasmania at the time of the Port Arthur massacre. Mr Wells recalled that Tourism Tasmania immediately implemented a long-standing crisis contingency plan. The plan had been developed in response to previous crises, including the 1967 bushfires and the Tasman Bridge collapse of 1975. The most urgent priority from a tourism perspective was to manage media relations on behalf of the Tasmanian tourism industry. All media inquiries relating to the impact of the crime on Tasmanian tourism were handled either by Mr Wells or Tasmanian Tourism Minister Ray Groom. An informal tourism task force/think-tank was rapidly established to devise a general marketing strategy to assist the recovery of tourism to Tasmania and a specific approach to Port Arthur.[3]

The massacre and its implications were subject to intense international media scrutiny. Malcolm Wells recalled that CNN actually had a news crew reporting the events before the emergency services had secured the crime scene. The Tasmanian government, police and emergency services regarded media management as a major priority. The Tasmanian government and tourism authorities were especially concerned that coverage of the Port Arthur site and contacts with Port Arthur residents, surviving victims and their relatives were handled with sensitivity.

Tourism Tasmania's immediate response was to undertake a brief moratorium on media promotion of the state and Port Arthur in particular, primarily because it would be seen as counter-productive while the state was under intense media focus for reasons which were anything but conducive to tourism.[4]

The moratorium on promoting Tasmania remained in force for three weeks (six weeks for the Port Arthur site). The Tasmanian government, in conjunction with Tourism Tasmania, its wholesale arm Tasmania's Temptation Holidays, the major domestic carriers Qantas and Ansett, domestic tour wholesalers and local and regional tourism authorities, met at what was dubbed the 'Port Arthur Summit'. The meeting, held on May 22, 1996 examined cooperative strategies between the Tasmanian government tourism authorities and the private sector to restore tourism to Tasmania in general and Port Arthur specifically.[5] As both Malcolm Wells and Marketing Director of Tourism Tasmania John Pugsley pointed out, tourism numbers to Tasmania at the macro level were not greatly affected. Port Arthur recorded a significant drop in visitor numbers in the three months following the massacre, and the pattern of visitation changed for a much longer period. Prior to April 28, 1996, many visitors to Port Arthur tended to stay in the area overnight. From May 1996, the pattern of visitation was dominated by day visitors and it would take an energetic marketing campaign to restore Port Arthur and the surrounding Tasman Peninsula region as a popular region in which to stay overnight.

Malcolm Wells outlined a number of immediate actions which were undertaken in response to the event:

- Destination TV advertising was briefly suspended as a mark of respect to victims and loved ones.
- The wholesale arm of Tourism Tasmania, Tasmania's Temptation Holidays, relocated clients who were affected by the event, especially from those places with a large media or police presence.

- In addition to the summit meeting, a state government committee was formed which involved Tourism Tasmania developing appropriate responses to the tragedy.[6]
- A public relations consultant was appointed.

It is significant that the Port Arthur massacre was a notable example of a one-off, aberrant event. The challenge for destination authorities and marketers was to reinforce this fact to the travel industry and to consumers. Mr Wells stated that the media attention had both positive and negative repercussions. The international coverage, while primarily focusing on the massacre and subsequent related developments, brought many foreign correspondents to Tasmania who began to include descriptive coverage of the state in their reports. This coverage was beneficial in creating international awareness of Tasmania on a scale beyond the resources Tourism Tasmania could have purchased. Although a chain of causation cannot be precisely ascertained, between 1996 and 2000 the proportion of overseas visitors to Tasmania increased by 25 per cent; part of this growth can be attributed to increased awareness of Tasmania after the events of 1996.

On a local level, many Tasmanians visited Port Arthur as a gesture of support and solidarity with the community. One of the most significant impacts of the event from a tourism perspective was the intense degree of cooperation between the public-sector travel authorities, private-sector tour operators and airlines in restoring the tourism markets. At a human level, John Pugsley recalled the sensitivity and 'raw nerves' of some Tourism Tasmania staff when they were involved on the Tasmanian tourism stands at consumer travel expos in Sydney and Melbourne in June 1996, having to fend off 'is it safe?' and 'what are you going to do about crime?' questions from the public. It is certainly understandable that sales and marketing representatives of traditionally 'crisis-free' destinations such as Tasmania perhaps would be less emotionally equipped to deal with negative public perceptions of their destination than those constantly dealing with traditional 'hot spots'. In fact, if one accepts the basic definition of a crisis as dealing with an event which is outside the norm, the Port Arthur massacre certainly fits within that definition.

The events of April 1996 led to Tasmania reimaging itself in the market. The Port Arthur tragedy occurred at a time when Tourism Tasmania was 'between CEOs'. The appointment of Mr Robin Giason as CEO of Tourism

Tasmania in late August 1996 would provide the impetus for a significant rebranding of Tasmania.

TOURISM RESTORATION MANAGEMENT IN TASMANIA: A MARKETING PERSPECTIVE 1996–97

Overall, the Tasmanian tourism industry's management of the Port Arthur massacre is an exemplary role model in managing a one-off crisis. The key elements of its success were:

- the high level of cooperation between the Tasmanian tourism industry's public and private sectors. This included state, local and regional tourism authorities and private tour operators, owners of resort attractions and accommodation facilities;
- the support of the major domestic airlines, Qantas and Ansett, and the operators of the car ferry *Spirit of Tasmania*;
- the high level of cooperation between Tourism Tasmania and the Australian Tourism Commission;
- the support of a state government which recognised the significance of tourism as a key economic and social driving force;
- a clearly defined public relations approach which indicated that the event was aberrant, its impact localised, and Tasmania was a safe and desirable destination;
- the fact that the Port Arthur massacre was a catalyst successfully applied to redefining Tasmania's marketing image and message directed to its Australian and overseas source markets.

Malcolm Wells outlined a number of measures adopted by Tourism Tasmania within three months of the Port Arthur massacre. Tourism Tasmania commissioned a market research project involving 400 telephone interviews with Sydney and Melbourne residents to ascertain whether their attitude to travelling to Tasmania had been affected by the massacre. The survey revealed a minimal impact, with only 3 per cent of respondents affected; of these, one-third stated that it would make them more interested.[7]

Groups of Australian travel writers travelled to Tasmania in May 1996 under Tourism Tasmania's Visiting Journalist Program. Later, in December 1996 and February 1997, two overseas groups were hosted in Tasmania under the Australian Tourism Commission's Visiting Journalist Program. These programs were supported by Qantas and the Australian Tourism Commission (ATC). Tasmanian land content was hosted by Tourism Tasmania.

A Tasmanian Tourism Task Force was formed to recommend cooperative marketing initiatives. The major domestic carriers, Qantas and Ansett offered discounted holiday airfares of up to 65 per cent off full-fare seats and the TT shipping line offered a limited discount level of 45 per cent for specific periods. It is notable that discount offers were the exception rather than the rule. Operators tended to promote value-added deals for travellers in preference to discounts, inducing travellers to stay longer, extend their itineraries or visit an attraction. Tourism Tasmania also undertook specific projects to restore interest in the areas most directly affected by the massacre, namely the Tasman Peninsula and the Port Arthur Historic Site. The projects included a re-signage of the Tasman Highway which links Hobart and Port Arthur, the construction of new food and beverage facilities at Port Arthur to replace the Broad Arrow Café where most of the massacre victims were killed, and a revamping of the evening ghost tours through the historic site which lost popularity after the tragedy.[8]

The ATC undertook management of the international impact of the event. The ATC's Managing Director in 1996, Mr Jon Hutchison, recalled that the day after the massacre he convened a meeting of all state and territory tourism commissions to determine a unified approach. From a national perspective, the ATC decided to adopt a low-key approach which gave prime focus to Australia's humanitarian concerns for victims, their families and the Port Arthur community. Tourism comments to the media from the national perspective (as opposed to those of a local or Tasmanian concern) were made by Mr Hutchison in the weeks following the massacre.[9]

Following the appointment of Mr Robin Giason in August 1996 Tourism Tasmania became a statutory authority as opposed to a government department. This required the organisation to restructure as a marketing-orientated and commercially driven body.[10]

Tasmania's new marketing campaign from mid-1996 to October 1996 included several elements. One highlighted the special discounts and value-added offers available to tourists, although this was a relatively short-term campaign. Of long-term significance was the 'Fresh New Look' campaign launched in September 1996, which highlighted natural fresh food and wines, water, air, environment, peace and excitement. Allowing for its inherent contradiction, the campaign was highly successful in rebranding Tasmania to the Australian market. It refocused the previous dominant images of convict history, apples and mountains. The new campaign also suggested a more universal appeal which would have the potential to attract greater international visitation.

The campaign was conducted in conjunction and consultation with many tour operators, who adjusted content in the packages to match the state's tourism campaign. Tours offered more adventure options, information on flora, fauna and the environment and inclusions which enabled participants to sample Tasmanian wines and foods.

The Australian federal government's subsidy of car transport costs on the car ferry *Spirit of Tasmania* was designed as a further inducement to independent travellers, especially from Victoria, to visit Tasmania.[11] The result of these marketing initiatives was a rapid recovery of tourism to Tasmania and a more gradual recovery of tourism to Port Arthur and the Tasman Peninsula. Overall tourism numbers to Tasmania changed little between 1995 and 1997. In 1995, a total of 480 500 adult tourists (fourteen years of age and older) visited Tasmania; in 1996 there were 476 600 visitors and in 1997, 489 400.[12]

IMPACT OF THE MASSACRE ON TOURISM TO PORT ARTHUR

Brian Finlay, a tourism student at Southern Cross University in Lismore, New South Wales, conducted a survey ascertaining the impact of the Port Arthur massacre on attitudes of prospective tourists. Finlay states that there is a strong relationship between safety, tranquillity, peace and successful tourism. In dealing specifically with Port Arthur, the survey revealed that there was a fear of intruding on people's grief and discomfort about holidaying in a place where so many lives were lost.

Finlay emphasised the role of the media's portrayal of events at Port Arthur in shaping attitudes to visiting the area. In his opinion, the media played a prime role in influencing public perceptions about Port Arthur. Although he does not directly specify whether media coverage was positive or negative, the majority of the 73 people interviewed in his survey believed that media coverage of such an event could not be expected to be positive for tourism. Finlay refers to extensive supporting documentation that, during 1996, visitation to the Port Arthur Historic Site and the Tasman Peninsula region decreased in terms of actual numbers, and more significantly in terms of the proportion of tourists who stayed overnight.[13]

According to the Tasmanian Visitors Survey between May 1996 and March 1997 overall tourism to Tasmania increased by 0.5 per cent. Visitor numbers to the Port Arthur site declined by 4 per cent and overnight stays declined by 14.9 per cent in comparison with figures for the same period in 1995–96. It is noteworthy that, while Australian visitations and overnight stays declined during this period, there was a growth in visitations and overnight stays to Port Arthur by overseas visitors, which in part reflects the interest in the region generated by international media coverage.[14]

Craig Coombs, CEO of the Port Arthur Historic Site in 1996, outlined the response of the site's management to the massacre. Coombs stated that there was no set disaster contingency plan to work from, but that the site's management, which became a 'Government Business Enterprise' in 1995, managed the tragedy to the best of its ability. The authority controlled the historic site, ran site tours, a harbour cruise and an evening 'ghost tour'.

The initial response of Coombs' staff to the massacre was disbelief and confusion. Mr Coombs gave a detailed recollection of the events of April 28, 1996. From his paper, published in *Australian Emergency Management*, it was clear that the Port Arthur Historic Site was ill-equipped to manage an emergency on the unprecedented scale it encountered. There was no PA system to transmit messages to visitors and emergency medical and communication facilities were limited. Coombs was highly critical of what he described as the media's conduct being dominated by a 'search for ratings' and 'undisciplined by a respect for victims'. Coombs referred to the 'intrusive, penetrating and all-pervasive attitude the media took to the human tragedy in a sleepy corner of the world'. He claimed that the media subjected his overworked and still grieving staff to intrusion, criticism and confrontation. Although they sought to cooperate with the media, Coombs described the media's pressure on his staff as traumatic. Maria Stacey, who worked at the Port Arthur Historic Site at the time and is still employed there, claimed that, while the events were indeed traumatic, in her experience the overwhelming offers of trauma counselling gave rise to as many problems as they solved.[15]

Eventually the site appointed external PR consultants to manage media coverage. The site management was faced with a multiplicity of challenges. These included responding to inquiries and messages of sympathy, establishing a memorial for the victims and, most significantly, attempting to restore a sense of normality to the historic site, resuming business and marketing activity. One of the major problems the site management encountered was dealing with insurance issues arising from the massacre and renegotiating coverage for the site and its staff.[16]

The marketing problems of the Port Arthur Historic Site and the Tasman Peninsula were considerable. Although day visitations recovered relatively quickly, overnight stays continued to decline, as did participation in the evening ghost tours, a feature of the site. Ansett Airlines and several tour operators offered either discounted or value-added overnight arrangements in the Port Arthur area during 1996. While recovery of tourism to Tasmania was rapid, the revival of tourism, especially overnight stays to the Tasman Peninsula and Port Arthur was a far slower process. According to Malcolm Wells, the entire marketing of Port Arthur was changed from September 1996 in line with the reimaging of Tasmania. From late 1996, the Tasman Peninsula was described as a 'natural escape' with focus shared between the Port Arthur Historic Site and the environmental attractions of the region with its bush-walking, fishing, coastal scenery and wildlife.

The Port Arthur Historic Site and the Port Arthur region have established informative and detailed websites which give both travel professionals and prospective travellers a detailed coverage of activities, events and accommodation in the region. The new marketing strategy and reimaging of Port Arthur and the Tasman Peninsula successfully facilitated a full recovery of tourism to the region by 1998.

TOURISM TASMANIA'S MARKETING BEYOND PORT ARTHUR

The Port Arthur massacre proved to be a severe challenge for Tasmania's tourism authorities and the Tasmanian tourism industry. Overall, they succeeded in meeting it. The marketing of Tasmania is multi-faceted, with an active media campaign in Australia and selected overseas markets—notably New Zealand, the United Kingdom, and continental Europe. Tasmania actively promotes itself within the Australian tourism industry and plays an active role in both travel industry and consumer marketing overseas in association with the Australian Tourism Commission. In November 2001, Hobart hosted the World Tourism Organization Conference on Sustainable Tourism. This was one of the first gatherings of world tourism leaders after the September 11, 2001 attacks on New York and Washington DC. Although the main theme of the gathering was to discuss environmental issues relating to tourism (an issue which complements the overall tourism aims of Tasmania), crisis management was a significant element in that meeting. Tourism Tasmania's management of the Port Arthur massacre was of interest to many of the delegates who were facing their own destination marketing crises.

CONCLUSION

The Tasmanian tourism authorities were highly effective in most departments of managing an aberrant one-off crisis. Tourism Tasmania, under the direction of Malcolm Wells and his staff, rapidly gained control of media coverage; a crisis management unit was quickly established; and there was a high degree of cooperation between the Tasmanian and federal governments, state and national tourism marketing authorities and the public and private sectors of the Tasmanian tourism industry.

It was correctly decided to establish a brief moratorium of advertising and promotion of the state and the Port Arthur region to allow time for the immediate impact of the tragedy to abate. In the case of a one-off crisis, there is little point in destination marketing during the crisis and this break provided time to develop an effective and innovative marketing approach for the state. The price and value-added incentives in the months following the Port Arthur massacre successfully stimulated domestic tourism to Tasmania. However, Port Arthur and the Tasman Peninsula experienced a long-term decline in overnight stays, and it can be argued that this region could have benefited from a more actively focused campaign to restore tourism involving subsidised stays in the region for a six-month period until market confidence was restored.

It is noteworthy that Tasmanians were encouraged to show solidarity with the Port Arthur community by visiting and supporting the community. The extreme and aberrant nature of the tragedy directly impacted on the management of the Port Arthur Historic Site. Comments made by its CEO indicate that the site's management lacked sufficient outside support to relieve his staff of the intense media pressure they endured during the crisis. While the state tourism authority actively promoted the Port Arthur Historic Site and the Tasman Peninsula, it is clear that the provision of outside on-site consultancy may have helped ease the remarketing process and taken pressure off the traumatised staff.

The only major apparent weakness in the marketing recovery was the lack of success in stimulating a higher level of growth in the international market. Tasmania attracts a very small portion (2 per cent) of international travellers to Australia. The events of Port Arthur created (for all the wrong reasons) a significantly increased awareness of Tasmania yet, despite this, it took over six months for the Australian Tourism Commission to organise a visit from a group of visiting overseas travel writers, as opposed to less than one month for Australian travel journalists. While it is completely under-standable—given Tasmania's inbound tourism demographic—to prioritise access for Australian travel writers, an urgent approach to the international market may have been beneficial to redressing the negative images of Tasmania portrayed internationally. Tourism Tasmania should have capitalised more effectively on the high international profile Tasmania had already attained through the extensive coverage of events during and immediately after April 1996.

Tourism Tasmania especially deserves a great deal of credit for the professional and responsible manner in which it managed the 1996 crisis and the marketing recovery process. The program was a model of outstanding voluntary cooperation between government and private sectors of the tourism industry in the best Australian tradition—a spirit of cooperation in the face of adversity.

Part
VI | **WAR**

12 | CROATIA: THE CROATIA–YUGOSLAV WAR, 1991–95

Post-war recovery and tourism development

CRISIS RANKING: **DESTCON 2**

BACKGROUND

As a tourist destination, Croatia has been blessed by some of the most dramatic coastal scenery in Europe. Croatia's walled city of Dubrovnik is considered by many to be one of the most beautiful Renaissance cities in Europe, rivalling Venice in its historical, cultural and economic influence. Of all the Balkan countries, Croatia has the longest Adriatic coastline and its coastal area includes around 1000 islands, 69 of which are inhabited. Croatia's Dalmatian coast has a long history of attracting tourists from all over Europe, and was for centuries regarded as a playground of the European aristocracy. Its Adriatic resorts have made it the most popular tourist destination in the Balkans, easily accessible by road, air and sea from all parts of Europe. The country's scenic attractions are enhanced by the fact that, by European standards, accommodation, food and tourist services are relatively inexpensive. Croatia's inland capital of Zagreb is one of Europe's most attractive capital cities, located in the heart of a country with many historical treasures and diverse scenery.

Croatia has been cursed by a turbulent history and a long-standing enmity between its predominantly Catholic population, the Orthodox population of neighbouring Serbia, and Muslim-dominated Bosnia Herzegovina. Croatia has been a powerful state within the Balkan region and a reluctant state within the former Yugoslav Federation which, between 1945 and 1980, was ruled with

an iron fist by Croatian-born communist leader Josip Broz—or as he was better known, Marshall Tito.

An indication of Croatia's cultural distinctiveness from its southern neighbouring countries, Serbia and Bosnia Herzegovina, is the use of Latin lettering as opposed to the Cyrillic alphabet used in Greece and Serbia. Serbia has traditionally sought its political, religious and cultural inspiration from the East and identifies with Slavic Russia. Croatia has drawn its cultural, political and religious values from the West. The sharp divisions within this small area have fuelled intense rivalries within the Balkans for centuries. Throughout history, these have been exacerbated by the fact that Croatia and its neighbours have for centuries been a battleground for competing empires. As recently as the beginning of the twentieth century, Croatia formed the boundary between the last vestige of the Austro-Hungarian Empire and the Ottoman Empire prior to the outbreak of World War I in 1914, which redefined the political map of Europe.

Aerial view of Dubrovnik. Photo courtesy of the Croatian Ministry of Tourism Board.

For 500 years, the Ottoman Empire, the Austro-Hungarian Empire, Russia and Germany have competed to dominate this politically fractious region. Over a far longer period of time, the invasions of ancient empires, including Greece and Rome, contributed to the historical tapestry which imposed varied historical and cultural influences on Croatian society and its wealth of archaeological sites. Within modern Croatia, the Dalmatian coast tends to be influenced by Italy while the interior regions reflect the cultural influences of Austria and Hungary. Croatia's location as a crossroads between Eastern and Western powers has resulted in historically brief periods of autonomy and independence. During World War II, Croatia became a German-dominated state ruled by the nationalistic anti-Serbian and anti-Semitic Ustasha under the leadership of Ante Pavelic. Following the defeat of Nazi Germany by the Allies, Tito's communist partisan forces emerged as the dominant power in what was to become post-World War II Yugoslavia, the only country in Europe in which partisan forces drove the Germans out without the direct intervention of allied troops. Although Croatia was able to exercise a limited form of regional autonomy under Tito's regime, the expression of separatist Croatian nationalism in common with Serbian, Bosnian and other regional nationalisms was severely curtailed. Tito sought to impose a unified Yugoslavian national identity. Although he succeeded in establishing Yugoslavia as a communist state with policies independent from the Soviet Union, his attempts to impose a new Yugoslav nationalism met, at best, with superficial success. After Tito's death in 1980, the various nationalisms gradually reasserted their separate identities.

THE WAR ACCOMPANYING THE ESTABLISHMENT OF MODERN INDEPENDENT CROATIA

The collapse of communism in Eastern Europe and within the former Soviet Union from the end of the 1980s heralded a period between 1989 and 1991 in which communist regimes were (for the most part peacefully) overthrown or voted out of office. From 1989, Yugoslavia began to break up. Slovenia declared independence in 1989. Civil strife in Kosovo in 1989, in which the majority Albanians sought independence from Serbia (an issue which would lead to war in 1999–2000), led to calls from the various nations within the Yugoslav Federation for autonomy and independence. In the Croatian elections of April 1990, the Croatian Democratic Union led by Franjo Tudjman defeated the Communist Party and promulgated a new Croatian constitution which changed the status of Serbs from that of a constituent nation to a national minority. Many ethnic Serbs were dismissed from government jobs after the elections as the Tudjman government sought to assert an independent Croatian national identity. In a referendum held in May 1991 (boycotted by most of Croatia's Serbian minority), 91 per cent of voters supported Croatian independence. Independence was declared in 25 June 1991. On the same date, Krajina, a Serbian enclave within Croatian territory, declared its own independence from Croatia.

Between 1991 and 1995, Croatia was in a state of war against the Serbian dominated federal Yugoslav government. NATO, the United Nations and the EC nations sought to resolve the conflict, but apart from brief periods of truce the war continued for four years. The war included a relentless attack on the magnificent historical walled city of Dubrovnik. The Croatian–Serbian war introduced a new and sinister term—'ethnic cleansing'—into the vocabulary of human conflict; in practice, it meant the wholesale massacre of entire towns and villages populated by rival ethnic groups. The bloody conflict between Serbs and Croats involved atrocities committed by both sides. The battle for the Croatian frontier city of Vukovar, in which thousands of Croat civilians were killed by the Yugoslav army and by Serbian irregulars, resulted in more casualties than any other single action. The Croat offensive against the Serbian-dominated region of Krajina resulted in massacres of Serbian civilians and the flight of most Serbs from the region. The political resolution of this bitter war was the Dayton Agreement (signed in Dayton, Ohio), between Yugoslavia and Croatia, signed off in December 1995 under the sponsorship of the European Union and NATO. The agreement recognised the traditional borders of Croatia and, while it did not resolve the mutual antagonisms between Serbs and Croats, it put a stop to armed conflict in this region of the former Yugoslav Federation. Tragically, the formal resolution of the Serbian–Croatian conflict shifted the epicentre of the Balkan conflict to Bosnia Herzegovina.[1]

The intensive, extensive and unpredictable conduct of the Croatia–Yugoslav war between 1991 and 1995 was to prove disastrous for the Croatian tourism industry. Apart from the notable exception of Dubrovnik (close to the border with Yugoslavia), Croatia's coastal regions were largely spared any direct involvement in and damage from the fighting. Tourism numbers to Croatia dropped dramatically between 1991 and 1995. The combined impacts of the disintegration of Yugoslavia and the Serbian–Croatian war crippled the Croatian tourism industry. Hall and O'Sullivan[2] note that some source markets responded very differently to the war. During 1992, the British and French tended to avoid Croatia's northern coastline. Italians, Austrians and Czechs continued to visit. This was partially explained by the latter groups' greater familiarity with Croatia, compared with the British and French, and by more accurate media coverage of the war which explained where the fighting actually occurred. British media coverage reported all of Croatia as a war zone. In the case of the Czechs, Croatia's low-priced North Adriatic destinations made Croatia's northern Adriatic region an irresistibly affordable and relatively safe holiday destination.

In 1985, Croatia attracted 8.35 million international tourists. By 1990, this had fallen to 7.05 million and in 1995 just 1.23 million people visited Croatia.[3] While the tourist industry began to recover very quickly after 1995, civil war in neighbouring Bosnia Herzegovina hampered the pace of recovery. In 2001, the figures released by the Croatian Ministry of Tourism showed that, despite healthy growth since the 1995 Dayton Agreement, tourism numbers to Croatia (at approximately 7.8 million for 2001) were still below 1985 levels.[4] The external factors of instability in the Balkans (especially in Macedonia, Kosovo and Albania), while not directly impacting on Croatia, reinforced an image of Croatia as being located in an unstable region. Media coverage of tourism destinations has often led to what may loosely be termed 'collateral image damage', when the desirability of a destination is hampered by its perceived proximity to a 'hot spot'. Jordan has experienced this problem in relation to Israel since September 2000 and after the events of September 11, 2001 many destinations in the Indian subcontinent and Middle East suffered a decline in their inbound tourism due to their perceived proximity to Afghanistan.

The confluence of establishing sovereign independence in Croatia during a violent civil war involved a twin handicap for the Croatian tourism industry. The fledgling state economy was immediately on a war footing and consequently the Croatian government was in no position, economically or politically, to engage in an active tourism marketing campaign. Western media coverage depicted Croatia as a war zone and many governments in Europe and worldwide advised their citizens to defer non-essential travel to the country. The Serbian artillery and air attacks against Dubrovnik, Croatia's most popular tourist attraction and a World Heritage listed city, were subject to widespread international condemnation. Although contemporary media reports overstated the extent of damage to Dubrovnik, the wanton attacks against this historic city, which had little value as a military target, were one of the enduring images of the Yugoslav–Croatian war. From a tourism perspective, the attacks on Dubrovnik caused more harm to Croatia's tourism image than many of the more bloody battles and massacres in other parts of the country.

CROATIA'S ARDUOUS PATH TO TOURISM RECOVERY, 1995–2001

In contrast to other case studies examined in this book, Croatia's government and private sectors were severely hampered in attempting to devise and implement an in-crisis marketing strategy. This was largely due to Croatia's primary national task of militarily defending its own independence. The war effort dominated all Croatian economic activity between 1991 and 1995. Prior to independence, the Yugoslav Federation was active in promoting tourism which, under a communist regime, operated under strict government controls and subject to substantial government subsidy. The privatisation of tourism all over pre-1991 Yugoslavia following the overthrow of communist rule forced the private sector into an era of self-reliance. The outbreak of war, coinciding with Croatian independence, forced the private sector to labour under the twin handicap of lacking government subsidies in a marketing environment, a situation inimical to the promotion of tourism.

Consequently, during the war, many Croatian tourism enterprises, hotels and resorts were forced to close. In 1990 there were 863 000 hotel beds in Croatia. By 1995 this had been reduced to 609 000 representing a decline of close to 30 per cent. Foreign tourist numbers, which were just over 7 million in 1990, dropped to 1.23 million by 1995.[5] In 1992, the nadir of the war years, Croatia attracted only 1.27 million foreign tourists. Many foreign airlines and tour operators either ceased or radically reduced services to Croatia between 1991 and 1995. After signing the Dayton Agreement in December 1995, the Croatian government treated the recovery and restoration of the tourism industry as a high priority. Prior to 1991, tourism was Croatia's largest source of foreign currency earnings. In 1990 tourism officially accounted for 6.1 per cent of GDP, 62.2 per cent of service exports and 6.2 per cent of employment in Croatia. Due to an extensive unregistered, cash-only and tax-evading 'black economy' associated with tourism in pre-independence Croatia, the real figures are likely to have been much higher. In peaceful times, tourism was an industry which had the potential to spearhead rapid economic recovery for Croatia. An effectively managed recovery program had the potential to be a major provider of peacetime employment.[6]

As Rachel Treharne has demonstrated,[7] tourism to Croatia did indeed begin to grow rapidly from the low levels of 1995. The 1996 inbound figures were double that of 1995 and by 1997 international arrivals were nearing 4 million. In 1998 the rate of recovery slowed, largely due to Croatia's proximity to the conflict in Bosnia, and in 1999 tourism numbers dropped largely due to Croatia's perceived proximity to the Kosovo crisis of 1999–2000. In fact, only the southern Croatian coast was near the conflict zone. The major tourism-related project undertaken by the Croatian government (with considerable support from the United Nations) after its war with Serbia was the restoration of the thirteenth-century port of Dubrovnik which had sustained extensive damage as a result of the 1991–95 war. The Croatian government received a substantial amount of international assistance for this project. This support was significant for Croatia as a tourist destination, but especially so for Dubrovnik's status as a World Heritage site.[8]

One factor which enabled Croatia to achieve a relatively rapid recovery of inbound tourism was the demography of its principal source markets. Croatia's top ten source markets were from Continental Europe, in most cases within less than 24 hours' driving distance of Croatia. Croatia's five largest source markets—Italy, Germany, Slovenia, the Czech Republic and Austria, representing 74 per cent of Croatia's inbound tourism—were all within easy driving distance of Croatia's most popular tourist resorts on the Adriatic. Only the United States, ranked at thirteenth and Canada, in twentieth position were significant source markets outside Europe.[9]

The proximity of its key markets has enabled Croatia to centralise its tourism marketing infrastructure locally in order to service its main source markets. The Croatian Ministry of Tourism has not sought to establish offices in other countries, except for London, but has established links with key tour operators with substantial Croatian content and worked in conjunction with them. The proximity of Croatia to its principal tourism markets enabled the Croatian Ministry of Tourism representatives to service these markets from Croatia and consequently save the money which would have been required to establish and maintain offices and staff abroad. Private operators, Croatian Airlines and the airline's General Sales Agents (GSAs) have served as de facto Croatian tourism representatives in many key European, North American and other international source markets. The role of the national carrier has been limited to Europe and Israel (the carrier's only non-European destination).[10]

Meler and Ruzic assert that Croatia has an ill-defined tourism image, making it difficult to market a unique and attractive Croatian image—a vital element in restoring a destination after a crisis. Within its European environment, Croatia's main marketing advantage was its low-price accommodation, but this was counterbalanced by a reputation for inferior standards of comfort, hotel food, restaurants and cafés. Meler and Ruzic believe that developing a powerful positive image is an important stimulus for tourism demand.[11]

Aside from Dubrovnik, Croatia's Adriatic coastal resorts suffered relatively little damage during the war. Most of the wartime damage was inflicted in the east of the country, a region far less visited by tourists. As the Adriatic coast is the prime attraction for tourists to Croatia, the Croatian Tourist Board actively promoted this popular region for sailing and cruising holidays. Naturist (nudist) tourism has been an important niche market since the early 1930s, when European aristocrats (most notably the late King Edward VIII of England) regarded Croatia's Adriatic coast as the ideal location for an al fresco wardrobe-free holiday. As the late King was a style-setter in the 1930s, naturist holidays in Croatia developed a strong following and by the 1990s over 100 000 tourists were annually participating in naturist holiday packages.[12] The Croatian Ministry of Tourism spent most of its postwar budget on the repair and upgrading of tourism infrastructure, especially on roads, communications and improving ferry services between the mainland and the inhabited Adriatic islands. There has also been a shift towards the privatisation of hotels, resorts and guesthouses. During the communist years, many accommodation facilities were state owned. The sale of state-owned resorts and hotels have funded marketing, infrastructure and other investment programs.

The post-1995 priority for Croatia's tourism recovery program was to improve infrastructure to a level enabling Croatia to attract a larger portion of upmarket tourism and an extended length of stay. Tax breaks were offered to investors in hotel and resort property, and many of the major international hotel chains invested in Croatia. For practical reasons, far greater emphasis was given to improving road and rail links between Croatia and its northern neighbours than to upgrading airports, largely because the vast majority of foreign visitors to Croatia arrived by land. In the United States, Canada, Germany, the United Kingdom and Australia—all of which have large émigré Croatian communities—solidarity-based tourism was encouraged, although this traffic mainly involved visits to friends and family, and would not have contributed greatly to hotel patronage.

The Croatian tourism authorities sought to attract convention and incentive tourist traffic and to build a reputation as an eco-tourism destination. By European standards, a relatively large part of Croatia is set aside for national parks and state forests. Croatia has also sought to attract new niche markets, especially sport-orientated tourism (aside from water sports). The victory of Croatian tennis player Goran Ivanisevic at Wimbledon in 2001 was readily adopted as a symbol of Croatia's sporting prowess and Ivanisevic eagerly cooperated in becoming an internationally familiar face promoting tourism to Croatia.

The Croatian National Tourist Board's website is indicative of the direction the Croatian tourist authorities seek to take. The website actively promotes coastal-based tourism (including sailing), but includes sections on congress tourism, health tourism (focused on a number of inland spas), pilgrimage tourism, various types of eco-tourism and sporting tourism such as diving, climbing, hunting and sports fishing. There is also a growing Catholic-orientated pilgrimage market. Croatia is home to a number of important Christian holy sites.

The Croatian Tourist Board has utilised its website as a means to conduct market research on attitudes of both actual and intending visitors, although Internet market research has many methodological limitations, the greatest of which is the inherent unreliability of the statistical data which arise from a very limited sample population. The results of such polls are certainly helpful to Croatia's tourist authorities. In a series of questions to visitors to the Croatian Tourist Board's site in December 2001, polls covered attitudes to food, service by hospitality and travel industry staff, key attractions, decisive influences on choosing to visit, and factors deterring a visit. Although the results of these polls should not be considered to have any statistical validity, they did make some relevant observations. Scenery and price were rated by those surveyed as the major attractions. Food was rated by over 80 per cent as good to excellent. Previous holiday experience was the prime motivation to visit Croatia. While almost two-thirds of those who completed the survey were not deterred from visiting Croatia, the proximity of the country to Serbia/ Kosovo and the 1991–95 war remained as deterrents to 27 per cent of participants in this survey. 'Bad press' deterred 29 per cent of those surveyed from travelling to Croatia. In response to a US government offer to provide US$150 000 to Croatia to help improve the tourist industry, the Croatian National Tourist Board polled website visitors about their attitudes to Croatian hospitality and tourist staff. Of the small number who responded, 87 per cent rated them as average or better, with 58 per cent rating them very good to excellent.[13]

Other than Internet polls, there is little readily available evidence that the Croatian tourism authorities have conducted extensive professional market research. Even Croatian tourism statistics do not analyse tourist arrivals into identifiable market segments. Consequently, it is difficult to fully establish the motivation for visits and devise appropriate marketing strategies to appeal to specific market segments. Such information is an essential element in a crisis recovery program.

Croatia's tourism authorities have been forced to respond to the challenges of recently gained independence, a war during the country's first four years of statehood and Croatia's location within a politically unstable region. In addition, Croatia's tourism infrastructure has been obliged to undergo the transformation from a communist, state-controlled tourism system to a privatised tourism industry. Faced with this combined set of challenges, in addition to a limited budget, it would be unreasonable to expect that every aspect of post-crisis management and marketing could be handled with equal skill. Nevertheless, the Croatian government has recognised that tourism is a major element in establishing and maintaining economic independence, and consequently it has been in the national interest to manage the tourism recovery phase and advance to a growth phase.

TOURISM GROWTH IN CROATIA 1995–2001

There has been a significant recovery in tourism to Croatia since the end of the Croatian–Yugoslav war 1991–95. Table 12.1 provides some indicators.

With the exception of the downturn of 1999, due largely to fears about safety in Croatia aroused by Croatia's perceived proximity to the conflict in Kosovo (only the very southern coastal regions were actually near the conflict zone), the basic tourism indicators were revealing growth. However, it appears that tourists to Croatia were opting for shorter stays in 2000 than they were in either 1985 or 1990. Figures available to October 2001 indicate that international tourist numbers from January to October 2001 had reached 6.4 million.[15] Allowing for the fact that November and December are low season months for Croatia, it can conservatively be calculated that tourism numbers for 2001 would have exceeded 7 million, thus restoring Croatia's international tourist numbers to their pre-war levels, although the number of bed nights in 2000–01 appears to be somewhat below the 1990 levels.

Table 12.1: Basic indicators of tourism development, 1985–2000 ('000s)

	1985	1990	1995	1997	1998	1999	2000
No. beds	820	863	609	683	724	719	759
No. international tourists	8335	7049	1325	3834	4112	3805	5832
No. overnight stays by int. tourists	67 665	52 553	12 885	30 314	31 288	21 885	34 045

Source: Croatian Central Bureau of Statistics[14]

The statistical trends towards shorter stays by foreign tourists have led the Croatian Ministry of Tourism to treat both privatisation and up-selling of Croatia as its top priorities in order to optimise financial yield from each tourist and maximise the benefits and financial attraction for investors in the private tourism sector. In 2001, Croatia's Tourism Minister, Ms Pave Zupan Ruskovic, invited investors to buy formerly state-owned hotels, campsites and travel companies which, until purchased, were owned by the Croatian privati-sation fund.[16] Investors were invited to either purchase shares in tourist enterprises or acquire them outright. There are three phases of the sale process. Shares or enterprises can be purchased either at the nominal value, at a discount sale price or at a conditional price. Clearly, the Croatian Ministry of Tourism seeks to maximise the price it can obtain, but there is flexibility on pricing as the government's long-term holding of tourist properties—some of which are in a poor state of repair—is a greater liability than it is an asset. Once privately owned, the government has assumed that the owners will

Table 12.2: International tourist arrivals in Croatia showing principal and other selected markets of origin, 1996–2000 ('000s)*

Year	1996	1997	1998	1999	2000
Origin market					
Italy	467.1	688.3	750.8	630	1011
Germany	448.7	640	720.5	627	1048
Slovenia	437.6	577.9	636.7	717	849
Czech Republic	345.5	579.1	498.5	422	711
Austria	341.5	447.4	456.9	478	640
Slovakia	83.9	153.9	161.7	110	188
Bosnia Herzegovina	80.4	106.6	131.6	157	182
Poland	35.6	97.8	131	108	205
Netherlands	41.7	65	88.3	75	104
United Kingdom	31.2	50.6	68.3	60	84
France	26.8	34.6	41.9	34	57
United States	57.5	47.7	41.1	37	52
Canada	7.7	12.3	10.7	10	14
Total	2649	3834	4111	3805	5832

* Figures for 1996–98 are from the WTO and the 1999 and 2000 figures are from the Croatian Bureau of Statistics. There are some differences between the two bodies. Figures provided by both bodies for 1998 have substantial discrepancies.[17]

restore hotels/resorts to a standard which will maximise their desirability for tourists and, of course, profits to the owners.

In terms of its tourism recovery program, Croatia is fortunate that the overwhelming majority of its inbound tourism source markets are located in Europe and most of these are from neighbouring countries. This has enabled Croatia to focus on rebuilding its core market utilising a single base of operations. The source market structure has also facilitated a rapid recovery, as awareness of Croatia's security and political situation would necessarily be far greater in neighbouring countries than in more distant source markets which rely on frequently inaccurate media reports.

The proximity of Croatia's major source markets has enabled the Croatian National Tourist Board to organise media and travel industry familiarisation tours for representatives of key source markets at relatively low cost. The hostings have been a key element in the marketing recovery program. In 2002, the German Association of Travel Agents chose to hold its annual conference in Croatia, giving the country considerable positive exposure to the travel industry of its second largest source market. While there is a potential benefit for Croatia to more actively promote in other non-European markets, the Croatian tourism authorities have treated this as a secondary priority and focused their efforts on restoring their prime markets.

THE RESTORATION OF DUBROVNIK

As mentioned, the most significant restoration project of Croatia's postwar period was the successful restoration of the ancient walled city of Dubrovnik on Croatia's southern Adriatic coast. The funding of the restoration project of the World Heritage-listed port city, the country's most popular tourist attraction, was heavily supported by the United Nations, many foreign governments and private supporters.

The old city of Dubrovnik sustained considerable damage during the Croatian–Yugoslav War from Yugoslav aerial and artillery attacks which were viewed widely around the world as an act of military vandalism. The attacks caused damage to 60 per cent of buildings in the old port city.

By 2000, virtually all buildings and the sea wall had been restored. Events such as the annual Dubrovnik Festival attracted top-line international performers, many of whom donated their services free of charge to assist in financing the restoration project. The restoration of Dubrovnik attracted worldwide support and interest, and also attracted many tourists to witness the city's restoration for themselves. While the momentum of Dubrovnik's tourism recovery was temporarily slowed by the 1999 Kosovo conflict, tourism to Dubrovnik recovered to pre-war levels and tourism properties in the Dubrovnik area were privatised and upgraded.[18]

In November 2000, Dubrovnik was the host city for a major conference, Tourism in Transition. Many leading tourism academics from Croatia, nearby countries and further afield, including the United Kingdom, United States and China, attended. The dominant theme of the papers presented tackled the issues of transforming the structure, marketing and operations of the tourism industry in an environment of post-crisis recovery, globalisation and tourism during economic transition—all issues of relevance to the Croatian tourism industry.[19]

CONCLUSION

During Croatia's initial years of independent statehood, the country's tourism industry experienced four years of crisis which have been almost unprecedented in a European setting since the end of World War II. The country's initial years of independence were marred by war while the country sought to transform its political and economic system from a state-run, one-party system to a free market democracy. The war thrust upon this newly independent state made it all but impossible for Croatia to manage any tourism marketing recovery program during the crisis. Only after the war ended was Croatia able to develop and implement a recovery program.

In the context of Croatia's difficult situation and lack of financial resources, the recovery of the inbound tourism industry has been highly successful. Within six years, tourism numbers returned to pre-war levels and the country's privatisation program has made significant progress. The Croatian Ministry of Tourism and the Croatian National Tourist Board correctly focused their recovery program on re-establishing Croatia's core source markets.

However, there are some areas of the recovery marketing process which could have been better managed and which, in retrospect, may have accelerated the recovery process. These include:

- *Market research and strategic planning.* From available evidence, the Croatian tourist authorities appear to have conducted little in the way of serious analytical market research. Even national tourist statistics provide minimal analytical data that would enable the Croatian tourism authorities to conduct a focused marketing campaign to those market segments which would be responsive to visiting Croatia. According to Sandra Weber, the Zagreb-based Institute of Tourism has produced a number of strategic marketing plans for Croatia. In fact, the institute has been seeking to develop separate plans for all 20 counties of Croatia. Each county plan is designed to optimise the competitiveness of each Croatian county. By the end of 1999, seven of these strategic plans had been completed. The institute had completed a series of annual studies on attitudes and expenditures of tourists in Croatia since 1994, but according to Weber the lack of useful national statistical data had been a handicap to producing an effective national strategic plan. In her 1999 paper on destination marketing planning in Croatia, Ms Weber outlines a comprehensive framework for designing strategic marketing plans. Weber's four main themes are tourism demand and supply, the marketing environment (competition), the marketing position of the nation/county according to a SWOT analysis and the actual strategy. She also makes the salient point that a successful strategic tourism plan needs to be made in consultation with the tourism industry and the community. This point is as relevant to Croatia as to anywhere else in the world in which environmentally and socially sustainable tourism has become a major issue in tourism planning.[20]

- *Media campaign.* Croatia's tourism authorities have placed a high degree of reliance on private tour operators to promote the country to the travel industry and the travelling public. Croatia's largest tour operator, Atlas Travel, has links with many major tour wholesalers in Europe and around the world. While certain operators, like Atlas, have been able to focus primarily on Croatia and have been highly successful, most tour operators market Croatia in association with many other destinations and few have a singular commitment to Croatia. In crisis situations, over-dependence on private-sector support is an unreliable marketing strategy.

Croatia has been an active participant in consumer and travel industry expos and shows in Europe and in specific parts of the world. However, it appears to have done little in its key source markets to use the media to conduct concerted national tourism campaigns. In fact, it was not until Goran Ivanisevic won the Wimbledon tennis title in 2001 and offered his services as a tourism ambassador at large that the Croatians gave much practical attention to utilising the media to promote tourism. As part of a broader public relations campaign, Croatia's tourism authorities have done little, even on their website, to directly respond to some of the negative images about the country. The perception of Croatia held by many partially informed people on the periphery of Europe, especially from potential non-European source markets such as North America, Japan, Southeast Asia and Australasia, is one of a war zone.

- *Positive national recognition.* The key challenge Croatia faces in an increasingly competitive global travel market is establishing a recognisable identity as a tourism destination. This is not to suggest that Croatia is lacking in compelling tourism attractions but, apart from Dubrovnik (which is not a household name outside Europe), the Croatian tourist authorities have failed to promote a compelling Croatian image to draw people to the country.

Croatia has responded with a high degree of success to the challenge of recovering its tourism market, lost due to the four-year war forced upon it on attaining independence in 1991. The country's leadership recognises that tourism is a key element in Croatia's economic independence. Consequently, it is a national imperative for the tourism industry to not merely restore its market but to expand. An expansion program will involve seeking to popularise Croatia within Europe and develop new markets outside Europe. Croatia has access to a vast potential market in the Middle East, North America and Asia which could be the foundation of future growth—as many of Croatia's near neighbours, Greece, Turkey and Italy, have found to their financial advantage. Croatia's proximity to Athens and the 2004 Olympic Games presents a major opportunity for Croatia to broaden its marketing base for the future.

Part VII | COMBINATION CRISES

13 | PHILIPPINES: COMBINATION CRISES, 1990–2001

Managing terrorism, natural disaster, crime and political instability

CRISIS RANKING: **DESTCON 3–2**

BACKGROUND

The Philippine islands have 300 000 years of human habitation. A Pacific archipelago located to the east of the Malay Peninsula and north of Indonesia, the Philippines comprises 7107 islands (of which over 900 are inhabited), lush tropical rainforests, dramatic mountainous scenery and volcanoes (five are active). The Philippines has a diversity of cultural and religious traditions and a wealth of tourist attractions. It is among the most visited tourist destinations in Southeast Asia, with inbound tourist numbers exceeding 2 million per annum since 1996. Between 1990 and 1997, international tourist arrivals to the Philippines more than doubled from just over 1.025 million in 1990 to 2.2 million in 1997,[1] the country's record year for inbound tourism. By 2001, a combination of factors, dominated by political instability, resulted in a brief decline in overseas tourist numbers. Based on January–September figures for 2001, total tourism for the year would have reached about 1.9 million.

Tourism growth to the Philippines was erratic between 1990 and 2001. This was partly due to external factors, the most important of which was the brief economic collapse experienced in South Korea, Taiwan and Japan during the late 1990s, which impacted heavily on overseas tourism to all destinations from these key source markets. The Philippines has been exposed to several

internal problems including the destructive eruption of Mt Pinatubo in 1991, savage typhoons throughout the 1990s, and political instability in 2000–01, during which popular opposition supported by the Church and the military establishment ousted the Estrada government in January 2001. Muslim insurgents on the island of Mindanao have been waging a guerrilla war against the central government marked by acts of terrorism, including occasional abductions of tourists. In addition, the spread of AIDS as the deadliest of the sexually transmitted diseases greatly reduced the attraction of 'sex tourism', which was a popular—though socially problematic—niche market in the Philippines. A further predicament, which the Philippine tourist authorities had been forced to confront for many years, was a high crime rate by Asian standards. The 'sleaze element' as a niche market in the Philippine tourism industry has resulted in a greater likelihood of tourists being exposed to local criminal problems than is the case with most other international tourist destinations.[2]

Mount Pinatubo, Luzon. Photo courtesy Philippines Department of Tourism.

The Philippines tourism industry has concurrently experienced more of the typologies of tourism crisis than any other destination covered in this book. It was obliged to market the destination against a backdrop of frequently occurring natural disasters and episodes of terrorism in which tourists were targeted. Despite political instability—especially during the early 1990s and between 1998 and 2001—as well as crime and sexually transmitted diseases which impact on that segment of tourists whose prime motivation to visit has been to experience what we may euphemistically term 'night-life tourism', the tourism industry of the Philippines has had to demonstrate a high level of resilience to maintain its equilibrium and continuity. The tourism industry has prevailed in the midst of events which have had the potential to cause lasting damage to the appeal of the destination.[3]

Tourism is regarded as a strategically important industry in the Philippines. Successive governments have regarded a strong tourism industry as a solution to many of the country's economic and social problems. Mather and Bailey, reporting in *Travel and Tourism Intelligence* in 1998, observed that tourism represented an 8.7 per cent contribution to total GDP, up from 5 per cent in 1990. These figures represented the high point of growth in tourism to the

Philippines during the 1990s. They also noted that tourism represented the second largest source of foreign exchange earnings for the country after electronics and overseas remittances from Filipinos working abroad.[4]

The country has undergone a massive increase in population from 62 million in 1991 to 76.5 million recorded in the May 2000 Census.[5] The Philippines has the largest Christian community in Asia, with the majority of its people (82 per cent) adherents of the Roman Catholic Church, which was introduced to the country with the arrival of the Portuguese explorer Ferdinand Magellan in 1521 and throughout 333 years of Spanish rule between 1565 and 1898. In fact, the name 'Philippines' derives from King Philip II of Spain, reigning monarch after the Spanish conquest of the country. The period of American rule over the Philippines between 1898 and 1942 resulted in the country having the largest English-speaking populace in Southeast Asia.

The Philippines has a long history of socioeconomic inequality, with a small and incredibly wealthy elite and a vast impoverished majority. Within the capital Manila, an immense, rapidly growing city of 12 million people, there are enclaves of tremendous wealth which abut vast, sprawling slums. The visible social inequality in Philippine society is a festering source of political instability, crime, corruption and exploitation.

The social problems and consequential political problems are the primary factors hampering tourism growth in the Philippines. Opposition political militant groups and Muslim militants based in the south of the country have, at times, committed abductions and attacks on foreign tourists as a means to attract international publicity to their cause. In May 2001, a Muslim group known as the Abu Sayyaf Group abducted a group of Philippine and foreign tourists. The abductees, including two Americans, were detained by their captors who publicly threatened their decapitation.[6] The Philippine military ended the abduction by attempting to rescue them in June 2002. Several Philippine troops, terrorists and two of the abductees were killed. Throughout the 1990s, similar abductions took place.

HISTORICAL BACKGROUND

The Philippines has experienced a relatively short and turbulent period of political independence. Between 1565 and 1898, the country was a colony of Spain. The Spanish introduced and spread Roman Catholicism. As a consequence, the Philippines is home to the largest Christian population of any country in Asia. The Philippine independence movement supported the United States during the Spanish American War of 1898 but, rather than rewarding their support with independence, the United States paid Spain's US$20 million of debts and took control of the country. In 1935, the United States recognised the country's calls for independence and Manuel Quezon was sworn in as an elected transitional president in 1935. Between 1942 and 1945, Japan imposed a brutal occupation upon the Philippines until it was reconquered by US forces led by General Douglas Macarthur in 1945, fulfilling Macarthur's famous 1942 promise following Manila's fall to the Japanese: 'I shall return.' The massive naval engagement between US and Japanese naval forces fought in Leyte Gulf within the Visayas Islands in 1945 paved the way for Japan's ultimate defeat in the Pacific War.

In 1946, the United States recognised the full independence of the Philippines. Ferdinand Marcos came to power as an elected president in 1965, leading the dominant post-World War II regime. Marcos imposed martial law in 1972, ruling the country as a virtual dictator until he was removed in 1986, when Mrs Corazon Aquino led the largely peaceful, though military-backed, 'People's Power' uprising. Mrs Aquino is the widow of former opposition leader Benigno Aquino, assassinated by Marcos's soldiers at Manila International Airport in 1983. The blatant corruption and ostentatiousness of Marcos and his wife Imelda finally exceeded the stoic tolerance of the Filipinos, the Catholic Church and, significantly, the military leadership. Marcos and his wife were exiled to the United States. Much of the wealth acquired by the Marcos family during their years in power also remained in foreign hands. Succeeding governments made strenuous attempts to recoup the money, but were met with indignant denials from the Marcos family that such wealth existed. The case remains *sub judice.*

Mrs Aquino sought to restore democracy to Philippine political life, but she was hampered by the military and economic power elite who regarded her as a threat to their control over the Philippine economy. Aquino's more left-wing colleagues sought to reduce the US military presence in the Philippines. The eruption of Mt Pinatubo in 1991 damaged the US Clarke Air Force Base near Manila (which was not replaced or re-sited). Then the Aquino government refused to renew the US lease of its major Pacific naval base at Subic Bay. The perceived anti-Americanism and anti-capitalism of the more leftist elements of the Aquino government was deemed a handicap to the

Philippines attracting foreign investment. Initially popular, Mrs Aquino was eventually replaced in 1992 by President Fidel Ramos, with the backing of the military and the economic elite and, significantly, strong support from the Bush administration in the United States.

An *apparent* political success of the Ramos regime was the signing of a formal agreement between the central government and the Moro National Liberation Front in September 1996. The agreement officially ended 24 years of the MNLF's struggle for autonomy in the island of Mindanao and granted a high level of political autonomy for the second largest island in the country. Unfortunately, splinter groups opposed the agreement and the Moro National Liberation Front continued anti-government activity which also occasionally included attacks against tourists and tourism infrastructure. The agreement was a political achievement tarnished by the actions of splinter groups.

In 1998 the Philippines elected Joseph Estrada as president. Estrada was a 'B' grade Hollywood 'star' but a major celebrity in the Philippines. Ronald Reagan had been a famous Hollywood actor but he was a highly experienced politician with a well-developed conservative political program prior to his election as president of the United States. Mr Estrada had been Mayor of San Juan, a Senator and vice president to Fidel Ramos. However, his political program was vague, though he exuded considerable charisma and public appeal. Estrada's promises of great economic benefits to the Filipino people during the campaign were quickly forgotten after he assumed power and the 'economic benefits' did not extend beyond his immediate circle. By the end of 2000, the coalition of church, military and 'people power' which had overthrown Marcos demanded Estrada's dismissal on the grounds of corruption. Estrada was subjected to impeachment, in which he was almost acquitted by his allies in the Senate. He reluctantly agreed to step down following massive protests in January 2001. His deputy, Vice President Gloria Arroyo, succeeded him. The resignation of Estrada ushered in another period of political instability between January and May 2001, much of it involving demonstrations mounted by residual supporters of Estrada. Elections were held in May 2001 at which Ms Arroyo was elected president. During this period, acts of political terrorism occurred, mainly in Mindanao. The attacks sometimes manifested in bombings in Manila (including an attack on a Manila hotel with no casualties), deterring many tourists from visiting the country.[7]

TOURISM INFRASTRUCTURE IN THE PHILIPPINES

Until the 1990s, much of the tourism development in the Philippines was conducted on a relatively *ad hoc* basis. Manila and major resort cities, including Cebu and Davao, attracted considerable foreign investment for hotel and resort construction. During the Marcos years 'adult tourism' thrived in Manila and other popular resort cities. The mixture of pornography, prostitution and gambling brought with it the growth of organised crime and government and police corruption. During Marcos's imposition of martial law between 1972 and 1986, the nexus of crime and corrupt government crept into part of the tourism industry. Throughout this period, there was a sense of alienation between the traditional conservative Philippine society and the tourism industry, which became associated with the exploitation and objectification of the Philippine people.

The proliferation of 'introduction services' to introduce Philippine women to foreign men with a view to marriage and emigration was one of the more dubious tourism schemes tolerated under the Marcos regime. Many of the Filipino 'brides' used their 'marriages' as a means to secure citizenship in Western countries and in turn used their acquired citizenship to bring in members of their families. The immigration ministries of many Western countries, Japan and Saudi Arabia pressured the Philippines government to clamp down on this practice. Conversely, there were many instances in which Filipino brides and children from such marriages suffered abuse and exploitation at the hands of their foreign spouses. The Philippine website of the United People Against Crime documented an extensive case history of sex crimes and sexual slavery crimes in which the victims were Filipinos. This form of criminality remained prevalent well past the fall of the Marcos regime.[8]

There were some positive features of the deregulated tourism industry. Free-enterprise tourism resulted in the construction of excellent hotels and resorts throughout the Philippines. There was a strong retail sector and 'jeepneys', a popular form of tourist transport, added colour to Philippine streets. Philippine Airlines established a strong global network and cut-price internal airfares made many resorts in the Philippines accessible to foreign tourists. However, as Richter points out, indiscriminate marketing of the Philippines and its corrupt links to Marcos created internal opposition to tourism development; the public image of tourism in the Philippines as 'sleazy' and corrupt ultimately resulted in the tourism industry becoming a focus of protest, which in turn reduced inbound tourism demand.[9]

Under the Aquino regime, and more zeaously during the presidency of Fidel Ramos, there was a campaign to clean up the tourism industry and its image. Corazon Aquino's attempt to clamp down on sex tourism altogether only succeeded in driving such establishments underground. Even within the Aquino government, enthusiasm for this crackdown was cool. A former Tourism Minister during the Marcos years, Jose Aspiras, owned a number of hotels which were widely alleged to be venues for the sex tourism industry. The outbreak of AIDS ultimately did more to dampen enthusiasm for sex tourism than any government legislation could have achieved.[10]

During both the Aquino and Ramos presidencies, the government formulated a Master Plan for tourism. This was adopted and signed as Presidential Proclamation 188 in June 1991, thus giving the Philippines its first attempted coordinated strategic direction for the tourism industry since independence. Its formulation involved the combined efforts of the Philippines Department of Tourism, UN Development Program and the World Tourism Organization. The Master Plan was intended to serve as a guide for sustainable tourism development for 20 years.[11]

The main assumptions underlying the Master Plan were that tourism would undergo considerable growth and would inject US$20 billion into the economy and directly create 150 000 new jobs between 1991 and 2010. The key elements of the plan were that tourism growth would become environmentally and culturally sustainable and sensitive, enhance social cohesion, and be economically justifiable and geographically diverse in order to minimise exposure to internal or external threats to tourism activity. In 1996, Tourism Secretary Eduardo Pilapil predicted that the number of foreign visitors would double, reaching 5 million in 1998.[12] This optimistic prediction was justified on the grounds that, during the mid-1990s, tourism was growing steadily.

Beatrice Ang, writing in *Asia Travel Trade* in March 1998, described the development of new resort sites on the island of Mindanao and resorts on Samal Island near Davao as flagship developments. She also wrote of new gateway points into the country, including a second terminal at Manila International Airport. The tenor of her article at that time was that many of the elements of the Master Plan were being achieved and were achievable.[13] The Department of Tourism sought rapid growth of international, inbound and domestic tourism sectors to bolster broader national economic objectives. The combination of external economic problems and internal political confusion which affected the Philippines in 1998 proved a major obstacle in the path of the tourism master plan and predictions of quantum growth.

The last of the three elements of the Master Plan were especially applicable to the Philippines of 1991, the year volcanic Mt Pinatubo erupted with massive force. The eruption caused extensive damage to large areas of rural Luzon and ashes from the eruption blanketed Manila. The large US Clarke Air Force Base, which was slated for closure by presidential order of Corazon Aquino, was rendered inoperable by the debris from Mt Pinatubo. In addition, during 1991 typhoons caused far greater than normal damage to coastal settlements. While there was constant awareness of the Philippines' vulnerability to natural disasters, there was a strong socio-political motive for dispersing tourism enterprises throughout the Philippines.

The projects cited in the Master Plan included the development of 'satellite destinations', cultural tourism programs, agri-tourism, health tourism, sporting and adventure tourism, eco-tourism projects and island developments including the proposed Samal Casino Resort. One of the key infrastructure projects was the Philippine Tourism Highway, which involved construction of a world-class road linking Manila to Laoag in the north and Manila and Davao via Bicol and Eastern Viayas in the south, thus connecting many of the most popular tourist sites in the country. The southern road involved bridging several islands. Commencing in 1997, it was a most ambitious undertaking. Apart from facilitating tourism traffic, the highway had a broader strategic agenda: to strengthen central government control and influence over outlying regions of the Philippines.[14] The Tourism Master Plan is detailed on the website of the Philippines Department of Tourism, <www.tourism.gov.ph>, and outlines a number of specific projects which fit the main themes of socially, environmentally and economically sustainable tourism.

The formulation of a Master Plan was an important development in attempting to manage the development of the tourism industry in the Philippines, but it was not without its critics. Bing Jaleco, writing in *Asia Travel Trade* in August 1993, expressed concern that the development of luxury hotels in the Philippines was far outstripping demand, especially in the face of sluggish European economies at that time. Jaleco also pointed out that the government's attempt to 'de-sleaze' the tourism industry and close establishments in Manila's red-light district was proving a disincentive to elements of the Japanese source market.[15] The implicit marketing problem, principled though it may have been to crack down on 'red light tourism', was that source markets attracted to sex tourism needed to be convinced there were compelling alternative reasons to visit the Philippines. Jaleco pointed out that improvements of air links and land infrastructure in the southern resort city of Cebu had resulted in a tourism boom to Cebu—evidence that an element of the Master Plan was working, although much of this infrastructure had been developed and financed primarily by Japanese private capital during the 1980s. Jaleco viewed Cebu as the exception to the rule and observed that provincial development was hindered by disputes between the provincial governments and the Department of Tourism. As Elizabeth Nelle points out, implementation of the Master Plan involved extensive consultation between regional authorities which acted in consultation with local communities and the national government. Funding constraints often restricted implementation.[16] There was also a significant level of dispute between the Philippines Tour Operators Association and the Department of Tourism. In some cases, personal disputes between leading personalities in the government department and private industry associations obstructed implementation of the Master Plan.

The problems mentioned by Jaleco in 1993 were manifested in succeeding years. During the second half of the 1990s, the national carrier, Philippine Airlines (PAL), experienced severe financial losses and was virtually bankrupt by late 1998. Accusations ranging from mismanagement and corruption to operational and marketing incompetence were cited as reasons for the carrier's problems. The financial crisis in Japan, South Korea and Taiwan resulted in a severe slump in tourism from these countries to the Philippines during 1998, and also had a major impact on the viability of a number of PAL's principal routes during that year. Some services were closed. By 2000, an urgent restructuring of Philippine Airlines' routes resulted in a resumption of many of the routes formerly closed in 1988. Corruption during the short period of the Estrada government also resulted in the Tourism Master Plan being treated more as a statement of ideals for the tourism industry than as a strategic blueprint.

PERFORMANCE OF THE PHILIPPINE TOURISM INDUSTRY, 1990–2001

The 1990s began with a drop in tourism numbers, partly due to the impact of the 1991 Mt Pinatubo eruption, political destabilisation of the Aquino regime, the clampdown on sex tourism and the growing incidence of AIDS. From 1992 to 1997, inbound tourism to the Philippines achieved significant growth. There were several contributing factors. The Ramos regime was perceived as relatively stable. The major source markets were experiencing buoyant economic growth and the Philippines was perceived as a low-cost, high-value destination. By Southeast Asian regional standards, the Philippines was able offer high-grade accommodation and tourist services at lower prices than Singapore, Malaysia, Thailand and Hong Kong. The government was also perceived to be taking firm action against crime and corruption, and generally improving the reputation and image of the Philippines. The diversity of resorts and destinations within the Philippines was widely perceived as highly marketable.

In 1997, the Philippine tourism authorities ran the campaign 'Best of the Islands' which focused on the variety of tourism product the country offered. An energetic promotional campaign led into the Centennial year 1998, marking 100 years since the end of Spanish colonialism in the country. The successful ongoing campaign 'Bring Home a Friend' was predicated on the large number of overseas Filipinos returning on vacation with a friend from their country of residence. Twelve overseas offices promoting the Philippines abroad were centred in key source markets: two offices in Japan, four in the United States and one in each of London, Paris, Frankfurt, Sydney, Hong Kong and Singapore. In 1998, marketing representatives were appointed in several 'potential markets', including South Africa, Israel, Italy, Sweden, Spain, China and Taiwan.[17] Well-targeted and active international representation combined with specific national marketing campaigns were significant factors in assisting tourism growth during the period 1991–97.

The extensive media coverage of the Philippines political problems and the 1991 eruption of Mt Pinatubo aroused curiosity and interest from many prospective tourists who wanted to see the region. Between 1998 and 2001, inbound tourism to the Philippines suffered a downturn based on a number of factors. The 1998 decline was related to the severe economic recession occurring in South Korea, Taiwan and to a lesser degree Japan. Whereas most other source markets remained steady or grew during 1998, the severe drop in tourism from three of the Philippines' key source markets ended six consecutive years of inbound tourism growth. The period 1999–2001 was one of decline due to the return of political instability during the period of President Estrada's administration and internal economic problems within the country.

Table 13.1: Visitor arrivals in the Philippines 1990–99: key source markets and totals ('000s)[18]

Source market	1990	1991	1992	1993	1994	1995	1996	1997	1998	1999
ASEAN	47.8	48.7	55.5	68.1	84.0	92.9	139.3	155.2	134.8	138.4
Hong Kong*	70.6	55.7	66.2	76.6	93.7	107.2	149.5	159.6	162.7	160.2
Japan*	202.0	197.5	221.6	243.4	277.8	323.2	350.2	376.7	361.6	387.5
South Korea*	36.5	40.5	54.1	69.5	97.9	121.6	173.9	170.1	82.0	133.1
Taiwan*	56.7	52.5	122.2	169.3	157.4	190.4	206.7	246.4	185.9	143.8
Australia/NZ	51.0	47.9	55.4	65.8	76.6	83.7	96.9	104.0	95.9	88.1
United States*	203.9	192.5	221.6	270.0	310.2	342.2	374.0	427.4	468.8	463.6
Germany	26.9	28.2	36.0	41.8	46.5	50.8	60.4	62.6	64.2	62.0
United Kingdom	33.5	36.0	38.9	51.4	61.0	70.6	83.5	95.0	97.7	89.0
All Europe	112.1	117.2	136.7	162.9	183.1	205.8	243.2	263.8	277.6	263.6
Filipino Nationals	130.8	101.9	109.8	125.7	159.2	149.9	142.8	134.5	174.3	199.3
Grand total	1025	951	1153	1246	1415	1760	2049	2223	2149	2170
Growth rate %	-13.9	-7.1	21.19	19.01	14.70	11.84	16.43	8.45	-3.3	0.98

* largest primary source markets

The figures in Table 13.1 quantify inbound tourism trends to the Philippines. The largest source market is the United States, which grew consistently throughout the 1990s. Japan is the next largest single country market. Korea and Taiwan were source markets which underwent massive growth during the mid-1990s, a growth arrested by the economic slump experienced by both countries at the end of 1997. Hong Kong and Australia are significant regional source markets. Europe, dominated by Germany and Britain, represented just over 12 per cent of the Philippines' inbound market. Filipino nationals living abroad are another significant market.[19]

Two main events or crises which disrupted tourism growth to the Philippines between 1991 and 2001 were the eruption of Mt Pinatubo in 1991 and the Estrada regime and its overthrow from 1998–2001. The latter period was accompanied by heightened terrorism (especially Islamic terrorism) concentrated on the island of Mindanao. Some acts of terrorism were targeted at tourists and tourism infrastructure. The Estrada regime coincided with a period in which the economies of some of the Asian 'tigers', notably South Korea and Taiwan, experienced a sharp recession from which they recovered by 2000. The recession impacted on a number of East Asian countries and led to a sudden dip in tourism demand from several critical source markets.

MT PINATUBO'S ERUPTION AND THE MARKETING CHALLENGE

Mt Pinatubo is located on the Island of Luzon just 100 kilometres northwest of Manila. It is one of five major active or potentially active volcanoes in the Philippines. Mt Pinatubo is geologically defined as a composite or strato-volcano—a steep-sided mountain constructed of alternating layers of lava flows, ash and other volcanic debris which gives rise to an explosive eruption.[20]

Mt Pinatubo had been dormant for 500 years until a severe earthquake in June 1990, almost 100 kilometres northeast of the mountain, shook and squeezed the Earth's crust beneath the mountains and led to a chain of events which, on June 15, 1991, resulted in the twentieth century's second most powerful volcanic eruption.[21]

Vulcanologists and seismologists rapidly assessed the potential for eruption after the June 1990 earthquake. The Philippine government, with the cooperation of United States civilian and military officials, prepared the towns, cities

Table 13.2: Visitor arrivals in the Philippines, January–September, 2000 and 2001: key source markets and totals

Source country	Jan–Sept 2000	Jan–Sept 2001	% share total	Growth rate
United States	348 639	312 225	22.3	–10.4
Japan	304 056	283 668	20.2	–6.7
South Korea	126 216	150 919	10.8	19.6
Hong Kong	111 025	103 175	7.4	–7.4
Taiwan	55 358	64 372	4.6	16.3
Australia	54 500	49 926	3.6	–8.4
United Kingdom	61 257	47 929	3.4	–21.8
Canada	44 967	40 169	2.9	–10.1
Singapore	34 438	31 391	2.2	–8.8
Germany	40 047	31 073	2.2	–22.4
Malaysia	33 435	23 144	1.7	–30.8
China	11 266	13 665	1.0	21.7
Total	1 516 699	1 401 069	100.0	–6.6

and villages for evacuation and resettlement in the months before the eruption. The volcano gave many signals of its impending eruption from April 1991. Utilising GPS (Global Positioning System) technology, the scientists were able to pinpoint the epicentre of the eruption. Between April and June, over 200 000 people from the lowlands surrounding the volcano were evacuated in addition to 20 000 indigenous Aeta people who lived on the slopes of the volcano.[22]

The eruption sent ash some 19 000 metres above sea level. An avalanche of hot ash and gas (pyroclastic flows) extended to a radius of 25 kilometres from the mountain. The US naval base at Subic Bay was damaged by debris and Clark Air Base was partially buried by rain-soaked ash and rendered inoperable. Manila was spared the worst effects of the eruption, but the air was dense with volcanic ash for many days. Commercial aircraft heeded warnings of the eruption and most avoided the area. So powerful was the eruption that global temperatures fell by 0.5°C during 1992. The eruptions also altered a large area of central Luzon. Evacuations and rescue efforts before and after the eruption ensured that casualties were kept to a minimum. While the death toll from the eruption of 350 people was serious, the preventative measures were estimated to have saved many thousands of lives.

From a tourism marketing perspective, the eruption of Mt Pinatubo was far from catastrophic. The dramatic eruption was one of the major news stories of 1991 and heightened international awareness of the Philippines. While much of the coverage focused on the destruction caused by the volcano, there was praise for the efforts of the government in saving lives and in its approach to contingency planning. The massive scale of the eruption ultimately led to Mt Pinatubo becoming a significant tourist attraction. The high profile that news of the eruption gave to the Philippines provided both the national carrier and tourism authority with an opportunity to promote other attractions in the country to an attentive audience.

In the aftermath of the eruption, tourism numbers temporarily suffered due to uncertainty about the region surrounding Mt Pinatubo. Severe disruption was caused to airline services, especially to the country's major gateway, Manila. However, the rapidity and numerical strength of the inbound tourism recovery during 1992, representing the largest year of growth for inbound tourism ever recorded in the Philippines, demonstrated that, although the eruption upset tourism in the short term, it focused positive interest on the Philippines during subsequent years. The eruption of Mt Pinatubo coincided with Fidel Ramos's inaugural year as president and the release of the Tourism Master Plan. The massive civil recovery program in the region surrounding Mt Pinatubo coincided with this tourism recovery program. The international community focused considerable international goodwill on the Philippines, partially translated into a growth in tourism interest.

OTHER NATURAL DISASTERS

The Philippines is subject to an average of nineteen typhoons per annum, which routinely cause extensive damage to coastal areas. As an equatorial archipelago, large areas of the country are vulnerable to violent weather conditions. The Philippines is frequently threatened by tidal surges, high winds, floods, landslides, mudslides, tsunamis and occasionally drought. In addition to Mt Pinatubo, there are five other volcanoes deemed very active among a total of seventeen active volcanoes. Located on the geological 'Ring of Fire', the Philippines is exceedingly vulnerable to earthquakes. Between 1589 and 1990, 64 earthquakes caused major destruction. The most recent major earthquake measured 7.8 on the Richter scale and occurred in northern Luzon on July 16, 1990, causing extensive damage and resulting in the loss of 1600 lives.

The country's frequent exposure to extreme climatic events has resulted in the Philippines establishing a series of contingency plans including preventive measures to minimise casualties and loss of life from typhoons and other natural threats. The National Disaster Coordinating Council centralises weather reporting and action plans to evacuate and accommodate people who may be in the path of typhoons. Despite the many warning systems and contingency plans, typhoons—including one which struck Manila in November 1995, resulting in the loss of 500 lives—continue to threaten coastal towns and cities.[23] While there have been many natural disasters causing loss of life and extensive damage to agricultural infrastructure, the tourism industry in the Philippines has sought to ensure that most major resorts are constructed in areas unlikely to be flooded or washed away by storm-induced landslides or mudslides.[24]

The frequency and predictability of extreme climate and destructive natural phenomena are necessarily treated by the tourism industry as a background risk to visitors and citizens alike. Although typhoons in the Philippines normally occur between May and November, and thus travellers can choose a time to avoid the likelihood of exposure to them, tectonic movements and vulcanological events are less predictable. The country's exposure to the forces of nature means that these occurrences fall outside the realm of crisis, notwithstanding the gravity of some specific events.

CRISIS DESTINATION MARKETING: THE PHILIPPINES

Marketing destination Philippines is a significant challenge, requiring the ability to account for a range of obstacles which may occur individually, in tandem, or in clusters. The Philippines Department of Tourism has sought to focus on the positives rather than tackle the negatives. Natural phenomena such as typhoons are due to the country's geological and geographical location. According to Elizabeth Nelle, socio-political problems require long-term solutions anchored in political upliftment.[25] This raises the question of whether a Philippine tourism marketer needs to treat the country's many problems as an individual crisis—or indeed as a crisis at all.

A destructive typhoon in a location where typhoons are rare becomes a crisis because the victims are unaware of how to respond. However, the frequency of certain climatic events in the Philippines can be viewed in two ways: depicted as a hazard a traveller may avoid by timing a visit to minimise the risk of exposure to the event; or marketed as one of the wild natural risks taken in visiting the country. The tourism authorities in the Philippines provide foreign embassies in Manila with briefing information to provide a geographical perspective on travel advisories issued by foreign governments to their citizens. Crime is a problem in the Philippines, but tourists who avoid high-risk areas face minimal threat. Since 1990 the Department of Tourism has sought to dissuade tourists from visiting the red-light districts of Manila and other seedier tourist traps and has publicised the risks involved. The 'sleaze element' in the inbound tourism market to the Philippines has declined since 1990.

The political instability of the Philippines can be depicted as either a minimal risk to tourists or evidence of a robust democracy. It is noteworthy that the overthrow of Ferdinand Marcos in 1986 and Joseph Estrada in 2001 were both achieved with minimal violence. The most serious direct threat to tourism safety since 2000 has been the targeting of tourists by Islamist terrorist groups based in Mindanao. Abductions of Western tourists from Mindanao resorts, and even from resorts in eastern Malaysia, has been a particularly serious problem for Philippine tourist authorities due to the intense negative publicity generated by these incidents. In security-sensitive United States and Japan, the two largest source markets for the Philippines, representing 42.5 per cent of inbound tourism, the abductions attract more negative media coverage about the Philippines than a year's worth of typhoons, earthquakes or political demonstrations. The Philippine military and security services have made well-publicised attempts to combat this form of terrorism. The Philippine tourism authorities were reticent about abductions. Following the September 11 attack on New York and Washington DC and the ensuing United States-led war against Islamist terrorism, the Philippines received considerable support from the United States in its own military campaign against Islamist terrorist groups in the Philippines, some of whom were alleged to be linked to the Al-Qaeda terrorist network. In early 2002, US forces returned to the Philippines to train the military authorities in combating the Islamist groups based in Mindanao.

The Philippines Department of Tourism adopted the broad marketing strategy of promoting the cultural and scenic attractions of the country and the relatively low cost of the Philippines in comparison with many of its neighbouring destinations. The main marketing tools of the Department of

Tourism, including its website, brochures and audiovisual presentation, have little to say about potential threats to tourist safety. Both the government tourist authority and the private sector are well aware that consumers and the travel industry in key source markets are sensitive to numerous negative attitudes towards the Philippines. The Philippines Ministry of Tourism's main marketing arm, the Philippines Convention and Visitors Corporation (PCVC), has chosen to host large numbers of travel writers and travel industry professionals to act as *de facto* ambassadors of tourism to the Philippines rather than respond directly to traveller concerns about terrorism, crime and natural disasters. Traditionally, this approach has had mixed success. Travel journalists, especially from Western democratic countries, are not readily predisposed to act as automatic promoters of the destinations which host them. The PCVC has adopted a more proactive role with the international travel industry, particularly from key source markets. The intention is to equip travel industry professionals with the necessary information and promotional material to enable them to sell the Philippines to their overseas colleagues and their retail market. The PCVC is heavily involved in promoting the Philippines at trade and consumer travel shows and expositions.

Tourism Secretary Richard Gordon convened a meeting of the Philippines' first Tripartite Tourism Industry Conference held in Manila on August 30, 2001. The conference involved representatives of the government and private sector of the Philippine tourism industry. Key bodies represented were the Department of Tourism, the government-controlled Philippines Convention and Visitors Corporation, the Philippine Tourism Authority, the Philippines Hotel Association, the Airport Authority and several other private and government organisations. The meeting attracted 700 delegates, all of whom sought to address the issues of security and progress in achieving the aims of the 1991 Master Plan. President Gloria Arroyo opened the meeting.[26] The conference was a response to the lack of direction in marketing the Philippines during the late 1990s and heralded a new beginning towards a more coordinated approach to marketing and promoting the Philippines beyond 2002.

CONCLUSION

The tourism authorities of the Philippines have been obliged to contend with one of the most challenging marketing environments in the world. Between

1986 and 2001, there were frequent episodes of political instability, terrorism, natural disaster and (to a far smaller degree) epidemics, any one of which had the potential to cause damage to the country's tourism industry. In addition the late 1990s was a period of economic recession in Japan, South Korea and Taiwan, all of which were significant source markets for the Philippines. Outbound tourism to all international destinations from these countries plummeted drastically between late 1997 and 1999.

In the context of this challenging environment, Philippine tourism authorities displayed remarkable resilience. Although the Tourism Master Plan of 1991 was premised on a growth rate of 800 per cent between 1991 and 2004, the plan made no allowances for the various crises the Philippines experienced during the 1990s and in the opening years of the twenty-first century. During the 1990s, inbound tourism increased by 110 per cent from 1990 levels—a significant achievement but well short of the targets the government had set for tourism to lead the country towards economic recovery.

While the 1991 Master Plan was a guide to tourism development, it had no real contingency plan to deal with aberrant factors. The Philippines Department of Tourism and the Philippines Convention and Visitors Corporation have actively marketed the benefits of visiting the Philippines and have maintained a strong presence and active marketing campaigns in their principal source markets. The achievement of significant growth between 1990 and 2001 was testament to the overall effectiveness of the campaign and the inherent demand of the destination.

The level of tourism growth the Philippines could have achieved under more ideal domestic circumstances will remain a matter for speculation, but there were measures which the tourism authorities and the tourism industry failed to adopt in managing the range of crises which afflicted the Philippines. The 'ostrich approach' to a crisis is both uncomfortable and inelegant. Unlike some other countries discussed in this book, the Philippines failed to address the various crises in any of its official publications. One of the golden rules of effective crisis marketing is to acknowledge there is a problem and advise the target audience (in this case, the travel industry and prospective tourists) of what measures to take to either avoid or minimise exposure to that problem.

Whereas the Philippine government established institutions which brilliantly minimised the impact of various crises (especially natural disasters) within the country, tourism authorities carried on as if crises and disasters simply didn't exist. While familiarisation trips for travel professionals and the media may well have addressed the various problems, the tourism authorities failed to use their own media, brochures or websites to address travel concerns. There was no apparent crisis response message disseminated to travel professionals or consumers. The failure of Philippines tourism authorities to refer to issues such as the 2001 abductions of tourists implicitly—if unintentionally—communicates a range of negative messages. These include a total lack of concern for tourist welfare. While it is difficult to quantify the number of tourists lost through these acts of omission, other case studies have demonstrated that implementation of a crisis contingency plan accelerates tourism recovery following a crisis.

It is clear that by 2001, at the domestic level, the Philippines government and tourism industry recognised that there was a need for a more coordinated approach to marketing the Philippines between the public and private sectors. As a country that is vulnerable to many problems which negatively impact on inbound tourism, it is clear that the Philippines tourism industry would greatly benefit from a tourism crisis contingency plan.

NOTES

Chapter 1

1 Bill Faulkner and Roslyn Russell, 'Turbulence, Chaos and Complexity', in Bill Faulkner, Gianna Moscardo and Eric Laws (eds), *Tourism in the Twenty First Century*, Continuum, London, 2000, pp. 333–4.
2 Sehymous Baloglu and Ken McCleary, 'Model of Destination Image Formation', *Annals of Tourism Research*, Vol. 26, No. 4, 1999.
3 Martin Bryant was convicted of the mass murder at Port Arthur, but there are many claims he did not act alone.
4 Interview with Rupert Murdoch, Chairman, News Ltd, New York City, June 20 1987. This interview was part of the author's research on the Arab–Israeli conflict. Mr Murdoch's comments remain relevant to this study.
5 A. Pizam and Y. Mansfield (eds), *Tourism, Crime and International Security Issues*, John Wiley & Sons, New York, 1996.
6 World Tourism Organization and World Meteorological Organisation, *Handbook of Disaster Reduction in Tourism Areas* WTO/WMO, Geneva, 1999.
7 Anthony Concil, of IATA's Strategic Management Team in Japan, presented two papers on crisis management at the PATA/Southern Cross University Tourism Executive Development Conference, Ballina, NSW, Australia, June 28–29 2001.

Chapter 2

1 Christian Nielsen, *Tourism and the Media*, Hospitality Press, Melbourne, 2001. This is an excellent reference for specialists dealing with media relations with tourism authorities.

Chapter 3

1 US government tourism statistics. It is notable that the majority of visitors to France and Italy arrive across land borders. Most foreign visitors to the United States arrive by air.

2 NYC and Co website, <www.nyc.visit> 2002.

3 US government statistics website, <www.info.gov>.

4 Interview, Barry Schipplock, CEO Visit USA, Australia, November 2001.

5 ibid.

6 There is a new school devoted to dark tourism which has been established in Scotland. Dark tourism refers to tours devoted to exploring acts of criminality, disaster, war or other horror. Transylvanian authorities are currently seeking to cash in on Dracula.

7 CNN website. Background on terrorism USA, Sepember 12, 2001.

8 Casualty figures released to international media by US government, October 1, 2001.

9 Sites which contain such assertions include David Icke's website and Konformist. There are many more in this genre.

10 Richard Tomkins, 'An Eerie Quiet at the Airports as America Runs on Empty', *Financial Times*, September 26, 2001.

11 Brian Hale, Simon Mann and Michael Millett, 'Gone to Ground', *Sydney Morning Herald*, 6–7 October 2001, pp. 49 and 56.

12 Statement, Mayor Giuliani, September 17, City of New York 2001 website, <www.nyc.gov>.

13 Details of US Senate legislation to provide tax breaks for travel, October 2001.

14 World Tourism Organization, 'The Impact of the Attacks in the United States: An Initial Analysis', September 18, 2001.

15 <www.ehotelier.com>, October 24, 2001.

16 Statement by World Tourism Council, October 7, 2001.

17 Website, Travel Industry Association of America, <www.tia.org>

18 *Travel America Now Act:* Quotes from preamble, US Congress, October 2001.

19 Quotes from Mayor Giuliani's speech to the UN General Assembly, October 1, 2001, printed in full on New York City government website, <www.nyc.gov>.

20 Mischa Schubert, 'New York State of Mind', *Weekend Australian*, October 20–21, 2001, pp. 26–7 provides a very effective insight into post-September 11 marketing of New York City.

21 Strafor, *The Post September 11 Outlook for Travel and Tourism in East Asia and the Pacific*, Pacific Asia Travel Association, 14 October 2001.

22 <www.hotelier.com>, 4 July 2002, quoting from the June 2002 issue of *Lodging Magazine*.

Chapter 4

1 The author visited Egypt in June 1999 and flew with EgyptAir and Air Sinai Sydney–Cairo–Tel Aviv–Cairo–Sydney. These observations are by definition subjective, although the comments about Cairo Airport are widely shared by virtually all Australian-based operators which operate programs in Egypt, some of whom are Egyptian nationals.

2 Interview, Essam Karaash, Manager Misr Travel, North America and Australia, January 2001.

3 Fawaz A. Gerges, *America and Political Islam: Clash of Cultures or Clash of Interests*, Cambridge University Press 1999, Cambridge, pp. 172–3.

4 Salah Wahab, 'Tourism and Terrorism: Synthesis of the Problem with Emphasis on Egypt', in A. Pizam and Y. Mansfield (eds), *Tourism, Crime and International Security Issues*, John Wiley & Sons, New York, 1996, pp. 175–7.

5 Gerges, *America and Political Islam*, pp. 174–7.

6 Adrian Swincoe, *Travel and Tourism Intelligence No. 4, 1999, Egypt*, p. 27.

7 *PATA Travel News*, September 1996, pp. 6–8. The author met with the management of Burson-Marsteller in Melbourne in May 2001, and was briefed on the Egyptian case.

8 Wahab, 'Tourism and Terrorism', p. 180.

9 Gerges, *America and Political Islam*, pp. 174–80.

10 Swincoe, *Travel and Tourism Intelligence No. 4*, pp. 25–6.

11 Gerges, *America and Political Islam*, pp. 183–6.

12 ibid., p. 30.

13 ibid., p. 31.

14 The author worked closely with Essam Karaash of Misr Travel and with Mahmoud Khalek, Mohamed Moneir and Rob Howard of EgyptAir, plus Elahamy Elzayat, Chairman of the Egyptian Travel Agents Association, on an extensive range of Israel–Egypt and Eastern Mediterranean joint marketing seminars between 1995 and 2000. Insights gained from working with them on these programs have been of much assistance in the preparation of the Egyptian case study.

15 In addition to those mentioned in the preceding footnote, liaison with Zain El-Sheikh, Director of the Egyptian Tourism Authority (Tokyo Office) has been helpful in gaining an insight into Egypt's marketing activities, along with my Australian travel industry colleagues from such operators as Insight, Trafalgar, Contiki, Adventure World, Abercrombie and Kent, International Destinations and Yalla Tours, to name just a few. *Note:* The Egyptian government is notoriously slow in releasing tourism statistics, even on the Internet. The lack of recent statistics has made it difficult to quantify the extent of Egypt's tourism recovery from 1998–2001 and beyond.

Chapter 5

1 Israel Ministry of Tourism, *Statistical Abstract 1996*.

2 Prime Minister's Conference on Peace Tourism, September 1995, Israel Ministry of Tourism.

3 Documentation from the Israel Ministry of Tourism PR conference, Jerusalem, June 1999. Conference delegates, including the author, were taken to view all the developments cited, including the developments in PA-controlled Bethlehem.

4 D. Beirman, 'The Marketing of Israel in Australia and the SW Pacific', *Journal of Vacation Marketing*, Henry Stewart Publications, London, April 2000, pp. 145–53. This paper also explains the Israel Ministry of Tourism's overall global strategy for marketing Holyland 2000 and areas of cooperation with the Palestinian Authority.

5 The Israel Ministry of Tourism, on its website <www.goisrael.com>, presented a wealth of information on the papal visit. Events were widely reported in the international media.

6 The PA had made extensive plans to find a trigger to launch the Al Aqsa Intifada. The Sharon visit had been conducted with the approval of the Islamic religious authorities of the Haram El Sharif (Temple Mount) and the Israeli government.

However, Sharon's unpopularity among Palestinians and the wider Arab world made it easy to turn his visit into an 'invasion of an Islamic sacred site', conveniently ignoring the fact that this site had been sacred to Jews 2610 years before Mohammed was born.

7 Palestinian Ministry of Tourism website, June 2001.

8 David Beirman, *Surviving Negative Travel Advisories*, PATA Compass, Bangkok, December 2001, pp. 46–9.

9 Interview, Iain Ferguson, Manager, Australia Royal Jordanian Airlines, April 3, 2001. The Jordanian Tourist Board's website also contains material on the impact of the 'Palestinian' [sic] crisis on Jordan's tourism industry.

10 *Travel Daily* (Australia), May 12, 2001.

11 *Travel Week* (Australia), March 28, 2001, pp. 26–31.

12 The author commenced regular contact with all Australian-based travel insurance companies at CEO level from September 28, 2000. The observations are based on these contacts.

13 The Israel Ministry of Tourism sent an email to all Israel Government Tourist Offices on January 23, 2000 which detailed over 40 conferences and conventions cancelled from October 1, 2000 involving approximately 40 000 delegates.

14 Israel Department of Foreign Affairs, *Facts About Israel,* 1999, p. 72.

15 *Source:* Israel Ministry of Tourism.

16 At the Israel Ministry of Tourism PR Conference, January 14–17, 2001, Ruder Finn presented a paper on 'Image Management During Crisis' to delegates on January 16: Jeff Kahn, Manager, Ruder Finn Israel.

17 The source of information for the marketing strategies of Israel Government Tourist Offices in the United Kingdom, Europe and Japan is IGTO Reports for the Israel Ministry of Tourism PR Conference, January 14–18, 2001. Published by the Israel Ministry of Tourism 2001.

18 D. Beirman, 'Marketing of Tourism Destinations During a Prolonged Crisis: Israel and the Middle East', *Journal of Vacation Marketing*, Henry Stewart Publications, London, March 2002.

19 There is extensive documentary and visual evidence to back the assertion of Palestinian media manipulation. A selection of sources follows.

The Jewish website <www.aish.com> contains literally hundreds of examples of pro-Palestinian anti-Israel media bias but, more importantly, examples of stage management of events. The website for the Washington Institute for Near East Policy <www.washingtoninstitute.org> (a policy advisory body founded by former United States President Clinton's chief adviser on Middle East Affairs, Martin Indyck) contains many articles and papers dealing with this issue.

Two of the most cogent articles dealing with this issue are David Schenker's 'An Arab Debate on Child Sacrifice', *Jerusalem Post*, November 15, 2000, and David Makovsky's 'Arafat Sows Blame, Reaps Nothing', *Newsday*, April 3, 2001. Daniel Mandel's article 'The First Casualty', published in the November 2000 issue of the *Australia–Israel Review* (Melbourne), is but one of an extensive series of articles covered by this magazine analysing media coverage in the Israeli–Palestinian conflict. The June 2002 issue of the *Australia–Israel Review* was also largely devoted to the media war.

The reader may be forgiven for taking the view that, as many of the above sources cited are organisations friendly to Israel, *ipso facto* they are biased. However, the most damning exposé of media manipulation during the current Palestinian uprising ironically comes from one of Israel's most consistent critics in Australia, *60 Minutes* reporter Richard Carleton. Carleton's report, 'The Friday War: A tragic way of life', *60 Minutes*, March 4, 2001, graphically illustrates and validates every point the author has made about the media stage management of Palestinian protest, while simultaneously supporting the Palestinian position.

20 The five travel advisories cited appeared on the websites of the US State Department, Canadian Ministry of Foreign Affairs, Foreign and Commonwealth Office UK, Department of Foreign Affairs New Zealand and Department of Foreign Affairs and Trade Australia, checked on June 27, 2001.

21 Presentation by Dwight (Butch) Maltby, Touchstone Solutions, to Israel Ministry of Tourism PR Conference, January 16, 2001. Mr Maltby analysed the propensity of various Christian denominations to visit Israel during a crisis period.

22 Taskir Report, Israel Ministry of Tourism, 1995. This report, which involved interviews with almost 1 million inbound tourists to Israel in 1994, is the most reliable survey ever conducted on the Israel tourism market. Follow-up surveys using far smaller samples in each year since 1995 have confirmed, with minor variations, the findings of the Taskir Report.

23 The Birthright Program was an initiative of the Jewish Agency, which is largely funded by Jewish communities from around the world. It either subsidises or fully funds (subject to means) the travel arrangements of young Jews who have never visited Israel and was initiated in 2000 primarily to assist group study tours of Jewish youth by Jewish tertiary students from countries outside Israel.

24 All statistical information used in Tables 5.1 and 5.2 is based on monthly statistical reports on inbound passengers compiled by the Israel Ministry of the Interior and distributed to all Israel Tourism Offices by the Israel Ministry of Tourism.

25 Presentation by Mr Avi Rosenthal, Executive Director, Israel Hotels Association, to Israel Ministry of Tourism PR Conference, January 15, 2001.

26 The Palestinian Ministry of Tourism and Antiquities has not furnished official statistics since September 2000. However, its website claims in a April 23, 2001 press release that the PA has lost about US$150 million in tourism revenues since October 2000. The closure of most PA areas, coupled with the fact that the majority of world governments have advised their citizens to defer travel to the West Bank and Gaza, has virtually isolated the PA from all but the most determined international visitors (not including media and UN aid workers).

Chapter 6

1 Neelam Mathews, *Sri Lanka: Crisis Management as Tourism Reels,* Anderson Consulting Real Estate and Hospitality Resources, September 20, 2001.

2 Neelam Mathews, *Sri Lanka,* Tourism Report Travel and Tourism Intelligence No. 1, 2000, p. 79.

3 Foreign and Commonwealth Office, *UK Travel Advisory, Sri Lanka*, November 10, 2001.

4 Vijitha Yapa, 'Sri Lanka Strains to Fight Back', *PATA Travel News*, Bangkok, September 1996, pp. 15–16.

5 Mathews, *Sri Lanka*, pp. 80–2.

6 Ceylon Tourism Board website <www.lanka.net>.

7 Lonely Planet website, 'Brief History of Sri Lanka'.

8 Mathews, *Sri Lanka*, pp. 97–102

9 Ceylon Tourist Board website.
10 ibid.
11 Interview between Ms Ram and Renton de Alvis, Chairman, Sri Lankan Tourist Board, Express Travel and Tourism, Mumbay, India, October 16–31, 2001.
12 British, Australian and US government advisories on Sri Lanka, December 10, 2001.
13 Linda K. Richter, 'After Political Turmoil: The Lessons of Building Tourism in Three Asian Countries', *Journal of Travel Research*, August 1999, p. 43.
14 Yapa, 'Sri Lanka Strains to Fight Back', p. 15.

Chapter 7

1 Tracey Berno and Brian King, 'Tourism in Fiji After the Coups', *Travel and Tourism Analyst No. 2*, 2001, p. 77.
2 Interview, Josaia Rayawa, Director, Fiji Visitors Bureau, Australia, July 2001.
3 Berno and King, 'Tourism in Fiji After the Coups', p. 77.
4 Brian King and Mike McVey (Fiji), *EIU International Tourism Reports No. 2*, 1994, p. 10.
5 *Travel and Tourism Intelligence: Fiji No. 1*, 1998, p. 10.
6 Paresh Kumar Narayan, 'Fiji's Tourism Industry: A SWOT Analysis', *Journal of Tourism Studies*, vol. 11, no. 2, December 2000.
7 Interview, Rayawa.
8 Website, Fiji Visitors Bureau.
9 Berno and King, 'Tourism in Fiji After the Coups', pp. 75–85.
10 Statistics extrapolated by the author from Fiji Visitors Bureau website.
11 Narayan, 'Fiji's Tourism Industry', p. 19.
12 ibid., pp. 20–1.
13 ibid.
14 Interview, Rayawa.
15 Bernot and King, 'Tourism in Fiji After the Coups', pp. 80–2.
16 Interview, Rayawa.
17 Narayan, 'Fiji's Tourism Industry', p. 16.
18 Interview, Rayawa.
19 *Mice Net*, magazine published by Asian Publications, Sydney, November 2000–January 2001. Half of this edition was devoted to the promotion of Fijian convention, incentive and conference venues and hotels.

Chapter 8

1 Helga Loverseed, *Country Report Turkey: Travel and Tourism Intelligence No. 4, 2001*, pp. 90–2.
2 ibid., p. 89.
3 Bulent Alarizia, Senior Associate, Centre for Strategic and International Studies, *Turkey and the Global Storm*, CSIS, Washington DC, October 12, 2001, <www.csis.org>.
4 Interview, Erdal Aktan, Director, Turkish Tourism Information Office, Sydney, January 14, 2002.
5 Central Directorate of Disaster Affairs, Turkey, Earthquake Research Department website <www.sismo.depre.gov.tr>.
6 Based on figures from Turkish tourism statistics, Turkish Ministry of Tourism website, January 2002, <www.tourismturkey.org>.

7 Interview, Erdal Aktan.

8 PATA (Pacific Asia Travel Association) report, *Chinese Outbound Tourism Market*, January 2002.

9 Loverseed, *Country Report Turkey*, p. 100.

10 This observation is based on the author's extensive dealings with Turkish government tourism representatives, diplomats and tour operators between 1994 and 2002.

11 Loverseed, *Country Report Turkey*, p. 95.

12 World Bank, *Turkey: Preliminary Assessment Report*, World Bank, Washington DC, 2000.

13 UN Residential Coordinator Report, *Recent Natural Disasters in Turkey: An Overview of the National Technological Capacity and Its Utilization*, July 5, 2000, p. 1, <www.reliefeb.int>.

14 ibid., pp. 5–9.

15 METU Disaster Management Implementation and Research Centre website, Turkey, <www.metu.edu.tr>.

16 Central Directorate of Disaster Affairs, Turkey, Earthquake Research Department website.

17 Ankara Declaration to Establish the Global Disaster Information Network, April 14, 2000, <www.deprem.gov.tr>.

18 World Bank, *Turkey: Preliminary Assessment Report.*

19 Rusdu Saracoglu, *Presentation on Turkish Economic Crisis*, Centre for Strategic International Studies, April 12, 2000.

20 Vulent Aliriza, 'Turkey and the Global Storm', produced for the Centre of International Strategic Studies, Washington DC, October 12, 2001. This paper details the reasons for the Turkish–United States alliance and its particular relevance to Turkey's alliance with the United States post-September 11, 2001.

21 David L. Phillips, 'Beyond Traditional Diplomacy', *US State Department Magazine*, November 2000. The author is a senior fellow at Columbia University's (NYC) International Conflict Resolution Program.

22 BBC News website, *Istanbul Warning for UK Tourists*, August 17, 1999.

23 John Cunningham, 'Analysis: Holiday Trade', *The Guardian*, London, August 19, 1999.

24 'Kurdish Rebels Threaten War on Tourists', *USA Today Travel Guide*, October 19, 1999.

25 Loverseed, *Country Report Turkey*, p. 98.

26 Interview, Erdal Aktan.

Chapter 9

1 British Tourist Authority website, <www.vistbritain.com>, July 2001.

2 Ian Avent, CANSAR website, March 1, 2002.

3 BBC News website, quoting Anthony Nicol, Director of Communicable Diseases, Surveillance Unit, Public Health Laboratory Service, April 25, 2001.

4 Foot and Mouth Disease Restrictions issued by MAFF, March 1, 2001.

5 BBC website, March 22, 2001, Report of Professor Roy Anderson's findings on the foot-and-mouth epidemic provided to MAFF.

6 BBC website April 24, 2001, report on figures released by Public Health Laboratory Service.

7   Victor Barry of Treloan Farm, Portscatho, Cornwall was among the first rural businesses to place a notice on his website stating that his holiday farm was free from foot-and-mouth.

8   BTA website <www.vistbritain.com>: foot-and-mouth restrictions, March 7, 2001.

9   *Travel Daily* (Sydney), Tuesday, April 19, 2001.

10 BTA website, Market Intelligence Section, August 3, 2001. Statistics from International Passenger Survey Office For National Statistics.

11 ibid.

12 David Quarmby, Chairman, British Tourist Authority, 'Fighting Fit', *Overview Magazine*, London, July 2001.

13 Interview, Fiona Turnbull, Marketing Manager, British Tourist Authority, Sydney, May 2001.

14 Quarmby, 'Fighting Fit'.

15 Quarmby, 'Fighting Fit'. The author is indebted to Ms Dierdre Livingstone and Mr Elliott Frisby, press officer, BTA, London for sending Mr Quarmby's article.

16 I would like to thank Dierdre Livingston, Marketing Manager (Tourism Recovery) Btritish Tourist Authority, and her staff, especially Mr Elliot Frisby, for checking over material in this chapter and kindly making suggestions, most of which were adopted by the author.

Chapter 10

1   Graham Matthews, 'South Africa', International Tourism Reports, *The Economist*, No. 4, London, 1994, pp. 64–7.

2   Interview, Virginia Haddon, Manager, SATOUR, Australia, June 2001.

3   John Seekings, *South Africa*, Travel and Tourism Intelligence Country Reports, No. 2, London 1999, p. 84.

4   Jonathan Bloom, 'A South African Perspective on the Effects of Crime and Violence on the Tourism Industry', in A. Pizam and Y. Mansfield (eds), *Tourism Crime and International Security Issues,* John Wiley & Sons, Chichester, 1996, pp. 91–6.

5   Seekings, *South Africa*, pp. 86–9.

6   ibid., pp. 83–4.

7   South African Tourism, *South African Travel Planner 2001*. In this detailed 96-page brochure for prospective tourists to South Africa, crime is briefly referred to under the item of safety on page 6 and travellers are advised to take specific precautions to minimise risk.

8   Media statement by Mr S. V. Tshwete, Minister for Safety and Security, Cape Town, May 31, 2001. Published on <www.saps.org.za>, South African Police Service website.

9   These figures are extrapolated from the South African Police Service website.

10 Murder rates from Australia and the United States come from the Attorney General's website in Australia and the US Department of Justice.

11 South African Police Service. Extrapolated from national crime statistics, on website <www.sap.org.za>, April 2001.

12 Interview, Virginia Haddon.

13 Ed O'Loughlin, 'Violent Streak', *Sydney Morning Herald*, September 1–2, 2001, Travel Section, p. 3.

14 Seekings, *South Africa*, pp. 98–9.

15 Interview, Virginia Haddon.
16 Seekings, *South Africa*, pp. 97–9.
17 ibid., pp. 83–4.
18 ibid., pp. 86–97.
19 Interview, Virginia Haddon.
20 South African Airways website, <www.flysaa.com>, 2001.
21 Interview, Virginian Haddon.

Chapter 11

1 Tourism Tasmania website, Tourism Data Tasmania, 1996–2000.
2 ibid.
3 Interview, Malcolm Wells, Deputy CEO, Tourism Tasmania, January 21, 2002.
4 Interview, John Pugsley, Marketing Manager, Tourism Tasmania, January 23, 2002.
5 *Traveltrade*, May 15–June 4, 1996, Reed Publications, Sydney, p. 1.
6 Malcolm Wells, 'Port Arthur: One Year On', paper presented to a conference held in Mount Eliza, Victoria, April 1997.
7 Interview, Malcolm Wells, January 26, 2002.
8 ibid., pp. 4–5.
9 Jenny Burns, 'Port Arthur Strategy Wins', *PATA Travel News*, September 1996, p. 10.
10 Bob Engisch, *Travelweek*, Tasmania feature, September 25, 1996, p. 19.
11 ibid., p. 19.
12 Tourism Tasmania website, 1999 Data Card, 1995–99.
13 Brian Finlay, *Port Arthur Massacre: How Has the Tourism Industry Been Affected?*, unpublished dissertation, School of Tourism, Southern Cross University, May 1997, pp. 5–21.
14 Malcolm Wells, *Port Arthur Rebuilding the Image*, pp. 2–3.
15 Interview, Maria Stacey, Port Arthur Historic Site, January 29, 2002.
16 Craig Coombs, 'Port Arthur Historic Site Management Authority Response', *Australian Journal of Emergency Management*, Autumn 1998, pp. 16–19.

Chapter 12

1 The historical summary of Croatia has utilised two prime sources: Lonely Planet's *Eastern Europe* and Martin Gilbert's *Challenge to Civilisation: A History of the Twentieth Century 1952–1999*, HarperCollins, London, 2000.
2 C. Michael Hall and Vanessa O'Sullivan, 'Tourism Stability and Violence', in A. Pizam and Y. Mansfield (eds), *Tourism, Crime and International Security Issues*, John Wiley & Sons, Chichester, 1996, pp. 113–14.
3 Rachel Treharne, 'Croatia Country Summary', *Travel and Tourism Intelligence*, No. 2, London, 2000, p. 73.
4 Croatian Central Bureau of Statistics.
5 Treharne, Croatia Country Summary, p. 72.
6 ibid., pp. 72–5.
7 ibid., pp. 75–81.
8 Dubrovnik Online website, <www.dubrovnik-online.com>. This site provides detailed information about Dubrovnik and the restoration project.
9 Croatian Central Bureau of Statistics.

10 Croatian Airlines website, <www.croatiaairlines.hr>.
11 Marcel Meler and Drago Ruzic, Marketing Identity of the Tourist Product of the Republic of Croatia, *Tourism Management*, vol. 20, Pergamon Press, London, 1999, pp. 635–43.
12 Croatian National Tourist Board website, <www.htz.hr>.
13 ibid., Surveys.
14 Croatian Central Bureau of Statistics.
15 ibid.
16 Croatian Ministry of Tourism website, <www.minit.hr>.
17 Figures quoted for 1999–2000 from Croatian Central Bureau of Statistics and for preceding years from Treharne, Croatia Country Summary.
18 Dubrovnik On Line website, <www.lgc.apt.org/balkans/dubrovnik/html>. The BBC broadcast an excellent radio program on Dubrovnik's recovery on January 3, 2002.
19 Croatian National Tourist Board website.
20 Sandra Weber, 'Destination Marketing Planning in Croatia: Problems and Perspectives', *The Tourist Review*, Frankfurt, no. 2, 1999, pp. 78–83.

Chapter 13

1 Philippines Department of Tourism website, <www.tourism.gov.ph>, 2001.
2 Linda K. Richter, 'After Political Turmoil: The Lessons of Rebuilding Tourism in Three Asian Countries', *Journal of Travel Research*, vol. 38, August 1999, p. 42.
3 *Manila Times*, Editorial, December 3, 2001.
4 Sue Mather and Murray Bailey, 'Philippines National Tourism Report', *Travel and Tourism Intelligence*, no. 3, 1998, pp. 71–2.
5 Philippines Department of Tourism website, <www.tourism.gov.ph>.
6 Lonely Planet website, <www.lonelyplanet.com>, Philippines, January 2002.
7 History of the Philippines.
8 Fact Book on Global Sexual Exploitation, The Philippines website, <www.uri.edu>.
9 Richter, 'After Political Turmoil', pp. 42–4.
10 'United Peoples Against Crime' in Alejandro Melchor, *Drug Addiction, Sex Addiction and Sexual Slavery,* UPAC website, August 29, 2001.
11 Philippines Department of Tourism website.
12 Sol L. Villa, 'Officials Expect to Hit Magic 2.2 Million Mark', *Asia Tourism*, November 1996.
13 Beatrice Ang, 'New Plans for an Old Friend' *Asia Travel Trade*, March 1998, pp. 18–20.
14 Philippines Department of Tourism website.
15 Bing Jaleco, 'Update: Philippines Paradoxical Paradise', *Asia Travel Trade*, August 1993, pp. 30–3.
16 A very special thanks to Elizabeth Nelle, Director of the Office of Product Research and Development, Department of Tourism, Philippines, in Manila who reviewed this chapter and provided the author with this and other relevant pieces of information.
17 Mather and Bailey, 'Philippines National Tourism Report', pp. 88–90.
18 Philippines Department of Tourism website, December 2001.
19 ibid.

20 USGS (Cascades Volcano Observatory) website. Wolff and Hoblitt, 'Overview of Eruptions,' in Newahall and Punongbayan (eds), *Fire and Mud Eruptions and Lahards of Mt Pinatubo*, Philippines Institute of Vulcanology and Seismology, Manila, 1996.

21 J.W. Eawart and C.N. Newall, *Volcanic Crisis in the Philippines: The 1991 Eruption of Mount Pinatubo*, US Geological Survey website, 1997.

22 ibid.

23 Worldwide Church of Good News, November 14, 1995.

24 Passport 2, Manila website, <www.passport2maila.com>.

25 Comments to author by Alan Canazil, Department of Tourism, Philippines, May 2002.

26 Department of Tourism website, Press releases, August 24, 2001.

SELECT
BIBLIOGRAPHY

David L. Edgell, *International Tourism Policy*, Van Nostrum Reinhold, New York, 1990.
Bill Faulkner, Gianna Moscardo and Eric Laws (eds), *Tourism in the Twenty First Century*, Continuum Press, London, 2000.
Joseph D. Fridgen, *Dimensions of Tourism*, Educational Institute American Hotel and Motel Association, East Lansing, 1996.
Fawaz A. Gerges, *America and Political Islam: Clash of Cultures or Clash of Interests*, Cambridge University Press, Cambridge, 1999.
Colin Michael Hall, *Tourism and Politics*, John Wiley & Sons, Chichester, 1994.
Israel Ministry of Foreign Affairs, *Facts About Israel*, Jerusalem, 2001.
Israel Ministry of Tourism, *Taskir Report on Tourism to Israel*, Israel Ministry of Tourism, Jerusalem, 1995. This report is subject to annual survey updates.
S. Medlick, *Managing Tourism*, Butterworth Heinemann, Oxford, 1991.
Christian Nielsen, *Tourism and the Media*, Hospitality Press, Melbourne, 2001.
A. Pizam and Y. Mansfield (eds), *Tourism, Crime and International Security Issues*, John Wiley & Sons, New York, 1996.
Greg Richards (ed.), *Tourism in Central and Eastern Europe: Educating for Quality*, Tilburg University Press, Netherlands, 1996.
Linda K. Richter, *The Politics of Tourism in Asia*, University of Hawaii Press, Hawaii, 1989.
M. Thea, S. Sinclair and M.J. Slaben (eds), *The Tourism Industry—An International Analysis*, C.A.B. International, Oxford, 1991.
World Tourism Organization, *Handbook of Disaster Reduction In Tourism Areas*, Geneva, 1999.

Academic journals

Annals of Tourism Research
Australian Journal of Emergency Management
International Journal of Vacation Marketing

Journal of Travel Research
Journal of Tourism Studies
The Tourist Review
Tourism Management
Travel and Tourism Analyst
Travel and Tourism Intelligence

Travel trade journals

Asia Travel Trade
Compass-PATA (Pacific Asia Travel Association)
Express Travel and Tourism
Mice-Net
Overview Magazine (UK)
PATA Travel News
Traveltrade (Australia)
Travel News (Australia)
Travel Week (Australia)

Websites

Anderson Consulting
<www.anderson.com>

BBC
<www.bbc.co.uk>

BTA (British Tourist Authority)
<www.visitbritain.com>

Bula Fiji (Fiji Visitors Bureau)
<www.bulafiji.com>

CANSAR (Campaign Against Nuclear Storage and Radiation UK)
<www.westcountrylinks.co.uk/cansar>

Ceylon Tourist Bureau (Sri Lanka)
<www.lanka.net>

CNN
<www.cnn.com>

Croatian Airlines
<www.ctn.tel.hr>

Croatian Central Bureau of Statistics
<www.dzs.hr>

Croatian Ministry of Tourism
<www.mint.hr>

David Icke (conspiracy site)
<www.davidicke.com>

Directorate of Disaster Affairs, Turkey
<www.sismo.depr.gov.tr>

Dubrovnik Online
<www.igc.apt.org/balkans/dubrovnik/hmtl>

Egyptian Tourist Authority
<www.egypttourism.org>

E Hotelier Com (International Hotels)
<www.ehotelier.com>

Go Israel
<www.goisrael.com>

Konformist (conspiracy site)
<www.konformist.com>

Lonely Planet
<www.lonelyplanet.com>

Mayor of New York City
<www.nyc.gov>

New York City and Co.
<www.nycvisit.com>

PATA (Pacific Asia Travel Association)
<www.pata.org>

Philippines Department of Tourism
<www.tourism.gov.ph>

Philippines Institute of Vulcanology and Seismology
<www.phvoics.gov.ph>

SATOUR (South African Tourism)
<www.southafrica.net>

South African Airlines
<www.saa.org.za>

South African Police Service
<www.saps.org.za>

Sri Lankan Airlines
<www.srilankan.lk>

Tourism Tasmania
<www.tourism.tas.gov.au>

Travel Industry Association (USA)
<www.tia.org>

Turkish Ministry of Tourism
<www.turkey.org/turkey>

United Peoples Against Crime (Philippines)
<www.upac.2000.com>

United States Government, Acts of Congress
<www.congress.org>

United States Government, tourism statistics
<www.info.gov>

US Geological Survey
<www.info.er.usgs.gov>

World Travel and Tourism Council
<www.wttc.org>

World Tourism Organization
<www.world-tourism.org>

Travel advisory websites

Australian Government, Department of Foreign Affairs and Trade
<www.dfat.gov.au>

British Government, Foreign and Commonwealth Office
<www.fco.gov.uk>

Canadian Government, Ministry of Foreign Affairs
<www.dfait-maeci.gc.ca>

New Zealand Government, Ministry of Foreign Affairs
<www.mfat.gov.nz>

United States Government, State Department
<www.travel.state.gov/tips>

Note: *There is more material relevant to the subject matter of this book available electronically than there is in print.*

INDEX